294

# *A Disastrous* HISTORY OF BRITAIN

## CHRONICLES OF WAR, RIOT, PLAGUE AND FLOOD

### JOHN WITHINGTON

SUTTON PUBLISHING

First published in the United Kingdom in 2005 by
Sutton Publishing Limited · Phoenix Mill
Thrupp · Stroud · Gloucestershire · GL5 2BU

British Library Cataloguing in Publication Data
A catalogue record for this book is available from the British Library.

ISBN 0-7509-3865-X

For the purposes of this book, I have taken 'Britain' to mean the United
Kingdom. Fuller accounts of some London disasters can be found in my book
*The Disastrous History of London*.

Typeset in Photina 10.5/15pt.
Typesetting and origination by
Sutton Publishing Limited.
Printed and bound in England by
J.H. Haynes & Co. Ltd, Sparkford.

# CONTENTS

For Anne, Tom and my Mother

 PART ONE

# HOSTILE ACTION

# CHAPTER ONE

# WAR AND INVASION

No doubt there were many disasters in ancient Britain destined to remain forever shrouded in the mists of time – floods, plagues, famines, massacres – but the first we find that is well documented came in AD 60 or 61 (historians cannot agree), about seventeen years after the Romans first settled. During that time, they had fought with and crushed many tribes, but with others, like the Iceni, who lived in modern-day Norfolk and southern Suffolk, they made alliances. The Iceni's King, Prasutagus, was 'renowned for his wealth', and had been able to construct a special relationship with the Romans. Then in, let us say, AD 61, he died; it seems without male heirs. In his will he shared out his property jointly between his two teenage daughters and the Roman Emperor Nero, and appointed his widow Boudicca (the popular alternative name Boadicea appears to have come from a miscopying of an ancient text) as regent. Leaving part of your property to the emperor was a common tactic, designed to ensure your wishes would be carried out.

If that was indeed the intention, on this occasion it backfired badly. Representatives of the senior Roman financial official of the province, the Procurator Catus Decianus, seized all the King's estates and treasures, while members of the royal family complained they were treated as slaves by the procurator's servile officers, and this seems to have been accompanied by a general plundering of the Iceni's territories. The nobility were evicted from their ancestral properties, and, in the words of the great Roman historian Tacitus, 'Kingdom and household alike were plundered like prizes of war'. When Boudicca protested, the Romans flogged her and raped her daughters.

The Iceni were not the only British tribe unhappy with their treatment at the hands of the Romans. Their neighbours, the Trinovantes, who were in southern Suffolk and Essex, had seen Colchester, then known as Camulodunum, turned into the first Roman *colonia* in Britain – a place where veterans were given land when they retired from the army. That was bad enough, but the veterans often took even more land than they had been granted. 'The settlers drove the Trinovantes from their homes and land,' wrote Tacitus, 'and called them prisoners and slaves.' The Romans had also built a temple to Nero's predecessor, the Emperor Claudius, and those Trinovantes unfortunate enough to be chosen as priests had to 'pour out their whole fortunes' serving the cult of the Emperor.

Not surprisingly, they were happy to make common cause with the Iceni, and joined their forces to Boudicca's. The Queen was probably in her thirties. The only description we have of her comes from the historian, Dio Cassius, who was born a century later. He says she was very tall, with a mass of red hair hanging down to her waist, 'in appearance almost terrifying.' Certainly, her deeds were now about to terrify Rome. When she marched on Colchester, the colonists sent a desperate plea for help to the Procurator, but all they got was 200 'semi-armed' men. The town had no wall, and the Britons quickly overran such defences as there were. For some reason, the colonists seemed to make no attempt to evacuate women, children or the old. Boudicca's host sacked the town, burning down the wattle and daub houses. The temple of Claudius held out for a couple of days, then the Britons broke in and destroyed it, putting Roman veterans and their families sheltering there to the sword. The town was taken so easily there were even suspicions that a fifth column of prominent Britons within had betrayed it.

When the Britons went to war, the Roman Governor, Suetonius Paulinus, was fighting far away in Anglesey with the XIVth legion, so it was left to another general, Petillius Cerialis, to try to intercept Boudicca's army as it marched from the ruins of Colchester towards London. At his back he had about 3,000 men of the IXth legion, but the Britons ambushed them and cut the Roman infantry to pieces, killing perhaps 2,000. Petillius fled with his cavalry. By now, Catus Decianus had also made himself scarce, taking refuge in Gaul. Suetonius hurried back from Wales, and arrived in London before the Britons, who may have been delayed by the important business of plundering. The Roman town was a bustling centre of trade, spread over 30 acres in the present-day City of London but, like Colchester, it had no defensive walls, and the Governor took the view that it could not be saved. So, wrote Tacitus, 'undeflected by the prayers and tears of those who begged for his help', Suetonius led his soldiers off to the north again, taking with him those Roman Londoners fit and willing to escape. The rest he abandoned to their fate. Some may have got away into the territory of neighbouring tribes still friendly to Rome, but many were reluctant to leave, and the old and infirm could not.

Boudicca's army took the undefended city, and embarked on an orgy of destruction. The timber-framed thatched houses, mostly owned by well-to-do Gauls and other foreigners, burned well, and Londinium was reduced to a ruin. From remains that have survived, like melted coins, it is clear that temperatures reached the kind of levels seen in the firestorms of World War Two bombing raids. The Britons did not just destroy. They also slaughtered – 'there was no form of savage cruelty' from which they refrained. Tacitus was shocked that they did not seem to want to take captives and make money from ransoms. He wrote: 'The Britons took no prisoners, sold no captives as slaves and went in for none of the usual trading of war. They wasted no time in getting down to the bloody business of hanging, burning and crucifying.' The Britons' tactics were straightforward – 'bypassing forts and garrisons, they made for where the loot was richest and protection weakest.' After London, the next obvious target was Verulamium (St Albans), inhabited by Britons friendly to the Romans. Suetonius made no attempt to save them either. A month after the sack of London, the town was burned and, as in the capital, to this day a tell-tale ribbon of red earth can be seen below the ground as testimony to the destruction. Tacitus estimates that 70,000 were killed by Boudicca's host during their devastating progress. It is almost certainly a huge exaggeration, but the slaughter was plainly terrible.

By now the Queen's ranks had been swelled by recruits from other tribes 'who had not yet been broken by servitude.' It probably included Coritani and Cornovii from the Midlands and Brigantes from north of the Humber, and some say they may by now have numbered more than 200,000. Suetonius, though, had managed to amass a force of about 10,000 legionaries and auxiliaries. Where he met the British tribes is unknown, but many historians favour a site at Mancetter on the edge of Atherstone in Warwickshire, just south of Watling Street, the Roman road that led from Anglesey to London. Wherever the battle was, the outcome is clear. In spite of his inferior numbers, Suetonius exploited the superior discipline and organisation of his troops to inflict a crushing defeat and massacre British warriors and the women and children they had brought with them. 'According to one report', as Tacitus meticulously notes, 80,000 Britons died and only 400 Romans. Boudicca took poison, but her followers were to suffer a longer ordeal. Now fire and sword were in the hands of the Romans, and they made full use of them. It was not just those who had taken up arms whose land and farms were ravaged. Those who had stayed neutral or were deemed to be 'wavering' were also at risk, and that could include pretty well anyone. The Britons also had to endure another disaster – famine. Counting on being able to live off commandeered Roman supplies, many had failed to sow their fields. Now, even if they could escape the marauding Romans, they faced starvation. The devastation seems to have stopped only when the new Roman Procurator began to worry that the damage being inflicted might affect the Britons' ability to pay their taxes. Many Iceni were enslaved and deported, and their lands remained waste into the next century.

The Romans often conducted brutal campaigns of repression. Governor Agricola, who was Tacitus' father-in-law, crushed the Ordovices of central Wales so ruthlessly he almost annihilated them. A Scot on the receiving end of Roman suppression complained, according to Tacitus, that what they did was 'to rob, kill and rape and this they call Roman rule. They make a desert and call it peace.' By the third century, though, the Romans in Britain faced many dangers. Saxon pirates were already attacking the south and east coasts of England, so that the area stretching from Norfolk to Hampshire became known as the 'Saxon shore' (all German invaders tended to be referred to as 'Saxons', even if they were actually Angles, Jutes, Frisians or from some other Germanic tribe). By the fourth century, there was clearly some large-scale settlement by Germanic tribes, for example around Pevensey in Sussex. These may have been mercenaries, invited in by the central authorities or by individual towns and landowners and given land in return for fighting when required, or they could simply have been uninvited visitors the Roman Britons were not strong enough to keep out. Whichever was the case, the Germanic raids continued, while the Picts and Scots remained a constant menace in the north. Then in 364 – according to one Roman historian – additional attacks came from the Attacotti, a rather mysterious group, perhaps from Ireland, who were said to be cannibals.

Three years later, the Saxons overran the south-east and looted London, while in the north, the Picts, Scots and Attacotti mounted concerted raids and plundered and killed at will. Renegade soldiers from the now demoralised Roman armies may have been doing the same. The Roman general Theodosius was sent by the emperor and set up a base at Richborough in Kent, from which he began attacking the looting bands. He caught up with them loaded down with plunder and driving along cattle and prisoners in chains. Theodosius won great affection by distributing only a small part of the spoils he recovered among his soldiers, and trying to restore the rest to its rightful owners. Before he left, he also improved Britain's defences, but once he was gone, the attacks soon picked up again. Around 405, we know the teenage St Patrick was captured in the north of England, perhaps at Carlisle, by raiders from Ireland, and enslaved.

By then, Rome was facing too many dangers close to home to worry about a remote outpost of the empire and, early in the fifth century, the Emperor Honorius withdrew the last troops from Britain and told the province it must provide for its own protection. In 410, in the words of the Anglo-Saxon Chronicle: 'the Goths took the city of Rome by storm, and never afterwards did the Romans rule in Britain.' For some time, the old ways survived. In 429 St Germanus was greeted by sumptuously dressed landowners surrounded by their tenants, probably at Verulamium. The effective ruler of Roman Gaul, Aetius, had sent him, and he led the Britons in a successful campaign against the Picts and the Saxons, partly by teaching them to shout 'Alleluia', which is said to have sent the enemy fleeing in dismay. However, over the next few centuries the Anglo-Saxon invaders would destroy most of Roman Britain, particularly its most prosperous areas in the south and east. According to genetic evidence, in some areas up to 90 per cent of native males were either expelled or killed. This, though, was not – like the Roman invasion – a systematic attack by a disciplined army; rather it was a series of raids by a seemingly endless procession of adventurers. At least at first, many may have been more interested in taking home loot than in taking over land, but in these, the Dark Ages, piecing together a comprehensive story of the disaster that befell Roman Britain is impossible. It seems clear, however, that one event of great importance took place in 449. 'Hengest and Horsa,' says the Anglo-Saxon Chronicle, 'invited by Vortigern, King of the Britons, came to Britain at a place which is called Ypwinesfleot' (probably Ebbsfleet in Kent).

Vortigern had brought in the Saxon brothers Hengest and Horsa to try to combat the menace from another quarter, and the Chronicle records: 'The King ordered them to fight against the Picts, and so they did and had victory wherever they came.' Vortigern got them to go back across the Channel and recruit more men, but they also told recruits 'of the worthlessness of the Britons and of the excellence of the land'. Saxons and also Jutes, Angles and possibly other tribes like the Frisians answered the call. There is a story that Vortigern fell madly in love with Hengest's daughter and, in return for her hand, granted Kent to the Saxons, and certainly the Chronicle records that he gave them land in 'the south-east'. What also seems to have happened, though, is that once they had dealt with the menace of the Picts, the Britons got fed up with paying their German mercenaries, and the hired soldiers took up arms against their employers. In 455, the Chronicle records that they fought against and killed Vortigern at Aylesford in Kent. Horsa was also killed, but Hengest 'succeeded to the kingdom.' Two years later, Hengest and his son Aesc fought the Britons at Crayford and 'there slew four thousand men; and the Britons then forsook Kent and fled to London in great terror.' This is the last reference in the Chronicle to London as a Roman city.

At least in the early stages of their invasion, the Anglo-Saxons seem to have been more interested in destroying Roman towns than settling in them, and places like Verulamium, Silchester and Wroxeter were abandoned. It looks as though Roman London met a similar fate for a time, though the incomers did build a thriving trading settlement to the west of it. Roman villas too were destroyed; their mosaic pavements covered with rubbish from collapsed roofs or the debris of squatters' camp fires. Most Roman farms seem to have gone completely out of use, and land that had been cultivated degenerated into wilderness.

The Britons sent an appeal for help to Aetius in Gaul, lamenting that 'the barbarians drive us to the sea and the sea drives us back to the barbarians,' but with the Romans now enmeshed in a desperate struggle with the Huns, no help was forthcoming, and the Britons had to go on defending themselves as best they could. At a battle in 465, Hengest and Aesc slew twelve Welsh nobles. In 473, the Welsh fled from them 'like fire' and the invaders 'captured innumerable spoils'. In 491, the Saxon Aelle and his son Cissa besieged Pevensey, which was then perhaps the last Roman stronghold on the south-east coast, 'and slew all the inhabitants; there was not even one Briton left there,' and so it went on. The Saxons often used their ships to sail up the great rivers and cut deep into British territory. Writing just before the middle of the next century, the monk Gildas lamented in his tract *The Ruin of Britain*: 'Every colony is levelled to the ground by the stroke of the battering ram. The inhabitants are slaughtered along with the guardians of the churches. . . . How horrible to behold in the midst of the streets the tops of towers torn from their lofty hinges, the stones of high walls, holy altars, mutilated corpses, all covered with lurid clots of coagulated blood . . . some flee to the hills, only to be captured and slain in heaps; some, constrained by famine, come in and surrender themselves to be slaves for ever to the enemy.' The cities were reduced to 'dismal and deserted ruins', and agriculture and trade collapsed.

The Britons seem to have secured some respite around 500, when they won a great victory at Mons Badonicus, perhaps Baydon in Wiltshire. Some even believe that the legendary King Arthur may have led their army. It appears to have halted the torment for perhaps forty years, and there is even some evidence of Germanic tribes migrating back to the continent, but then the attacks resumed. By 571 we read that Cuthwulf defeated the Britons and took the villages of Limbury, Aylesbury and Eynsham, and six years later, that Cuthwin and Ceawlin 'slew three kings' at Dyrham in Gloucestershire, and took Gloucester, Cirencester and Bath.

In the north, too, the Anglo-Saxons were taking over. They may have settled in East Yorkshire, perhaps given land in return for military service, as early as the fourth century, and by the late sixth century, there were well developed kingdoms like Bernicia between the Tees and the Scottish Lowlands, ruled by Aethelfrith, who, according to the Venerable Bede, 'had laid waste the nation of the Britons . . . for no one before him had rendered more of their lands either habitable for the English by the extermination of the natives or tributary by their conquest'. At Chester, between 613 and 616, Aethelfrith slaughtered a host of monks who had come from the monastery of Bangor Iscoed to pray for a British victory, and then proceeded to defeat the Britons too. By this time, most of Roman Britain had fallen to the ruthless invaders, apart from Devon and Cornwall, Wales and parts of the Pennines and north-west, and the foe seemed as fearsome as ever. The Saxons went on to take control of Devon in the early eighth century, though the Welsh were so formidable that the English kingdom of Mercia had to build Offa's Dyke to protect its frontier, and may even have had to abandon some territory. By now, however, a new and even more ruthless invader was ravaging Britain.

The Vikings came from Scandinavia, braving the hazards of the ocean in ships 70ft long. In 787, three vessels from Norway landed at Portland. The King's Reeve of Dorchester 'rode thither and tried to compel them to go to the royal manor, for he did not know what they were, and they slew him'. They then mounted an attack on Wessex. Monasteries were favourite targets. The raiders would steal treasure and massacre or enslave the monks. In 793, they plundered Lindisfarne and slaughtered the monks, who had the reputation of creating the finest books in Europe, and the following year they sacked Jarrow, where the Venerable Bede had written his great *Ecclesiastical History of the English Nation*.

Many of these early raiders passed around the north coast of Scotland to Ireland. They plundered Bangor and Downpatrick, and Iona was raided so often, the whole community moved to Meath, and built a new monastery. One monk noted in the margin of his manuscript:

> Fierce and wild is the wind tonight,
> It tosses the tresses of the sea to white;
> On such a night I take my ease;
> Fierce Northmen only course the quiet seas.

Unfortunately for those who lived in Britain, the seas were often quiet enough. One chronicler wrote that everyone 'suffered in common, both men and women, laity and clergy, old and young, noble and ignoble, of hardship and of injury, and of oppression, in every house, from these valiant, wrathful, foreign, purely pagan people'. The first raids were on coastal areas, but before long the Vikings moved inland along rivers. If they found the way barred by rapids or falls, they would pick up their ships and carry them. Soon they were setting up bases on Lough Neagh, from where they could plunder Ulster's estates and churches. Armagh suffered particularly badly. The Annals of Ulster records: '832: The first plundering of Armagh by the heathens three times in one month.' Then, in 840, 'Armagh was burned with its oratories and stone church.' Twelve years later, the city was laid waste again.

In England, the Norwegians were followed by the Danes, who mounted their first raid in 835, attacking the Isle of Sheppey. Over the next thirty years, they came at least a dozen times. Kent suffered most, but in 841, the Danes also devastated Lindsey and East Anglia. In 842, they sacked Southampton, and in 855 they devastated the country around the Wrekin. By the 860s, they had developed a systematic approach to pillaging. Ivar the Boneless and his brother Halfdan appeared with a great army. They would seize an area of land that was easy to defend, often close to a river so they could bring in reinforcements easily, and use it as a base to ravage the countryside around until the local people paid them to go away. Then they would move to another area and start the whole process again. Sometimes they stole horses and moved as a mounted force. When the Vikings attacked York in 866, there was 'an immense slaughter of the people there.' The city bought peace, as did Nottingham. Scotland suffered too. In the 860s Danes came from Ireland to ravage the Picts' territories and sack Dumbarton.

In 871, Alfred the Great was twice defeated in battle by the Danes and his kingdom of Wessex had to buy peace. Two years later, Halfdan raided as far north as Strathclyde, but by now his men had plundered Britain so pitilessly that pickings were growing slim, and the raiders became more interested in establishing settlements. In 876, they appropriated half the kingdom of Mercia in the Midlands, and Halfdan planted his men in Yorkshire. By 878, Alfred was close to losing his kingdom, and had been driven to seek refuge on the then remote and inaccessible Isle of Athelney in Somerset, where he is supposed to have allowed the cakes to burn. Gradually, though, he built up an army formidable enough to defeat the Danes and bring them to make a peace that gave them the land in England to the north of Watling Street, while Alfred ruled the rest. This settlement, however, did not prevent new Viking raiders appearing from across the sea. In 892, they came in 250 ships to the mouth of the River Lympne and dug in at Appledore, raiding into Hampshire and Berkshire. Alfred's son, Edward, intercepted them, but could not stop them joining the Danes in the north. Together they mounted a whole series of expeditions, attacking Chester and wide stretches of Wales. Eventually, Alfred and Edward established their power over the Danes in virtually the whole of England south of the Humber, but even that did not end Britain's ordeal. Fresh waves of fierce Scandinavians were soon mounting new raids. Norsemen from Ireland attacked the north-west coast, and in 919 a Viking named Raegnald stormed York and made himself its king, while his cousin Sihtric destroyed Davenport in Cheshire. In 939, Olaf Guthfrithson, the King of Dublin, launched a great raid on the Midlands, laying waste Tamworth and the surrounding country. Then in 941, he sacked the church of Tyninghame near Dunbar in East Lothian. The reaction too was often brutal. When King Dunmail of Strathclyde supported the Vikings, Edward ravaged his territory and had two of his sons blinded.

In 978, Aethelred the Unready became king at the age of 12, and the Vikings were quick to take advantage. They mounted attacks from Cornwall to Thanet as well as hitting Cheshire, at first coming in small groups and departing before any army stronger than the local countryside levies could be brought against them. They returned in 991, under the leadership of Olaf Tryggvason, later King of Norway, and Aethelred paid them off with 22,000 pounds of gold and silver. This became the prototype for the Danegeld, but as Kipling observed, once you have paid the Danegeld, you never get rid of the Dane, and in 994 Olaf was back, in alliance with Svein, son of the King of

Denmark. This time, after an attack on London, the price of peace was 16,000 pounds. Just three years later, another Scandinavian army appeared, prepared to spend years in systematic plundering of coastal Britain. In its first season of operations, the Vikings harried Cornwall, Devon, Somerset and south Wales. Over the following year, they also ravaged Dorset and Kent: 'they burned and slew everything they met . . . carrying off an indescribable amount of plunder with them.' Eventually, in 1002, Aethelred paid this army off with another 24,000 pounds. He then ordered a massacre of the Danes, and the victims included Svein's sister. Her brother retaliated, in the following years raiding through Hampshire, Berkshire and Wiltshire, and sacking Norwich, before pocketing another 36,000 pounds and sailing off.

In 1009, an even more formidable Danish army appeared. They burned down Oxford, and attacked Ipswich. The Anglo-Saxon Chronicle records that they also overran fourteen counties. After three years of killing and plundering, they were paid 48,000 pounds to leave, but they also demanded a separate ransom for Archbishop Aelfleah of Canterbury, whom they had captured. The Archbishop bravely ordered that no money should be paid for him, and the invaders murdered him. Perhaps realising that England had been bled too dry to offer much more in the way of satisfactory plunder, Svein now seems to have decided to seize the throne, but he died in 1014 before he could achieve his ambition. His son Cnut, though, returned with a great army and ravaged Wessex, Warwickshire, Staffordshire and Shropshire, before pursuing a journey of destruction along the Great North Road. By 1016, he was the undisputed master of England. The privations brought by the Vikings were accompanied by another disaster for England's peasants – the loss of their freedom. Impoverished by the devastation and the constant taxes raised to pay off the invader, many decided to put themselves under the protection of a lord, for whom they would have to labour, but who might at least provide food in hard times.

Fifty years after Cnut became king, England was conquered again. In September 1066, Duke William of Normandy landed at Pevensey while King Harold was still in the north of England, having beaten off yet another Viking attack. Duke William defeated Harold at Hastings and then, to encourage the rest of the country to submit, embarked on a circuit of destruction. The people of Romney were subjected to maimings and executions because they had had the temerity to attack some of William's soldiers who landed there by mistake. William told his followers to spare any town that surrendered without a fight, but he had recruited his followers by promising them England as spoil, so even though they had submitted, Dover, Canterbury and Winchester were sacked anyway.

Now the Conqueror felt ready to mount an attack on London, but he ran into resistance. So he burned Southwark over the river, then looped away from the capital, ravaging Surrey, Hampshire and Berkshire, crossing the Thames at Wallingford then heading back towards London again, destroying as he went. It had the desired effect. The English nobles met him at Berkhamsted to beg him to accept the crown. His hold was not completely secure, though, and in the autumn of 1069, a descendant of Cnut, Svein Estrithsson, King of Denmark, arrived in the Humber. Yorkshiremen rose to support him, and revolts also broke out in Dorset, Somerset, Staffordshire and south Cheshire. William easily quelled the rising in the west, but then he turned north. When he reached Nottingham, he learned the rebels had occupied York. He advanced on the city, devastating the countryside as he went, leaving no house standing and sparing no man his horsemen could find. Just before Christmas, he reached York and put it to the torch. Then, in its smouldering ruins, he celebrated Christ's birth. William bribed the Danes to go home, then split his men into small bands to continue the destruction, some going as far as Derby and Chester. To escape, desperate Englishmen fled into slavery in Scotland. The damage caused by the so-called Harrying of the North was still apparent when the Domesday Book was compiled seventeen years later, with scores of villages left uninhabited, and even some of William's admirers were shocked at his ruthlessness. A Norman monk described it as 'wholesale massacre', and complained that the Conqueror had 'levelled both the bad and the good in one common ruin'. A writer from the north recalled putrefying corpses left by the highway, leading to pestilence, while a chronicler at Evesham wrote of desperate, destitute refugees pouring into the town.

In view of the turmoil that Britain had seen to that point, perhaps the most surprising thing is that there now followed centuries during which most of it would be free from foreign invasion. True, there were occasional raids. The Vikings mounted one in 1151 on Whitby, and the French burned Winchelsea in 1449 and Fowey in 1457, while the Dutch attacked villages in Essex in 1667, but for the next 800 years the danger from hostile action to the people living in Britain came mainly from other Britons.

# CHAPTER TWO

# REBELLION AND RIOT

At the age of 12, King Henry I's daughter, Matilda, became an empress. That was in 1114 when she married the Holy Roman Emperor, but just over a decade later he died, and Matilda had to settle for a mere count as her second husband. Her father had managed to produce twenty illegitimate children, a record for any king of England, but only one legitimate son, who was drowned. So as far as children born in wedlock were concerned, that left just Matilda, and Henry was faced with the rather unpromising task of getting the turbulent and warlike barons of England to accept a woman as their ruler.

The King did his best, but within three weeks of his death in 1135, with Matilda away in France, his nephew, Stephen of Blois, had got himself crowned king at Westminster Abbey. Stephen was said to be the handsomest man in Europe, while Matilda was very beautiful, but their struggle for the throne would turn England into a very ugly place indeed. The Anglo-Saxon Chronicle did not have the heart to record 'all the atrocities nor all the cruelties which they wrought upon the unhappy people of this country', but noted that it 'was said openly that Christ and his saints were asleep'.

Trouble began in 1138 when Geoffrey Talbot took up arms against Stephen and set fire to Hereford. The following year, at a big meeting of the nobility in Oxford, a dispute arose between the Bishop of Salisbury and the Earl of Richmond over the quality of their accommodation. The argument escalated into an armed fight between the two retinues, in which a number of men were killed, and culminated in one of the Bishop's kinsmen devastating the country around Devizes. Further trouble came at Bristol, where Stephen's enemies laid waste to the hinterland so that he would not be able to feed his army if he decided to mount operations against them. At this point, in sailed Matilda. Her half-brother Robert of Gloucester was now also in revolt against Stephen, and attacking Worcester. His soldiers burned down houses and took away valuables, livestock and captives to be sold for ransom. The attackers then departed 'maddened and drunken'. Meanwhile, Stephen devastated the country around Dunster and Bristol 'leaving nothing at all, as far as it lay in his power, that could serve his enemies for food or any purpose'. The conflict was beginning to earn the name with which it has gone down in history – 'the Anarchy'.

The nobility threw up castles to establish local power bases. Said the Anglo-Saxon Chronicle: 'They sorely burdened the unhappy people of the country-side with forced labour on the castles; and when the castles were built, they filled them with devils and wicked men. By day and night they seized those whom they believed to have any wealth whether they were men or women; and in order to get their gold and silver, they put them into prison and tortured them with unspeakable tortures.' Among those of which the Chronicle does speak are that they put men into boxes full of sharp stones and crushed them until every bone in their bodies was broken, or that they tied 'knotted cords round their heads and twisted them till they entered the brain'. The warring nobles demanded protection money from villages, and if people did not pay, 'they plundered and burned all the villages, so that you could easily go a day's journey without ever finding a village inhabited or a field cultivated'. Even those who escaped from the fighting were often caught by the famine that came in its wake. William of Malmesbury wrote: 'The knights from the castles carried off both herds and flocks . . . pillaging the dwellings of the wretched countrymen to the very straw.' In many places, people moved out of their homes and built hovels close to churches so they could flee into them when trouble loomed, but this was not always a good solution. Neither side worried about setting fire to holy places, and those seeking safety inside were often killed as the buildings collapsed on them.

As the fighting went on, Matilda's supporters sacked Nottingham and 'the whole city was destroyed by the flames'. After winning a victory at Lincoln, the rebels began to cut down the citizenry. Some tried to escape across the River Witham, and 500 drowned in the attempt. Now Matilda herself began a progress through Kent, burning and ravaging the countryside as she went until it became 'a home only for the hedgehog'. In turn, Stephen's brother put Winchester to the torch, because it had been supporting Matilda. Among the buildings destroyed was the abbey, where a great jewel-encrusted cross given by King Cnut melted in the flames. The melancholy catalogue of disasters continued, with Wareham, Oxford, Cambridge and Bedford sacked by one side or the other. It was only after fifteen years of such horrors that a deal was finally struck. Stephen would remain king for the rest of his life (in fact, he died just a year later), but would be succeeded by Matilda's son, Henry. It had been a dreadful time. 'Every man who could robbed his neighbour,' lamented the Chronicle. 'Never did a country endure greater misery.' With farmland neglected, food prices rocketed, and many were reduced to begging, even 'some who had been great men', while thousands starved to death. Henry of Huntingdon put it in verse:

> Gaunt famine, following, wastes away
> Whom murder spares, with slow decay.

By 1381, the Hundred Years' War between England and France had been raging for more than forty years, and paying for it had become a major problem. Four years earlier, the government had imposed a poll tax of one groat (a bit less than 2p) on everyone over the age of 14, but the conflict continued to eat up money. So in 1380 the Chancellor, Simon Sudbury, who was also Archbishop of Canterbury, came up with a new poll tax, designed to raise £100,000. As before, and as with Mrs Thatcher's poll tax, a duke would pay the same rate as a dustman (though there was a vague suggestion that the rich should help the poor), but now it would be three groats (5p) for everyone over 15, which represented about a week's wages for a working man.

There was widespread evasion, with many families going into hiding. Indeed, judging by comparisons with 1377, a third of the adult population had disappeared, and instead of the expected £100,000, the tax brought in only £22,000. The government believed the collectors were falling down on the job and recruited new men, instructed to take a tougher line, like threatening non-payers with imprisonment. On 30 May 1381, one named Thomas Brampton rode into Brentwood with his clerks and a small armed escort. He summoned the people of the villages of Fobbing, Corringham and Stanford-le-Hope to appear before him. A hundred turned up, and stoned him out of town. Next the government tried sending a senior judge, Sir Robert Belknap. The people gave him a rough reception, too, and made him swear on the Bible that he would never again hold such sessions. Sir Robert quietly went home.

We do not know whether there was a prearranged plan or a spontaneous, simultaneous upsurge of feeling in many different places, but all over Essex and Kent, people began to leave their villages and assemble with whatever weapons they could find. It was the beginning of the Peasants' Revolt, though many of those who joined it were artisans or even lesser gentry and knights; they were often people on the up who wanted to be freed from archaic feudal practices that might restrict their ability to make money. They attacked landlords' homes, and monasteries and abbeys where the poll tax records were kept. They also beheaded a few clerks and lawyers. At Dartford, the Essex and Kent rebels got together and on 6 June they stormed Rochester Castle, freeing a number of people imprisoned for failing to pay the poll tax, together with a renegade priest named John Ball, who had a track record of denouncing the rich for exploiting the poor. In the words of one contemporary chronicler: 'He tried to prove . . . that from the beginning all men were created equal by nature and that servitude had been introduced by the unjust and evil oppression of men against the will of God.'

They proclaimed their loyalty to the 14-year-old King Richard II, but said they wanted to remove the 'evil counsellors' around him, and demanded freedom for serfs and villeins. They also elected a man named Wat Tyler as their leader. Little is known about him except that he was a tiler by trade and had served in the French wars. Then they moved on to Canterbury, where people greeted them with cheers. Tyler went into the cathedral while the monks were saying mass. He climbed into the pulpit and told them to find a new archbishop because the Commons had condemned Simon Sudbury. The rebels then ransacked the archbishop's palace and made a bonfire of records and accounts in the courtyard. They also executed three people they considered to be 'traitors'.

Next stop was London. It was said that by 12 June tens of thousands had assembled at Blackheath, 4 miles south-east of the capital. It may have been while they were here that John Ball delivered his famous sermon, posing the rhyming question:

When Adam delved and Eve span
Who was then the gentleman?

Meanwhile, the Essex men had settled down at Mile End to the north of the Thames. The rebels now embarked on a trail of destruction, burning down prisons and freeing the inmates. They also destroyed the Archbishop of Canterbury's Lambeth Palace, and the manor of the Treasurer Robert Hales ('Hobbe the Robber'), as well as highly profitable brothels, in which the Mayor of London, William Walworth, had invested heavily. Walworth now ordered the city gates to be barred and the drawbridge on London Bridge to be raised, to prevent the Kent rebels from entering the city, but the authorities were in a rather precarious position. The King's army was on the high seas on the way to Portugal and John of Gaunt, Richard's uncle, often seen as the real power in the land, was away in Scotland. The rebels had the effrontery to ask for a meeting with the King at Rotherhithe, and Richard, in a response that must have seemed extraordinary to most of his courtiers, obeyed this summons from the hoi polloi. He set off in the royal barge with Sudbury and Hales, but when they saw the multitude assembled by the Thames, the courtiers became alarmed. Richard was apparently willing to go ashore, but he was persuaded to turn back after a rather unsatisfactory attempt to hold a conversation across the water.

Many of the rebels were now growing anxious. There was work to be done in the fields if they were not to starve in the winter, but just as they were thinking of going home, suddenly, the drawbridge was lowered and the way into the city was open. It is not clear how this happened, though it may be that some of those inside the city who were opposed to the poll tax took a hand. The Essex men were also let in. Rebel leaders forbade looting under pain of death, and made their first priorities the destruction of legal records at Lincoln's Inn and the Temple, and the freeing of prisoners as they burned down the Fleet and Newgate prisons. They also set fire to the Hospital of the Knights of St John at Clerkenwell, where Hales was Prior. It is said to have burned for a week. Richard watched London in flames from the Tower and asked his courtiers what he should do, but, according to one chronicler: 'none of them knew, or was willing to advise him.'

John of Gaunt was a particular hate figure, and the biggest group of rebels headed for his Savoy Palace, one of the grandest in Europe, on the present-day site of the Savoy Hotel. They blew it up with gunpowder, threw furnishings, clothes, jewels and plate into the Thames, and ground precious stones into dust. They killed some of the Duke's servants, but when the rebels caught one of their number hiding some silver under his clothes they flung him into the flames as the palace burned. Some, however, clearly thought that the 'no looting' rule did not apply to the Duke's wine, and a number were killed when they had rather too much, and were trapped in the cellars beneath the burning building. The authorities were now so desperate that they decided Richard should have another go at talking to his unruly subjects, and on 14 June 1381, he set out for Mile End with a great retinue. The rebels, now perhaps swelled with recruits from East Anglia, Hertfordshire and Cambridgeshire, were said to have numbered up to 100,000. As the King approached, the crowd fell to its knees, and shouted: 'Welcome King Richard: we wish no other king but you!'

The rebels demanded that every man should be freed from bondage, and that there should be a general amnesty. Richard agreed to everything and said he would get his clerks to draw up charters making it law. The atmosphere was celebratory and soon rebels were fraternising with soldiers at the Tower of London. Before setting out, Richard had advised Sudbury to attempt to escape. It seems he tried, but was recognised by a woman and withdrew in confusion. Although there were supposed to be more than 1,000 armed men at the Tower, Tyler and his men were able to enter. They found Sudbury and Hales at prayer, and dragged them off for execution. The rebels impaled their heads on London Bridge, Sudbury's with his archbishop's cap nailed to his skull, while along Cheapside, trestle tables were set up for clerks to write the promised charters. Their objectives apparently achieved, some of the rebels began to melt away, but it was not just London that was in turmoil. Places around it like Clapham, Croydon, Harrow and Twickenham were also plundered and burned, and all over the country, similar risings were happening. At St Albans, rebels broke down the gates of the abbot's park, emptied his fishpond, killed his game, sacked the houses of his officials, and burned the charters by which he exercised his manorial rights. At Bury St Edmunds, they stormed the abbey and forced the monks to renounce any claims on the town. They also ransacked the house of a senior judge and summarily executed him together with a number of other notables. To the east of Norwich, a man named Geoffrey Litster gathered a band of followers on Mousehold Heath, and set himself up as the 'King of the Commons', being waited on by captured knights, while his followers looted the town. There were risings in Suffolk, Winchester, Lincoln, as far west as Bridgwater, and as far north as Scarborough. Meanwhile, in the capital, the rebels, and particularly perhaps the Londoners who supported them, gradually became more disorderly. They executed the warden of the Marshalsea prison, and massacred 160 Flemish weavers, piling up their headless bodies. Now the richer citizens grew alarmed.

Tyler had asked for a further meeting with the King to hear proposals for a new legal system. On Saturday 15 June, Richard and his courtiers set out again, but this time they put on armour beneath their sumptuous robes. The encounter was set for the hour of vespers at Smithfield, then a big open space to the west of the city. Tyler rode out to meet Richard, and is said to have shaken him by the hand and said, 'Brother, be of good cheer', which is not how you were meant to speak to the King. The rebel leader also presented a new list of demands, including one that the wealth of the Church should be shared out among the people of England. The King nodded his assent, but what happened next is not clear. Was there an argument that turned into a fracas? Was it a premeditated plot? Whichever it was, Walworth dragged Tyler from his horse and stabbed him. Then another courtier finished the rebel leader off, while the Mayor dashed off to the city to raise a volunteer force, which he managed to stiffen with some regular soldiers.

In the fading light, the rebels had probably not seen clearly what had happened to Tyler, but after a time they sent up a great cry and prepared to rush their assailants. At this point, the young Richard, showing great courage, as well as coolness that would not be much apparent in the rest of his reign, rode across to the rebels and exclaimed: 'Sirs, will you shoot your king? I am your captain, follow me.' The rebels obeyed, and went with him to an area called St John's Fields. Then he rode off, while Walworth's forces surrounded them. Walworth told the rebels their demands had been met, and made them disperse. They went quietly, and on London Bridge on the journey home, they would have seen Tyler's head in the place where the Archbishop's had been only a few hours earlier. Walworth, who was knighted by the King, promptly launched a reign of terror. A block was set up in Cheapside, and all night long, one suspected rebel after another was executed till the pavements were red with blood. Anyone who sounded like a countryman was in danger.

The government then put together an army, said to be the biggest ever seen in England, to pacify the realm. On 22 June, the King met a deputation from Billericay, who produced the charters bearing his seal which proved they were now free, but with the danger now passed, the King had changed his previously conciliatory tune, telling them: 'You will remain in bondage, not as before, but incomparably harsher. For as long as we live and by God's grace, rule over this realm, we will strive with mind, strength, and wealth to suppress you so that the rigour of your servitude will be an example to posterity.' In the face of this, some of the rebels decided to fight on, and about 500 were killed, while all over England, there were mass executions. In fact, so many were hanged, there was a shortage of gibbets, and sometimes the executioners had to suspend them ten at a time from the same beam. At St Albans, John Ball was among seventeen people despatched. Of course, the authorities did sometimes come across tiresome people who tried to remind them of the King's promises, so Richard simply declared the charters null and void.

In East Anglia, the Bishop of Norwich led the suppression with such relish it is said that he foamed at the mouth like a wild boar as he slashed at the rebels with his heavy sword. Among those he captured was the leader from Norwich, Geoffrey Litster, to whom he gave confession before having him executed. One estimate puts the number killed at 7,000 out of a total population of perhaps 2.5 million, and even some monastic chroniclers were shocked at the authorities' severity. With labour already short and wages consequently forced up due to the depredations of the Black Death [see Chapter 14], landowners may have begun to worry that if the slaughter went on, things would get even worse, so in November, Richard issued a general pardon, excepting only 287 rebels still at large. The one clear achievement of the rebels was that the poll tax was abolished. Richard had shown little mercy to them, and eighteen years later, he was shown little himself, when his cousin Henry (who became Henry IV) deposed and imprisoned him. At Pontefract Castle, Richard was murdered, or perhaps starved himself to death.

Soon after assuming the throne, Henry had to face a rebellion of his own. It all began with a quarrel over some common land which Reginald de Grey, lord of Ruthin in north-east Wales, had appropriated, to the anger of his neighbour, Owain Glyn Dwr. Now Glyn Dwr had fought for the English Crown, and to such effect that in the Scottish war of 1385, he was said to have driven the enemy before him like goats. He had studied at the Inns of Court for seven years, and had a fine mansion with a moat at Sycarth, but de Grey was a friend of the new King, and when Glyn Dwr appealed to Henry, he received an insulting rebuff. Incensed, on 16 September 1400 he raised his standard outside Ruthin, home to many English settlers. From that moment, his followers called him 'Prince of Wales'.

With a force of about 250 he burned Ruthin, leaving only three buildings standing, and stole food, weapons and livestock. Over the next week, he savaged another seven towns from Denbigh to Oswestry, while in Anglesey, Rhys and Gwilym Tudor joined the rebellion, and attracted more support as they burned towns and churches. Welsh labourers working in England and Welsh scholars studying at Oxford downed tools and pens, and headed off to join the revolt. Henry had been distracted by trouble in Scotland and Ireland, but now he took a huge army into Wales and burned and looted without mercy. Glyn Dwr's following was reduced to just seven, and it looked as though the rebellion had been defeated, but in the spring of 1401, the Tudors managed to seize Conway Castle, and it flared up again. Another royal army moved into Wales, but Henry's men could only travel by the main roads, and the Welsh guerrillas constantly mounted attacks on them, then melted away. By now few towns controlled by the English had escaped unscathed, and the great Marcher lord, Edmund Mortimer, decided to raise an army and hunt down the rebel. Instead, Glyn Dwr defeated and captured him at Pilleth in Powys, and when Henry proved reluctant to ransom him (perhaps because the Mortimers had a better claim to the throne), the Welshman made a match between Mortimer and his daughter and turned him into an ally. Now the great castles began to fall to Glyn Dwr. He captured Cardiff, then Aberystwyth and Harlech, where he made his headquarters, and by 1404, he controlled most of Wales. In 1405, with French help, he led an army of 10,000 into England as far as Worcester, but Henry starved him of supplies, and he had to march back again without ever bringing the English to battle.

The Welsh people were persecuted by both lots of combatants, with Glyn Dwr's men living by pillage, holding rich men and sometimes whole districts to ransom, then scorching the earth in retreat, while Henry sent in army after army to burn, loot and confiscate. By 1409, the King had recaptured Aberystwyth and Harlech, seizing Glyn Dwr's wife, daughters and granddaughters, and during the next two years, most of his soldiers accepted offers of pardon and went home. The failure of the English to capture Glyn Dwr, even in his most difficult times, had led them to credit him with occult powers, and to invoke him as a bogeyman to frighten disobedient children. Now, fittingly, he simply vanished. Henry V twice offered him a pardon, but the 'Prince of Wales' never emerged to accept it, and no one knows where or when he died.

In 1450, the Hundred Years' War was still going, but it was finally about to end in ignominy, with the loss of virtually all England's possessions in France. The throne was occupied by the pious, well-meaning, but feeble-minded Henry VI, who founded Eton College and King's College, Cambridge. By 1450, the government was bankrupt, and once again trouble erupted in Kent. A man named Jack Cade emerged as rebel leader, and led up to 45,000 of them, including a number of gentry, to Blackheath, where they camped at the beginning of June. They were well armed, and appeared to have plenty of money. The government sent a delegation to meet the rebels, who handed over 'A Bill of Complaints and Requests of the Commons of Kent' complaining about the King's advisers, corruption and excessive taxation. It also demanded the repeal of the Statute of Labourers, the first attempt in British history to impose a wage freeze. The King's response was to tell the rebels to disperse. When he heard that they had not, he set off on 18 June with an army, but a surprise awaited him at Blackheath. The camp was deserted, the rebels having apparently decided to return to Kent after all. Some of Henry's men set off in pursuit, but they were ambushed and routed near Sevenoaks.

When he heard the news, Henry fled to Kenilworth, ignoring the Lord Mayor's pleas for soldiers to protect London. Cade now led his men back to Blackheath, while a big contingent from Essex also set out for the capital, and trouble stirred in other parts of the country, like Wiltshire, where the Bishop of Salisbury was dragged out of his church and murdered. A hero of Agincourt, Sir John Fastolf, helped organise London's defences, and also sent his servant, John Payne, to Blackheath to find out what exactly the rebels wanted. They decided to behead him, and fetched an axe and block, but he managed to persuade them to let him go back and report their grievances instead. Their complaints about the selfishness and incompetence of the kitchen cabinet surrounding the King would be calculated to appeal to many Londoners.

Payne delivered the message, and also told Fastolf about the size of Cade's force, at which point his master retreated to the Tower. Cade's men promptly took possession of Southwark on 1 July. Uncertain about the loyalty of ordinary Londoners, and afraid of how much destruction might be caused if the rebels forced an entry to the city, the authorities decided that letting them in would be the lesser evil. As his men passed over London Bridge, Cade ordered them to cut the ropes on the drawbridge so that it could not be raised against them. The rebel leader rode in 'like a lordly captain', wearing a captured suit of armour, to the cheers of many of the townsfolk. He assured Londoners that their lives and property would be safe, and warned his followers that any caught looting would be executed, but soon they were ransacking the house of an unpopular merchant. They also beheaded Lord Saye and Sele, the Treasurer of England, then tied his body to a horse's tail, and dragged it across the bridge to Southwark. His son-in-law William Crowmer, Sheriff of Kent, met the same fate, as did about twenty royal servants and a few other unpopular characters.

There were now about 25,000 rebels inside the city, and soon there was looting of rich folk's houses, assault, robbery and rape, so that sympathy for them began to evaporate. On 5 July, after the rebels had retired to their Southwark headquarters for the night, another veteran of Henry V's wars against the French got to work. Captain Matthew Gough took a group of soldiers, killed Cade's sentries, and occupied London Bridge. When the rebels heard, they rushed to the bridge, and a fierce battle ensued, raging back and forth over its entire length. Many tumbled into the river as they grappled with each other, then drowned when their heavy armour dragged them straight to the bottom. The authorities had a new weapon of mass destruction, the cannon, which they fired from the Tower, but it was not sufficiently accurate to make an impact. A few of the bridge's inhabitants had fled, but most stayed behind to try to protect their property. Some were now burned alive as Cade's men set fire to their houses, while others were cut down in the street. After 10 hours of fighting, with about 200 people dead, including Gough himself, both sides agreed a ceasefire. An archbishop, a cardinal and a bishop brought pardons for Cade and his men, but they carried no royal seal. The leader was suspicious, but eventually signed an order for his men to disband.

Most left for home, often laden with loot, but Cade and a few others remained in Southwark, where they heard that the authorities were now saying Cade's pardon was invalid, and that the general one applied only to the gentry and landowning classes. This seemed a good moment to leave, but once Cade had gone, the King put a price of 1,000 marks on his head, with a reward of 5 marks for each of his followers taken. In Sussex, the hungry and exhausted rebel leader was cornered by a local squire who bundled him, wounded, into a cart to take him to London, but Cade died on the way. His naked corpse was mutilated and dragged on a hurdle over London Bridge, where his skull was put on show, while his quarters were displayed at Blackheath, Salisbury, Norwich and Gloucester. Twenty-eight of his followers were executed, but in the end, King Henry VI fared even worse than Richard II. He was deposed not once, but twice, and in 1471 he was murdered in the Tower.

By the middle of the next century, one of the most pressing concerns of Middle England was enclosure – the loss to ordinary folk of the right to graze their animals on common land, and the conversion of open fields that were cultivated by many peasants to meadows where only rich men's sheep grazed. It led to the graphic complaint that sheep were eating men. In the summer of 1549, the King of England was 11-year-old Edward VI, but the real power in the land was his uncle, the Duke of Somerset. Somerset seemed unhappy about enclosures, and issued a general pardon to protesters who broke fences and hedges. Perhaps he just wanted to buy off trouble in England while he pursued a war in Scotland, but his attitude did not endear him to the ruling class. The future Lord Privy Seal, Sir William Paget, reproached him for 'your softness, your opinion to be good to the poor'.

Whatever Somerset's motives, the dissent did not die down, and discontent was given an extra twist because a drought had led to the failure of the harvest and rocketing food prices. Country folk began to form leagues against landlords and to organise rent strikes, and rioting spread across seven counties. In Norfolk, at the Wymondham fair of July 1549, speakers began haranguing the crowd on the evils of enclosure, and so incensed them that many went off to pull down fences. One of the first miscreants they targeted was a tanner named Robert Kett. When the mob appeared, he declared, 'Whatsoever lands I have enclosed shall again be made common,' and then set to work demolishing the barriers himself. The next morning, beneath a tree known ever since as 'Kett's oak', the crowd elected him as their leader. Then they set to work clearing enclosed land, as they moved towards Norwich, at the time the third biggest city in England. A series of dignitaries tried to persuade them to disperse, but to no avail. Instead, Kett decided to establish a camp they could defend, and, like the rebels of 1381, settled on Mousehold Heath, a high area of rough ground with scattered coppices and woods that had a commanding view of the city across the river Wensum. On the heath was the Earl of Surrey's new palace, which the rebels now appropriated. New supporters kept joining them until they numbered an estimated 20,000, with their leader warning them 'there is no hope but in venturing boldly,' so the rebels fortified the camp with ditches and stockades, and confiscated food from the rich.

The community set up its own elected council, headed by Kett and his brother William, which sent a 29-point manifesto to the King, demanding an end to enclosures and the restoration of all common land, plus the freeing of all 'bond-men'. Somerset told them it would be considered when Parliament met again in October, but in the meantime, they should break up their camp and disperse. The community responded by strengthening the defences and bringing in cannons. In Norwich, the great merchants were beginning to be alarmed, and one rode hell-for-leather to London to ask for help, but the government was still embroiled in its war with Scotland, and faced unrest in more than a dozen counties from Yorkshire to the West Country. In Devon, people were also angry about church services being conducted in English instead of Latin and were demanding that nobles should hand back former monastic lands to the Church. Soon 10,000 rebels were besieging Exeter. In these straitened circumstances, instead of despatching an army, the best Somerset could do was to send the ceremonial York Herald, who gamely rode into the rebels' camp with a few men and tried to arrest Kett. He failed, but he did manage to persuade some of the rebels to drift away in return for a pardon.

Now the Mayor closed the gates of the city, mounted cannon on the battlements and fired on the camp. The rebel guns replied, but the sides were too far apart for either bombardment to have much effect. Next morning, though, Kett's men attacked and occupied Norwich, and they even managed to repel a royal army that the government had finally scraped together, although at the loss of 400 men. Perhaps surprisingly, the rebels made no attempt to link up with malcontents in other parts of the country, and on Saturday 25 August a rather different royal army appeared outside the city, stiffened with a force of merciless German mercenary cavalry. Its commander, the Earl of Warwick, promised the rebels a pardon if they handed over Kett. The offer was refused, and the royal army began bombarding the city. Their artillery beat down the gates, and there then followed many hours of street fighting, but at the end of it, the rebels were driven back to their camp. Warwick filled the market place with gallows, and hanged those he had captured. Kett's men knew the army could now lay siege to their camp and starve them into submission, so although the rebels knew they would be at a grave disadvantage, they decided to seek a pitched battle. As Kett had feared, the Earl's artillery pulverised his forces, and then his cavalry cut them down without mercy. A few made a last stand in a ring of wagons, and the Earl rode up in person to promise on oath that they could go home in peace if they would lay down their arms. They did and, for once, the authorities kept their promise, though rebels they had captured would enjoy little mercy.

More than 5,000 are said to have been killed in the battle, with many more wounded and maimed. Kett escaped the field, but was later captured. Nine of the ringleaders were hanged on an oak tree in their camp, then cut down while still alive, disembowelled and quartered. Another thirty suffered a similar fate outside Magdalen Gate, Norwich, while 300 more were left hanging around the walls until their bodies decayed. Kett was dragged through the streets on a hurdle to the castle, then slowly strangled on a rope from the battlements, but as so often happens, those who take the sword, perish by it, and within four years, both Somerset and Warwick would themselves be executed.

A hundred years later, England was in the throes of the most important civil conflict in its history – the Great Rebellion, the English Civil War. It laid the foundation of the parliamentary democracy we hold so dear today, but the conflict was a disaster for thousands of non-combatants who became caught up in it. It is estimated that 85,000 people were killed in military action, and another 100,000 died from disease. At least 150 towns were damaged, with around 11,000 houses destroyed, making perhaps 55,000 people homeless. That would represent little more than one in a hundred of the population, but in the areas where the war raged most fiercely, up to one property in four was damaged. Some villages like Boarstall in Buckinghamshire were completely destroyed, as was Belvoir in Leicestershire, the site of which was incorporated into the park of Belvoir Castle. Up to 200 country houses were also destroyed, with many more damaged.

If a town agreed to surrender, there was usually an agreement that there was to be no plundering, and this was generally respected. On the other hand, if the attackers took the town by force, then they considered they were entitled to sack it. Among the places that suffered worst after being captured were Liverpool and Bolton, known as the 'Geneva of the North' for its staunch Puritanism. Both were despoiled by the Royalists with considerable loss of life in 1643. Liverpool was said to be 'in a great part destroyed and burned,' while in 1651, when Parliamentary forces took Worcester, they plundered ruthlessly, 'all houses being ransacked from top to bottom, the very persons of men and women not excepted.' Newark was strategically important, being close to the point where the Great North Road crosses the Trent. It had to withstand three sieges and did not surrender until 1646, by which time one-sixth of the houses had been destroyed, while of the buildings at Banbury, Joshua Sprigge, a chaplain to the Parliamentary forces, found there was 'scarce the one half standing to gaze on the ruins of the other.' One particularly unfortunate town was Leicester. In May 1645, the Royalists captured and sacked it. Sixteen days later, Parliament's New Model Army arrived, fresh from its victory at Naseby, and called on the garrison to submit. The governor quickly agreed to surrender on terms, but some of the Royalist garrison left their posts to loot the town, and Parliamentary stragglers joined in. Nor did Scotland escape. In 1644, Montrose's Royalist army sacked Aberdeen, and after the Scots changed sides and joined the Royalist cause, on 1 September 1651, Parliament's General Monck pillaged Dundee, massacring 1,000 of its citizens, including 200 women and children.

Occasionally, places were destroyed out of revenge. So the Parliamentarians plundered Blandford Forum because they claimed it had betrayed a party of troops to the Royalists. Sometimes vengeance would be more targeted. When the Royalists took Cirencester in 1643, they set on fire only 'particular men's houses' – those they thought had given support to the enemy – while the following year when the Parliamentarians captured Newcastle upon Tyne, the home of the prominent Royalist and Mayor Sir John Marley was one of the few destroyed. In the chaos of war, there were sometimes misunderstandings. Dorchester agreed terms of surrender with a Royalist force in 1643, and was spared pillage, but soon after, another group of Cavaliers arrived, and plundered the town because of its previous allegiance. Soldiers from both sides would also threaten to burn down a town unless it paid protection money. Droitwich paid £40 to 'save the town'. Sometimes it might be an individual who faced extortion. A citizen of Oxford was confronted by a party of Royalists who threatened to blow up his house. To save it, he handed over plate and rings worth £300. There were also accidents, as in 1644, when a quarrel broke out among Royalist troops occupying Beaminster in Dorset. Someone let off a musket in a house in North Street, setting fire to it. The flames were fanned by a strong wind, and within 2 hours, most of the town was burned to the ground, with the loss of 144 houses, making it the most destructive fire in England in thirty years. When the inhabitants tried to save their possessions by carrying them into the street, soldiers ran off with most of them. Joshua Sprigge visited the town fifteen months later, and described it as 'a place of the pitifullest spectacle that man can behold, hardly a house left not consumed with fire'.

Buildings were also destroyed on occasion because one side wanted to make its position more defensible or to prevent the enemy from using them. So when Parliament's forces advanced on Donnington Castle in Berkshire, the Royalist governor destroyed the nearby village of thirty houses to prevent Parliament quartering there, and Parliament's army destroyed the village of Beachley in Gloucestershire in 1644 because it stood in a strategic position at the confluence of the Wye and the Severn, and the Royalists wanted to fortify it. Among other places that were badly damaged were Exeter, York, Hereford,

Worcester, Carlisle and Gloucester, where the Parliamentary defenders destroyed 240 houses as well as 'many barns, stables, outhouses, gardens, orchards.' At Bridgwater, Royalist defenders and Parliamentary besiegers between them destroyed about 120 houses out of 400. Retreating forces would sometimes scorch the earth to hinder their pursuers, as did the Royalists fleeing from the battles of Langport and Cheriton.

The victorious Parliamentarians authorised charitable collections for some places like Taunton – where much of the eastern part of the town was left in ruins after a fierce attempt by the Cavaliers to take it – and Faringdon in Oxfordshire, where the Royalist garrison destroyed 200 houses, reducing virtually the whole of the town to a small defensive perimeter around the church. The waterman poet, John Taylor, was moved to describe 'a good handsome market town turned into ashes and rubbish'. Land seized from Royalists was allocated to help towns like Liverpool, Lancaster and King's Lynn, but those like Oxford, which had been regarded as Cavalier strongholds, got little sympathy, and often had to wait until after the Restoration for assistance. Reconstruction of public buildings generally took priority over private houses, and while they were waiting for their homes to be rebuilt, the inhabitants of Faringdon had to stay in 'outhouses, barns, and other desolate places.' Individuals, though, were sometimes aided. At Coventry, John Frem's house was one of 100 that were destroyed, and he also lost most of his goods when they were thrown into the street. In view of his 'great age' and 'extraordinary poverty', he was awarded 5 shillings. The victors did not generally believe the Church should enjoy great wealth, so buildings in the cathedral close at Exeter were turned over to 'poor people . . . whose houses were burned down in the several sieges', and the bells of the demolished St Pancras Church at Chichester were sold to help those made homeless.

With the population reduced by perhaps one in twenty-five, there was often little incentive to rebuild in a hurry, so when the diarist John Evelyn visited Colchester in 1656, eight years after it had been besieged, he found it 'a fair town but now wretchedly demolished.' At Scarborough, which had been the scene of two destructive sieges, the population fell from an estimated 2,870 in 1640 to fewer than 1,600 in 1660, and by 1680 it was still only 2,380. In 1680, there were still vacant house plots in Exeter, and some of the suburbs of York and Gloucester were not rebuilt until the eighteenth century; indeed Gloucester had still not regained its pre-war population by 1696. To try to prevent their use in any future conflict, Parliament embarked on a systematic dismantling of castles. Some, like Pontefract and Banbury, were completely destroyed, while others were slighted, deliberately damaged so as to make them indefensible. Corfe in Dorset, which had twice been the object of long sieges, was left a spectacular ruin.

Perhaps the most disastrous riot in British history came in response to a modest relaxation of the laws discriminating against Roman Catholics. Anti-Catholic feeling was exploited by Lord George Gordon, a 29-year-old MP on the make, who was President of the Protestant Association. On Friday 2 June 1780, he roused 50,000 people to march on Parliament with a huge petition against the new law. This was not a rabble; rather they were 'the better sort of tradesmen' – journeymen, apprentices, labourers, small employers. Indeed, a great deal of 'respectable' opinion was against the liberalisation.

It was a very hot day, but Gordon told his supporters to dress in their Sunday best. The procession stretched for 4 miles, and as it reached Westminster, the marchers gave a great yell, and invaded the Parliamentary lobbies. It all seems to have gone to his lordship's head, and he dashed about addressing the Commons one moment, then haranguing the mob the next. His followers terrorised Lords and MPs until they heard that soldiers were on their way, then they dispersed. A body of Horse Guards captured a few of them and took them off to Newgate prison, but actually the government was very short of troops because of the American War of Independence, and that evening the mob gathered again. Londoners began to bar doors and windows, fearing the worst.

Obvious Catholic targets were soon under attack. The mob ransacked the Bavarian embassy, and burned the Sardinian embassy to the ground. Then they gutted a Catholic chapel and burned some priests' houses. The government believed, wrongly, that they could not open fire on the mob until the Riot Act had been read, and this required a city magistrate. Oddly, whenever the troops needed one, they seemed in short supply. Perhaps it was a reluctance to interfere with the city's libertarian tradition, or sympathy with the rioters' views, or simply a wish not to get one's house burned down. Certainly, the attitude of the city authorities was equivocal; one alderman supported Gordon in the Commons, and the Court of Common Council, the city's governing body, opposed the new law. So the rioters were left free to roam the streets with blue 'No Popery' cockades in their hats, and soon the violence spread beyond Catholic buildings. Also in the firing line were any magistrates who had dared to imprison rioters, and any politicians who had supported pro-Catholic legislation. The mob also attacked Bow Street police office and burned down Newgate prison, freeing more than 300 inmates, some of whom had been awaiting imminent execution. Sometimes mistakes were made, as when French Protestants, who had fled to Britain to escape persecution by Catholics, found themselves targeted.

By now, Gordon had completely lost control, and the rioters were choosing more and more alarming targets. They attacked the home of the Lord Chief Justice, and burned his furniture, his paintings and his law library. The Fleet and King's Bench prisons were opened, freeing about 1,600 debtors. Distilleries, sometimes owned by Roman Catholics, were set on fire, often taking houses with them. The rioters attacked the Bank of England, and there were threats to the Mint, the Royal Arsenal, and even royal palaces. At one time, thirty-six separate fires were raging. By Tuesday, King George III had decided that the mob must be suppressed with or without the city's approval. Fortunately for the King, London's authorities were also beginning to wonder whether their earlier rather relaxed attitude had been mistaken, and called out the militia and the Honourable Artillery Company, which freed the government's regular soldiers for more aggressive action. Even the great radical John Wilkes took up arms against the mob. On Thursday, the troops were finally ordered to fire on the crowd, and by that night, 285 rioters lay dead or dying, but order was not finally restored until the following Monday, by which time, according to some estimates, more property had been destroyed in London than in Paris during the week following the storming of the Bastille.

Gordon was arrested, but was cleared of high treason. Many of his followers paid a heavier price; twenty-five were hanged in addition to those shot down in the streets. Estimates of the number killed or injured during the ten days of rioting range up to 850. His lordship lived another thirteen years, and found time to be converted to Judaism, and to libel Marie Antoinette, an offence for which he was sent to the rebuilt Newgate prison, where he died.

Britain's worst disturbances since the Gordon Riots also had their roots in religious hatred. In June 1886, a fierce parliamentary debate resulted in defeat for a bill that would have given Ireland home rule. In Protestant Northern Ireland, people lit bonfires while Orange bands struck up Loyalist tunes. In Belfast's Shankill district, they also attacked pubs owned by Roman Catholics. Police with fixed bayonets tried to disperse them, but were met with a hail of stones and bottles, and it was only when buckshot was fired over their heads that order was restored. The next day, 2,000 rioters, helped by women carrying stones in their aprons, cornered seventy policemen in a small barracks. In desperation, the police opened fire, killing seven people. Soldiers from the Highland Light Infantry, who came to their rescue, found several children in the street unconscious from the effects of drinking looted alcohol. Sectarian mobs were out again the following month, and on 14 July, police killed two rioters, while a soldier was shot dead in the Shankill, and the head constable was mortally wounded. On 31 July, Catholics stoned children returning home from a Sunday school outing, and Protestants attacked Catholic children in retaliation. As the trouble escalated, thirteen people died in a weekend. The following Saturday, police trapped by rioters in Dover Street had to kill three people to escape, and twelve more died elsewhere in the city. It is estimated that fifty people were killed before the trouble died down in mid-September.

Three decades later, the argument over home rule was still raging, and there was serious sectarian trouble in 1920, when Unionists lost control of Londonderry Corporation for the first time. In April, fights broke out between Protestants and Catholics, then in May police had a 4-hour gun battle with the IRA, in which the head of the local police special branch was shot dead. Protestants then began mounting road blocks and manhandling Catholics. One who had returned from the First World War gassed and wounded was killed. In June, Protestants began setting Catholic homes on fire, and shooting down into Catholic districts from the city walls, killing a number of people and wounding a baby. The Catholics then began burning Protestants out of the predominantly Catholic Bogside, killing two. Eventually, the army intervened, imposing a curfew and opening fire on the Bogside, at a cost of six Catholic lives. Shootings, assassinations and reprisals continued until the death toll reached forty.

On 21 July the funeral was held for a senior police officer from Banbridge in County Down, who had been shot dead in Cork. After the funeral, Protestants in Banbridge and Dromore attacked Catholic homes and businesses, driving out virtually the whole population, while in Belfast, Protestants in the shipyards decided to drive out 'disloyal' workers. They tore open vests and shirts to look for Catholic emblems, then beat those who wore them or pelted them with rivets. That evening, Catholics stoned trams carrying Protestant workers home, and for three days and nights there was fierce inter-communal fighting. Troops fired on both sides, and by the time order was restored, there were thirteen dead. In addition, an estimated 11,000 people had been driven out of their jobs.

In August, a police inspector was shot dead in Lisburn, and Protestants tried to drive out Catholic homes and businesses. By the end of the trouble, one former soldier said Lisburn was like 'a bombarded town in France.' In Belfast, Protestants again tried to drive out Catholics, who they began increasingly to see as IRA supporters. In just one week, there were 180 major fires. There were hopes of a reduction in tension when the Irish Free State was set up in the South in June 1921, but if anything, it seemed to increase tension. In August, three days of fighting in Belfast left twenty dead. The following month, troops opened fire on Loyalist rioters and killed two, while Catholics and Protestants threw bombs at each other, killing another three people. In November, 27 were killed in a week, and the toll for the whole year was 109.

The next year, the conflict grew even more brutal. On 11 February, the IRA killed four Ulster special policemen as their train passed through the Free State on its way from Newtownards to Enniskillen. Belfast Protestants responded by attacking Catholic districts, Catholics bombed trams going to the shipyards, and Protestants killed six Catholic children in a bomb attack. Altogether, forty-four people died that month. Then in the early hours of 24 March, uniformed men, believed to be police officers, broke into the house of a Catholic publican and shot the family dead. Only the youngest child, who crept under a table, escaped. A week later, a bomb thrown into a Protestant's house killed two of his sons and severely injured him and his two daughters, while the attackers also fired shots at his wife, who was nursing a baby. Sixty-one people died in March.

In April, the fatal shooting of a police constable was followed within an hour by an attack by uniformed officers on Catholic homes, in which they beat one man to death with a sledgehammer, shot dead three others and mortally wounded a child. More Catholic homes were burned, and hundreds of refugees began arriving in Dublin, convincing Michael Collins in the Free State that an anti-Catholic pogrom was under way. He began arming the IRA in the North, as they launched a systematic campaign of arson, starting forty-one serious fires in Belfast in just over two weeks. They also burned down great houses like Shane's Castle by the shores of Lough Neagh, and Crebilly Castle near Ballymena, and set fire to railway stations and flax mills. This fomented another cycle of sectarian killings and burnings.

Then, in May, a Protestant MP was shot dead, and the northern government imposed a curfew and introduced internment, arresting 200 Catholics. It did not stop the violence. During the month, forty-four Catholics and twenty-two Protestants were killed. What did in the end make the North more peaceful was the outbreak of the Irish Civil War in the South, which diverted the IRA's energies into fighting the Irish government, but by the time something approaching peace was restored in 1923, 557 people had been killed in Northern Ireland – 303 Catholics, 172 Protestants and 82 members of the security forces. In addition, Catholic relief organisations estimated that up to 23,000 Catholics had been forced from their homes, and 500 Catholic businesses had been destroyed.

# CHAPTER THREE

# REPRESSION AND MASSACRE

When Richard the Lionheart was crowned King of England on 3 September 1189, religious passions were running high, with preparations under way for the Third Crusade, in which Richard would be a leading figure in the struggle to free the Holy Land from the grip of the infidel. London's Jews had not been invited to his coronation, but some turned up anyway with presents, hoping 'to find favour equal to the multitude of their gifts', according to the contemporary chronicler, William of Newburgh. In particular, they probably wanted a renewal of the charters of protection that some of Richard's predecessors had granted them. The Jews were useful because they could lend money, a trade Christians tended not to pursue as they were effectively banned from charging interest, and they were also regarded as the King's property, to be taxed at will. Revenue often took priority over protection, so when the Jews of Oxford were slow in paying up in response to a particularly extortionate demand from King Stephen during the Anarchy (see Chapter 2), he ordered all their houses to be burned down.

Richard's coronation began badly, when a bat entered Westminster Hall and flew round the throne in broad daylight. This was thought to be an evil omen. Meanwhile, some of the Jews 'mixed among the crowd' and tried to gatecrash the ceremony. According to William of Newburgh's graphic account, an angry Christian then 'struck a Jew with his palm and so drove him away from the entrance to the door . . . and many being excited by this sample drove away the Jews with insults.' The crowd's mood quickly turned uglier, and 'being more savagely enraged they brought sticks and stones. Then the Jews began to flee, some during their flight being beaten unto death or some of them even being crushed, perished.'

Among the unfortunate group were 'two noble Jews of York', Joce and Benedict. Joce escaped 'with difficulty', but Benedict 'was caught as he fled but tardily from the strokes laid upon him: in order to escape death, he was compelled to confess Christ and being led to the Church was baptised on the spot.' By then, though, he had been mortally wounded. Next, a 'rumour spread with incredible rapidity through all London, namely that the King had ordered all the Jews to be exterminated.' The mob by now was 'all armed', and the Jews fled to their houses, where they were besieged. 'Owing to their strong build', the mob could not break them down, so they set fire to the thatched roofs. The problem was that, as they spread, the flames did not discriminate on grounds of race or religion, and soon Christian homes and 'the best known places of the city' were burning too. 'The Jews', wrote Newburgh, 'were either roasted in their own houses or if they came out of them were received with swords. Much blood was shed in a brief space. But soon the lust after booty burning higher brought on a repletion of slaughter, and avarice got the better of cruelty. Thereupon leaving the butchery, their greedy rage betook itself to stripping the houses and snatching their riches.' At which point, the Christians began to fight among themselves over the spoils.

The King was furious when he heard what had happened, but not quite sure what to do. 'To pass over such a breach of the royal majesty without any example, and to dismiss it unavenged, seemed unworthy of a King . . . but on the other hand to exercise the rigour of the royal displeasure against such a multitude of criminals was plainly impossible.' According to Newburgh, virtually everyone apart from the nobles actually dining with the King had joined in the killing and plundering. Just three of the rioters were hanged – one for robbing a Christian and two because the fires they lit burned down houses owned by Christians. However, Richard did issue a royal edict protecting the Jews. Then, in December, he left for France to get ready for the crusade. Meanwhile, in nearly every town in England, brave men were preparing to set off on the long journey to do battle with the infidel, often finding it hard to raise the money they needed to fund the holy task. In the circumstances, many felt it was surely justified to plunder the race that had crucified Christ of their ill-gotten gains, and Jews everywhere found themselves under attack. At King's Lynn in February 1190, one who had converted to Christianity was allegedly insulted by other Jews, and had to take refuge in a church. This sparked a full-scale riot, possibly led by foreign sailors in port, and virtually all the Jews were either butchered or burned to death in their houses.

As news spread to Norwich, some of its Jews fled to the castle. Those who did not were murdered in their homes. Within a month, a large group of crusaders had gathered in Stamford. 'They were indignant that the enemies of the cross of Christ who dwelt there should possess so much when they had not enough for the expenses of so great a journey. They considered they ought to extort from them as unjust possessions whatever they could apply to the necessary uses of the pilgrimage.' As the mob attacked, several Jews escaped to the castle, but many were killed, 'their homes were pillaged and a great quantity of money captured'. Jews were also attacked in Colchester, Thetford and other nearby towns. In York, the houses of Joce and Benedict were 'like royal palaces, and there they dwelt like two princes of their own people and tyrants of the Christians'. In spite of Benedict's fate, and the pogroms in other towns, Joce and other Jews in the city were sufficiently reassured by Richard's edict 'to act confidently according to their old ways', but around York lived a number of nobles who had got heavily into debt to them, some so heavily they had had to forfeit their estates. A man named Richard Malebisse emerged as leader of these malcontents. One stormy night, they set fire to Benedict's house, where his widow and children lived 'with many others.' They died in the flames, while the robbers made off with their booty. As leader of the Jews in York, Joce begged for help from the authorities, but a few days later, the robbers also laid siege to his house, 'which rivalled a noble citadel in the scale and stoutness of its construction.' Joce, though, had prudently taken refuge in the castle with his wife and children and many other Jews, so that when the house was captured and plundered, 'only a few' were killed.

Jews still at large fell prey to mobs roaming the city, who offered them the choice of death or baptism. Those who refused the Christian alternative were cruelly murdered, but the rioters were also determined that Jews sheltering in the castle should not escape. Egged on by a fanatical hermit, 'the whole of the workpeople and all the youth of the town and a large number of country folk, together with soldiers', mounted a determined attack. The Jews withdrew to the stronghold of Clifford's Tower, which the mob attacked with siege towers, battering rams, and stone-throwing catapults. A 'most famous doctor of law' among the Jews spoke up eloquently, urging them not to renounce their faith to save their skins and 'to prefer a most glorious death to a very dishonest life.' We are told that 'very many' declined his advice and chose to throw themselves on the mercy of their enemies, but the rest started a fire to burn their richest garments and other valuable possessions, 'lest the enemy should be made rich by their wealth'. Joce then cut the throat of his wife and sons, before his own throat was cut – as were those of the other Jews who had chosen to die. At daybreak on Saturday, the crowd stormed the gates. Those Jews left alive threw down the bodies of the dead, and said that they wished to embrace the Christian faith. Malebisse and his followers said they could be baptised, but then massacred them as they left the safety of their stronghold. Altogether, about 150 Jews were killed. Next the mob made for the cathedral, where they demanded the records of Christian debts to Jewish money lenders, and made a bonfire of them. Then 'those of the conspirators who had taken the cross went on their proposed journey'.

Special messengers carried the news to Richard in France. He was furious, not just because of the implied rejection of his authority, but also because of the huge potential loss to the exchequer, and demanded action against those responsible. By then, those nobles who had not left for the crusade had fled to remote parts of England or Scotland, and the mob was too numerous to bring to justice, but the sheriff was sacked, and about fifty leading citizens fined, while hostages were taken to ensure future good conduct. No one was executed, but in March, a new royal charter was issued saying the Jews could live 'freely and honourably' in England, and that they could hold land and pledges. When Jews died, these pledges were 'taken into the king's hands'. They were sufficiently reassured to return to York in considerable numbers, and by the thirteenth century, they had settled in about seventy towns, as far west as Beaumaris, as far north as Newcastle upon Tyne, and as far south as Exeter. This did not mean that their sufferings were over. In 1210, King John imposed heavy taxes on them, and a number were banished for failing to pay, while he had others hanged for allegedly concealing their wealth. Fifty years later, many of the barons who supported Simon de Montfort in his rebellion against Henry III were heavily in debt to Jewish money lenders. Indeed, de Montfort used a promise to cancel Jewish debts to attract support. In February 1262, the Earl of Derby massacred most of the Jews of Worcester after storming the city, and in Easter week 1264, one of de Montfort's leading henchmen, John fitz John, led a massacre of 500 London Jews. Jews were also killed at Canterbury, Lincoln and Cambridge.

By the time Henry III's son, Edward I, became king in 1272, the Jews may have been bled so dry by penal taxes and forced loans that they were no longer a useful source of royal income, and in 1290, Edward expelled them from England. It may also have been a factor that his mother was a fervent believer in the blood libel – that Jews needed blood to bake their unleavened Passover bread, and got it by killing Christian children. Whatever the reasons for it, the expulsion was profitable, as Parliament and the clergy immediately voted money for the King, and Edward was also able to raise funds by selling off Jewish property. Most Jews were allowed to leave peacefully. At Queenborough in the Thames estuary, though, when one ship beached at low tide, the captain suggested to his Jewish passengers that they might want to stretch their legs. Then, when the tide turned, he would not let them back on board, and left them to drown, while others were killed and robbed when their ship drifted ashore at Burnham-on-Crouch in Essex. The captain of the Queenborough vessel was gaoled for two years. The Jews would not return in any numbers to England for three and a half centuries.

Edward was to have the words 'Hammer of the Scots' inscribed in Latin on his tomb, in recognition of the many wars he fought against them, and six years after he had expelled the Jews, he dealt Scotland a savage blow. Early in 1296, the Scots tried to take Carlisle. They failed, but did a great deal of damage in the surrounding country, so at Easter, Edward led an army of more than 25,000 to Berwick-upon-Tweed, then the richest and most populous town north of the border. He promised the burgesses good treatment if they surrendered, but instead they jeered at Edward's army. The town was defended only by a flimsy palisade, and when the English broke through at their first attempt, the Scots are said to have stood stupefied and offered no resistance. Edward hired the commander of the castle garrison to fight for him, and allowed the women to leave, but he was angry 'like a wild boar pursued by dogs' that the town had dared to resist, and for three days his army slaughtered the men until, according to one chronicler, 'blood streamed from the bodies of the slain so copiously that mills could be turned by its flow.' With no one left to bury them, the dead were thrown down wells or tipped into the sea.

Eventually, the clergy persuaded the King to call a halt, but by that time, according to one estimate, more than 11,000 people had been killed. Edward then colonised the town with English settlers, while the Scots retaliated by ravaging Tynedale and Redesdale, and were said to have burned 200 schoolboys alive in a Northumberland church. Conquest by Edward, though, was not the end of Berwick's troubles. It changed hands again several times, and was captured and looted by the Scots in 1355, then burned by the Earl of Douglas in 1405.

In history, said Oscar Wilde, 'one is absolutely sickened, not by the crimes that the wicked have committed, but by the punishments that the good have inflicted', and certainly, in many of the rebellions that have happened in Britain, any harm done by the rebels has been completely overshadowed by what the authorities did in response. In the 1530s there was much restlessness in the north of England, where people were still attached to Catholicism and disturbed by Henry VIII's breaking with Rome so that he could marry Anne Boleyn. Then, in May 1536, Anne fell from favour and Henry had her executed. It was said that church tapers spontaneously re-lit. Perhaps, but instead of restoring England to Catholicism, Henry dissolved the monasteries, and there were wild rumours that this was only the beginning – parish churches were going to be plundered of their gold, jewels and ornaments, many would be closed, and people would have to pay a tax to the government every time a child was baptised. So when Henry's commissioners rode into Hexham on 28 September to take possession of the abbey, they found the streets full of armed men, and the abbey gates locked and barricaded, while on the roof was a monk dressed in armour. The monk said there were twenty others armed with guns and cannons, and they would die before they would hand the abbey over. The commissioners withdrew.

Trouble was also brewing in Lincolnshire. On 1 October, Henry's officials arrived at Louth to collect taxes. The citizens hanged one, and killed the other by sewing him up in a cow's skin and giving him to the dogs to eat. Within a few days, the revolt had spread to Ancaster, Horncastle and the whole of Lindsey, and 30,000 rebels were marching on Lincoln. They proclaimed their loyalty to Henry, but demanded the removal of heretics like Thomas Cranmer, the Protestant Archbishop of Canterbury, and low-born men like Thomas Cromwell from his circle of advisers. In every place where they rose, they went first to the local squire and asked him to be their leader. Fearing for their safety and that of their families if they refused, many agreed, though some smuggled out letters to the King saying they were acting under duress. When they had secured the support of the gentry, the rebels would then approach the local nobleman, who often reacted in the same way.

Henry despatched the Lancaster Herald to deny the rumours about closing churches or stealing their ornaments, to tell the rebels they were impertinent to pass opinions on his advisers, and to order them to send him 100 of their leaders with halters around their necks to beg his pardon. Otherwise he would send an army that would burn and destroy their goods, their wives and their children. Trouble, though, was spreading, with Wensleydale and Beverley now in revolt. A barrister from the East Riding named Robert Aske persuaded people to take an oath to the 'Pilgrimage of Grace' for the removal of evil counsellors, and the restitution of Christ's Church. Within a couple of days, 40,000 were marching on York wearing badges of the five wounds of Christ and chanting anthems. Lord Darcy surrendered Pontefract Castle to them, telling the King he did not have enough men to resist.

Meanwhile, the Duke of Suffolk led Henry's army against the rebels in Lincolnshire. Most were genuinely loyal to the King, and had no wish to be in arms against him. Suffolk told the King that if he promised a general pardon, they would go home, and then he could move against the East Riding men. Henry wanted a few ringleaders executed, but allowed the duke to pursue his more conciliatory approach for the moment, with the proviso that if there was any new disturbance, he must 'destroy, burn and kill man, woman and child, to the terrible example of all others'. Suffolk had been right, and the promise of a pardon sufficed to get the Lincolnshire rebels to lay down their arms. Then the Earl of Shrewsbury led the army of 7,000 to the East Riding, but soon realised he could not take the field against Aske's 40,000. On 16 October, the pilgrims entered York, and the following day Doncaster. Shrewsbury was given the discouraging news that 'never sheep ran faster in a morning out of their fold' than did men to join the Pilgrimage, and by the third week in October, the rising had spread to Lancashire, Furness, Cumberland and Westmorland. At Sawley, near Clitheroe, the people went to the abbey, ejected the gentleman who had leased it, and put the monks back.

One of Henry's best soldiers was the Duke of Norfolk. Not a squeamish man, he had presided over the trial of his niece, Anne Boleyn, and had sent her to the block, and would help to procure the execution of another niece, Catherine Howard, when she too fell from the King's favour. Nevertheless, he was known to be attached to the old religion, and to resent counsellors of 'villein blood' like Cromwell. There were even rumours that at some point he would reveal himself as the rebels' real leader, but Henry now put him in command of Shrewsbury's army. Norfolk knew there had been whispers about his loyalty, and perhaps saw this as a good opportunity to still them, but when he met the rebels at Doncaster and saw how strong they were, he felt he had to offer similar advice to Suffolk – promise the East Riding pilgrims a pardon, and they too would go home. Reluctantly, Henry agreed, so Norfolk promised restoration of the suppressed abbeys, and got Lancaster Herald to read out the pardon. It worked. Aske proclaimed his loyalty to Henry, tearing off his badge of the five wounds, and declaring 'we will wear no badge but the badge of our sovereign lord'. The pilgrims went home, and Henry invited Aske to come to Greenwich for Christmas to discuss his grievances, giving him safe conduct until 5 January 1537. The King received him with courtesy and grace. He promised Aske he would visit the north, and hold a Parliament there to consider their complaints. Buoyed up by the good news, the barrister rode home. Within a few days, though, there was a new rising in the East Riding. For some reason, an anti-Catholic named Sir Francis Bigod, who had taken no part in the Pilgrimage, suddenly launched an attack on Hull, one of the few places in the north that had stayed loyal to the King.

Aske and gentlemen who had joined the Pilgrimage, like Lord Darcy and Sir Robert Constable, condemned the rising, and it failed, but, alarmingly, it was followed by another by 6,000 men near Cockermouth. Aske and Darcy wrote to Henry asking him to send Norfolk back to the north to reassure the people. The Duke did indeed return, and ordered people to wear the red cross of St George on a white coat to show their loyalty. To encourage compliance, he hanged eight people at York, and rumours swept the region that he was going to hang and draw from Doncaster to Berwick. Everyone, even children, hastily donned the cross. Henry's instructions to Norfolk were very simple: 'Our pleasure is that you shall cause such dreadful execution to be done upon a good number of every town village and hamlet that have offended as they may be a fearful spectacle to all others hereafter.' Norfolk recruited gangs of robbers from Tynedale and Redesdale to his army. When they looted Kirkby Stephen, people in the neighbouring villages attacked them. Privately, Norfolk admitted the robbers had caused the trouble, but he still ordered his troops to kill and burn houses because 'this pageant well played, the realm shall be the quieter'.

Now the Duke told the rebels that the only way to gain the King's mercy was to surrender. When they did, he selected seventy-four and hanged them in chains in their villages, leaving their bodies swinging from gibbets till they rotted. As more and more were executed, there was not enough iron to hang them all in chains, so Norfolk often had to make do with just hanging them. At Durham, where there had been no rising, he managed to get twenty-one people convicted of high treason and executed, and all the while, the earls of Sussex and Derby were hanging people in Lancashire. Henry demanded wholesale executions of monks, and among those chosen were the abbots of Whalley and Sawley. The earls pleaded for the life of one old monk who had fought three times for the King against the Scots. Henry just said that this made his crime more heinous. In March, Norfolk returned to York for more show trials. His speciality was making people sit on juries that would condemn their own kinsmen. Now, throughout the north, rotting corpses on gibbets were providing the 'example' the King desired.

Henry meanwhile thanked Aske, Darcy and Constable for their part in suppressing Bigod's revolt, and invited them down to London. When they arrived they were clapped in the Tower and charged with high treason. Aske protested that he had a safe conduct. Henry told him it had expired on 5 January. Cromwell was given the task of coming up with some evidence, and devised a case for the Crown that went like this: when Bigod had risen, the three accused had told people to stay in their homes. This, it was alleged, amounted to an instruction not to join the King's forces to suppress the rebellion, and was good enough to procure the execution of all three. Nearly all of the Yorkshire gentry had joined the Pilgrimage, and Henry realised he could not hang them all, but Bigod and a number of others were executed, as were the abbots of Jervaulx and Fountains and the Prior of Bridlington. The Lincolnshire rebels had gone home on the promise of a pardon, but now forty-six of them were executed. According to the Earl of Shrewsbury, Lancaster Herald deserved more credit than anyone else for ending the revolt in Lincolnshire, but now he too was condemned for treason, hanged, drawn and quartered, and had his head displayed on a gibbet above York Castle. Altogether, about 200 people were executed. By 1540, every monastery in England and Wales had been dissolved, and in the same year, Thomas Cromwell, now disgraced, was beheaded on Tower Hill. Norfolk too fell from Henry's favour, not a difficult feat, and was scheduled to be executed on 28 January 1547. On 22 January the King died and Norfolk was saved.

The agonies of conscience that drove so many to join the Pilgrimage of Grace would continue to make England an unhappy place on and off for the next century and a half. Sixteen years after the Pilgrimage, Henry's daughter, Mary, came to the throne filled with a fierce desire to restore England to Catholicism. She believed that some persecution might be necessary to achieve this, but that it should be directed against learned men who might mislead others rather than against ordinary people, and she hoped most Protestants would renounce their errors rather than face the flames. Her Catholic husband, King Philip II of Spain, offered her little encouragement, and the Catholic Holy Roman Emperor's ambassador warned it could cause a revolt. On the other hand, one of her advisers, Myles Huggarde, urged that burning a few heretics was just what was needed to make an impression on men's minds, because many people who would not bother going to hear a sermon would turn out for an execution. Bishop Bonner likened it to the action of 'a good surgeon [who] cutteth away a putrified and festered member for the love he hath to the whole body'.

So the heresy trials began in January 1555. First to be burned was John Rogers, prebendary of St Paul's; in the words of Foxe's *Book of Martyrs*, 'the first proto-martyr of all the blessed company that suffered in Queen Mary's time'. The initial victims were, as Mary had intended, Protestant clerics, among them Bishop Hooper of Gloucester, who was burned outside his own cathedral, and Rowland Taylor, the minister of Hadley in Suffolk. Ominously for Mary, Taylor was accompanied to his death by a great crowd of men and women 'with weeping eyes and lamentable voices'. The most famous martyrs were what we would probably today call 'the Oxford three' – the veteran preacher Hugh Latimer, who was nearly 70, the Bishop of London, Nicholas Ridley, and Thomas Cranmer, the Archbishop of Canterbury, who were all burned in the university city. At one point Cranmer recanted, but when he discovered Mary still insisted on his death, he withdrew his renunciation of his beliefs and thrust the hand that had signed it into the flames. Ridley and Latimer were burned together, and Latimer spoke the immortal words: 'be of good comfort, master Ridley, and play the man. We shall this day light such a candle, by God's grace, in England, as I trust shall never be put out.'

Although Mary had initially believed that burnings might make an instructive spectacle, it soon became clear they were having the opposite effect, and she tried to deny the martyrs the oxygen of publicity. In January 1556, the Privy Council told householders they must not allow their servants and apprentices out when burnings were scheduled, then barred all 'young folk' from attending them. It may have been Mary's intention to spare ordinary people from the flames, but of the 237 men and 52 women burned at the stake, only 25 were ministers and 8 gentlemen, while the rest were indeed ordinary folk like artisans and husbandmen; many of the Protestant clergy and the more prosperous Protestant laity had fled abroad. In addition to those burned, other Protestants died in prison. As the persecution grew more severe, some of Mary's circle, like Bishop Gardiner of Winchester, began to withdraw their support, but there were plenty of important people prepared to help, such as the Earl of Derby in Lancashire and Lord Darcy and

Lord Rich in Essex. Nor was there any shortage of informers. Nearly nine out of ten of the burnings took place in the south-east and East Anglia, where Protestantism was strong, but in spite of the persecution, Protestants continued to worship in secret, and when Mary's short, unhappy life came to an end in 1558, she was succeeded by her half-sister Elizabeth, who restored the reformed religion.

Much of the north, though, remained Catholic and unreconciled. The veteran royal adviser, Sir Ralph Sadler, remarked that 'the ancient faith still lay like lees at the bottoms of men's hearts, and if the vessel was ever so little stirred, came to the top.' The Catholics' great hope now was another Mary – Mary, Queen of Scots, who in 1569 was Elizabeth's prisoner at Tutbury in Staffordshire. Elizabeth's writ barely ran in the five counties of the north. She had never visited this part of her kingdom, and the people did not like her habit of leasing lands to absentee southern landlords. They generally felt more loyalty to the local nobleman than to the monarch, and the leading northern magnates like the earls of Northumberland and Westmorland were surrounded by Catholic advisers. When they heard that Westmorland's brother-in-law, the Duke of Norfolk (grandson of the duke who had suppressed the Pilgrimage of Grace), had been arrested for trying to marry Mary, they began mobilising retainers for their own protection, but the Earl resisted the advice of his supporters to take up arms, saying: 'I will never blot my house, which hath been preserved this long without staining.'

Elizabeth had heard rumours of rebellion stirring, and decided to summon Northumberland and Westmorland to court to explain themselves, though some of her advisers were against the idea, fearing it might push the earls into rebellion. Five days after receiving Elizabeth's message on 14 November 1569, the two noblemen rode into Durham with 300 armed horsemen. They entered the cathedral, tore down the communion table, ripped up the English bibles and prayer books, and declared that no more Protestant services would be held there. A huge crowd turned up for a Latin mass. The next morning, the little army marched south hoping to free Mary, who it wanted recognised as Elizabeth's heir, picking up support in the villages through which it passed. All over the north, people were setting up high altars instead of communion tables, and burning the prayer book. Elizabeth began raising an army, and she also took the precaution of moving Mary south to Coventry, but when the rebels reached Clifford Moor, near Wetherby, they halted. They had not attracted as many nobles and gentry as they had hoped, and their numbers stood at only 5,000. The King of France had given them some money, but by now they were short of funds and having to live off the land, which was beginning to alienate local people. Northumberland's wife tried to stiffen their resolve, but they decided to return to county Durham. On 11 December, the Earl of Sussex (grandson of the earl who helped suppress the Pilgrimage of Grace) started to advance with the Queen's army, and five days later Westmorland and Northumberland told their supporters to 'make shift for themselves', and fled to Scotland. Now the rebellion was effectively over, and the suppression could begin.

The Scots captured Northumberland and handed him over to Elizabeth to be executed, while Westmorland escaped to the continent. When the Queen's army captured more prosperous rebels, Elizabeth gave them a proper trial because then she was entitled to seize their property, but the 'common sort' could be summarily hanged. Sussex agreed that: 'The example shall be (as it is necessary it should be) very great.' Just as with Norfolk thirty years before, Sussex knew there were question marks against his loyalty, and he was constantly chivvying his lieutenants to hang more people. The Queen in turn chivvied him: 'We marvel that we have heard of no execution by martial law, as was appointed, of the meaner sort of rebels in the North. If the same be not already done, you are to proceed thereunto, for the terror of others, with expedition.' Elizabeth even wanted him to prosecute those who had merely stayed at home and failed to join his action against the rebels. More than 300 were marked down for execution in the Palatinate of Durham, though some may have escaped. Altogether, it is likely that at least 500 people were executed. Another army arrived from the south only after the rebellion was effectively over, and behaved with great ferocity, looting and pillaging. The Queen was furious, because she reckoned they helped themselves to £10,000 worth of property that she had her eye on for her own coffers. Elizabeth did, however, manage to raise £5,000 by selling pardons to some of the richer rebels, and the Crown also seized estates and goods belonging to about 200 of the gentry. After the rebellion, beggars became a much more common sight in the north, with whole families reduced to destitution by the seizure of their property or the execution of the breadwinner.

The last attempt to return England to the old religion came when the Catholic James II succeeded to the throne in 1685. Many Protestants had tried hard to exclude him, and four months after he became King, the favourite illegitimate son of his brother and predecessor Charles II, the Protestant Duke of Monmouth, landed at Lyme Regis with 150 soldiers. He had chosen the west because it was full of nonconformist Protestants and had provided many recruits for Parliament during the Civil War. Soon people were rallying to his banner, though the local gentry and the Anglican clergy and their flocks remained disappointingly aloof. Monmouth managed to gather an army of about 7,000, but they were short of muskets and pikes, and many were armed only with scythe blades lashed on to 6ft poles. They marched for two weeks, often in pouring rain and without any clear purpose, till they came to the sodden meadows around Bridgwater. James offered a pardon to any of Monmouth's men who would desert, though not to the Duke himself, and some did drift away, but on Saturday 4 July, Monmouth attempted a surprise night-time attack at Sedgmoor on the royal army under John Churchill, later the Duke of Marlborough. Though they were fewer in number, the royal soldiers were better equipped and they were soon cutting swathes through the rebels, but, as day broke, most of Monmouth's men were still fighting bravely. At this point, though, the Duke and his leading commanders threw off their breastplates and insignia of rank and rode for their lives, leaving their army to its fate.

The rebels are said to have lost more than 1,000 against perhaps fifty in the royal ranks in what was, in the words of the great historian Lord Macaulay, 'the last fight, deserving the name of battle, that has been fought on English ground'. By evening, the royal commander, Lord Feversham, had assembled 500 prisoners in the parish church of Weston Zoyland, and had set aside a considerable number for immediate execution. One who was locally renowned as a fast runner was told his life might be spared if he raced a colt. The story goes that he managed to keep up with it for an astonishing three-quarters of a mile before it pulled away, but he was still sent to the gallows. The next day Feversham set up a long line of gibbets along the road to Bridgwater, and hanged a rebel from each one, leaving some to rot in irons, while Monmouth, disguised as a shepherd, was soon run to ground in the New Forest.

When the Duke had taken up arms against James, he had accused the King of poisoning his own brother, Charles II, and had declared a war without quarter against him. Now he grovelled before his uncle, begging for his life in the most degrading manner, even saying that he would convert to Catholicism and turn informer. It was to no avail, and he was sentenced to death. On the day of his execution, he managed to mount the scaffold with a firm tread, and saluted the guards with a smile. Then he ran his fingers along the axe, and complained that it did not feel sharp enough, but he gave six guineas to the executioner John Ketch, and said: 'Do not hack me as you did my Lord Russell. I have heard that you struck him three or four times. My servant will give you some more gold if you do your work well.' Ketch's first blow, though, inflicted only a slight wound, and the Duke struggled up from the block and looked reproachfully at him, before settling down again. Blow after blow failed to kill the victim, and with his body still moving, Ketch flung down his axe, shouting: 'I cannot do it, my heart fails me.' By now, the crowd was baying for his blood, so Ketch picked up his weapon again, and with two more blows managed to kill off Monmouth, though the head had to be severed from the body with a sword. The spectators were in such a fearful rage that Ketch might have been torn to pieces if he had not had an armed escort.

Meanwhile, back in the West Country, Feversham put Colonel Percy Kirke in charge of the pacification. Kirke and his men had been schooled in brutality in Tangier, and were known ironically as 'Kirke's lambs', because they marched under the Christian emblem of the lamb. He took two cartloads of rebels with undressed wounds to Taunton, and a long drove of prisoners on foot chained two and two. He hanged a number without trial, and did not even let them say farewell to their loved ones. Kirke and his officers also hanged rebels from the sign of the White Hart Inn, while they were dining there. The story goes that every time they drank a health, one was hoisted up, and as the victim began to writhe in his final agony, Kirke would order the drums to strike up, saying he would give the rebels music to their dancing. So much quartering of dead bodies was done that the executioner stood ankle deep in blood. There are no exact figures, but it was thought Kirke despatched 100 in a week. He was also selling safe conducts, though, and the government recalled him because they felt he was being too lenient.

So in early September, Judge Jeffreys set out on the western circuit, with the promise of reward if he did his work well. The 'Bloody Assizes' started at Winchester, where he tried a woman named Alice Lisle. Her crime was to shelter two men fleeing from the battle. This may not have been a partisan act, as in the past she had helped Cavaliers in trouble, but soldiers had found the men, and she was charged with treason. Witnesses soon experienced Jeffreys's distinctive way of conducting cases. Anyone who spoke up for one of the accused was likely to get what he called 'a lick with the rough side of his tongue'. When one was so terrified by the Judge's ferocity that he stood silent, Jeffreys exclaimed: 'How hard the truth is to come out of a lying Presbyterian knave.' Alice Lisle said that she knew the men were in trouble, but she had not believed they had been involved in the rebellion, particularly as one was a man of God. Jeffreys was beside himself with fury. 'There is not one of those lying, snivelling, canting Presbyterians', he raged, 'but, one way or another, had a hand in the rebellion.'

The jury went out to consider its verdict, and remained in discussion for a long time. The Judge raged again. In such an open and shut case, he could not understand why they even needed to leave the box. He sent a messenger in to them, and told them that if they did not return instantly, he would lock them up for the night. They came back to say they doubted whether the case had been proved. Jeffreys raged yet again, and this time they came back with the required verdict. Alice Lisle was sentenced to death by burning. The clergy of Winchester Cathedral protested, as did some close to James, but the only concession he would make was to commute the sentence to beheading. Now Jeffreys moved on to Dorchester, where he ordered the court to be hung in scarlet, and let it be known that the only hope of mercy was to plead guilty. Clemency was in short supply, though, and seventy-four were hanged. Somerset, the heart of the rebellion, was saved till last. Jeffreys laughed, joked and swore. When one accused complained that the witnesses against him were a Papist and a prostitute, Jeffreys railed: 'Thou impudent rebel . . . I see thee already with the halter around thy neck.' Another produced testimony that he was a good Protestant. 'Protestant!' exclaimed the Judge, 'You mean Presbyterian. I'll hold you a wager of it. I can smell a Presbyterian 40 miles.' When it was pointed out that one of the accused was on the parish, Jeffreys remarked: 'Do not trouble yourselves. I will ease the parish of the burden.' Altogether on the circuit, he hanged 320, boasting that he had hanged more traitors than all his predecessors put together since the Norman Conquest. At every crossroads, market place or green of a village that had furnished Monmouth with soldiers, corpses in irons clattered in the wind, and quarters or heads were impaled on poles. The very rich, like Monmouth's cavalry commander, Lord Grey, could often make their peace for a price – in his case, £40,000. Those with less money had less chance of success. Churchill gained one woman admittance to the King to plead for her brother's life. As she went in, he laid his hand on the chimneypiece and warned her: 'I wish well to your suit, but do not flatter yourself with hopes. This marble is not harder than the king.' A Tory peer, Lord Stanwell, who complained of the butchery, found a corpse suspended in chains at his park gate.

Very few of those executed expressed any remorse. They composed hymns in prison, sang them on the scaffold, and prayed that England would soon be rid of the Antichrist. In addition to those executed, 840 were transported to the Caribbean. They travelled with wounds untreated below decks in tiny holds where there was not even room to lie down. One in five died on the journey. Jeffreys had earned his reward, and was made Lord Chancellor, but once again cruelty did not prosper. Just four years after the rebellion, James II had fled the country, and Jeffreys had died in the Tower. He was buried close to the Duke of Monmouth.

James and his descendants would make a number of attempts to recapture the throne. The most celebrated of these Jacobite rebellions was led by his grandson, Charles Edward Stuart, 'Bonnie Prince Charlie'. In 1745, the Prince was a handsome, charismatic 24-year-old. He arrived in Scotland in July, raised an army of 5,000, and soon controlled most of the country. Then he crossed the border and took Carlisle, and by 4 December, he had reached Derby. In London, according to Henry Fielding, there was 'a panic scarce to be credited', and the royal ladies began packing their bags to leave for the continent, but there was dissension in the Prince's ranks. Charles had hoped for a rising of English Jacobites and help from France, but neither had materialised, and many of his supporters were not much interested in England, believing he should concentrate on establishing a Scottish kingdom. As some of the Highland clansmen who made up so much of his army began to drift home, on 6 December the army turned around and headed back north.

At the same time, the government forces mounted an ever-tightening blockade of Scotland, and the Prince's army was forced to retreat to the Highlands. On 16 April 1746, at Drummossie Moor, north-east of Inverness, they met the government troops under King George II's son, the Duke of Cumberland. In what became known as the battle of Culloden, the last fought on British soil, the Jacobites were quickly defeated by the more numerous and better equipped government forces. More than 1,000 of the Prince's men were killed, but in spite of a £30,000 price on his head, he managed to escape to France after five months on the run in the Highlands. His followers would be less fortunate.

After the battle, the Duke's infantry combed the field, stabbing and thrusting at any man showing signs of life among the heaps of rebel bodies. Many people had turned out to watch the battle, or as Cumberland's soldiers looked at it, to see them killed. So as they rode towards Inverness, they cut down men, women and children, and shot at any curious face that appeared at a window. An old man was chased till he fell to his knees exhausted, begging for his life, then shot through the head. A 12-year-old boy had 'his head cloven to his teeth'. Some who did not even know there had been a battle were hacked down, like a man and his 9-year-old son at Inshes, 2 miles away. A woman at Mains of Gask who saw the dragoons coming ran into the fields carrying her newborn baby. The soldiers sabred her and flung her baby to the ground. It was said that James Wolfe, later the hero of Quebec, then an 18-year-old, refused to shoot a young rebel commander lying wounded, but that the government general just shrugged his shoulders and got another soldier to do it. A more common sentiment in the army was probably that expressed by another of the Duke's soldiers: 'This rebel host had been most deeply in debt to the public for all the rapine, murder and cruelty; and since the time was now come to pay off the score, our people were all glad to clear the reckoning.' Nor did the clansmen show much solidarity to each other. One who managed to kill a pursuing dragoon with a discarded sword got home to find his neighbour looting his house.

Next, Cumberland sent soldiers on a systematic search of all the cottages near the battlefield for any Jacobites who might be hiding. The army had been told, falsely, that the rebels had been ordered to give no quarter, and all through Friday and Saturday, they killed men found sheltering. On one occasion, a beggar had hidden with a group of rebels, but the soldiers just locked the door and burned them all. Another dozen wounded men who had taken refuge in a house were led away civilly by an officer who told them he was taking them to a surgeon, but a few minutes later they were all shot dead. Then there were the prisoners to be dealt with. By the evening of the battle, there were more than 300 in the gaols of Inverness, among them more than thirty who had originally fought on the government side and had then switched over after being captured. This was not unusual at the time, but now these men were regarded as deserters, and before the end of the month, nearly all of them had been marched to the gallows on the outskirts of the town and hanged – usually naked, their clothes being the property of the executioner. Many rebels died in prison from disease or gangrenous wounds, and their bodies were generally left with the living for a few days before being removed. Two loyal government supporters, the Lord Provost of Inverness and his predecessor, pleaded with a government general for a more merciful approach, but the general had them kicked down the stairs and into the street. As the days went by, more and more prisoners were brought in, and soon the gaols and churches in Inverness were full, and the gaols in Perth, Dundee, Aberdeen and Stirling too, so rebels were transferred to ships in the Moray Firth. A total of 125 were crammed into the tiny hold of the *James and Mary*, 'where numbers of them died every day, and were thrown overboard like so many dogs; and several of them before they were really dead.'

As the search for rebels spread beyond the immediate area of the battle, troops went burning, murdering and plundering in the glens, earning Cumberland the nickname 'Butcher'. Officially, clansmen who came in and gave up their weapons might be given a certificate and allowed to return home, but at the same time, those found in arms could be summarily executed, so it was risky for a clansman to try and give himself up, especially if he did not speak English. One officer wrote that they were 'carrying fire and destruction as they passed, shooting the vagrant Highlanders they met in the mountains and driving off the cattle'. Some soldiers tried to be merciful. One group who had been told to burn down a house set fire to damp straw outside instead, to try to make it look as though they had obeyed the order, but all through May and June, people were being made destitute, as the soldiers took their cattle, oxen, sheep and goats and shared out the proceeds when they sold them off to Lowland or English dealers. Officially, any soldier found looting could be flogged, but if officers could claim the victims were rebels or sympathisers, there was no punishment. By now people were beginning to starve. One officer wrote in a letter home: 'there were found last week two women and four children dead in the hills who perished through want, their huts being burnt.' Lord George Sackville's men blazed a trail of terror and destruction through Knoidart. When clansmen raided his baggage train, and stole his food, bedding and clothes, he and his men took their revenge at the next hamlet they came to, raping the women, and then forcing them to watch as they shot and bayoneted their menfolk. Everywhere, it was the same story of houses burned, men killed and women raped. HMS *Furnace* appeared off the isle of Eigg, and the captain threatened to burn it house by house unless Jacobite fugitives were given up. They arrested thirty-eight men, and then the sailors and marines raped women, slaughtered cattle and pillaged houses. The Highland militia did its share of cruel deeds too. After the soldiers had ravaged the island of Raasay, the militia mounted its own raid, burning 300 houses and slaughtering the islanders' livestock.

Jacobite prisoners were sometimes taken down to English gaols. At one time, in all, nearly 3,500 were being held – men, women and children, the youngest being a 7-year-old boy, while one in twenty of the men was over 70. Sometimes the only charge against them was that they had drunk Bonnie Prince Charlie's health or had wished the rebels well. Cumberland wanted whole clans transported, but the government came up with a more novel scheme. Some prisoners who were men of property or who had given evidence against their colleagues were exempted, but the rest would draw lots, and one man in twenty would stand trial for his life. Of the remainder, some would be sent to plantations in the colonies and others would be banished and left to find their own place of exile. Of the 3,500 prisoners, 120 were executed, including three lords, and twenty-four men of the Manchester Regiment, the only one that the Prince raised south of the border. Many met their end in England at places like Tyburn, York and Carlisle. Some escaped death by signing up to join the King's army. It is known that 936 were transported and 222 banished, while the fate of 684 is unknown. Many of these probably died in prison. By September, out of 560 being held on ships on the Thames, more than 150 had died, while 80 perished in Lancaster prison, where they had been fed only on hides and offal from butchers' yards. Of the hundreds who were put to death on or near Drummossie Moor after the battle, or who were murdered in the glens later, or who died of starvation in the winter that followed, there is no tally.

Six years after Culloden, George II declared an amnesty, but the government also forbade the wearing of Highland dress. The punishment for a second offence was transportation for seven years, but if a soldier saw you, he might simply shoot you. This measure was followed by the abolition of the hereditary jurisdiction of the Highland chiefs, many of whom received big payments in compensation. Then, with the help of soldiers, they cleared their crofts of men, women and children, and leased the empty glens to sheep farmers.

# CHAPTER FOUR

# AIR RAIDS

The First World War brought danger and destruction home to the British people in a new and terrible way. A foretaste of this new warfare came at about quarter past eight on the bright, clear morning of 16 December 1914, as the people of Hartlepool awoke to the sound of heavy guns. At first they thought it was the British fleet practising, but then the shells began falling, setting the gasworks on fire, and hitting the waterworks and the old church of St Hilda. The bombardment wrecked working-class homes in the old town, and grander houses on the cliffs. Buildings were also damaged at neighbouring Seaton Carew. The official death toll for Hartlepool was 55, with 115 injured, but some believed the true figures were higher.

It was the work of three German warships, which then moved on to attack Scarborough, killing seventeen, including a 14-month-old boy, and injuring twenty. Three hotels and the town hall were damaged, and a church was hit during Holy Communion. Many houses were said to have had their windows broken, but one damaged shop quickly put up a sign proclaiming 'Business as Usual'. It was to become a famous phrase. *The Times* reassuringly commented: 'At all three places there was an entire absence of panic and the demeanour of the people was everything that could be desired.' Eyewitness accounts tell a rather different story. One woman had been in bed when she had heard 'a noise like thunder. Plaster at once began to fall from the ceiling, and going to the door I saw crowds of people running along the street.' Many were carrying children. She joined them, hurrying past houses 'falling to pieces', and managed to board a train to Leeds. Others took refuge in country lanes. Finally, the ships moved on to Whitby, where they hit the ruins of the abbey, and killed two people. The Admiralty announced that the raids were 'devoid of military significance'. Indeed it seems they failed to disrupt work at Hartlepool docks, and most of the people who had left the bombarded towns quickly returned.

Most people had expected the first German attack to come from the air, and eight days later, on Christmas Eve, a sea-plane did drop a bomb near Dover Castle. It caused little damage, just breaking a few windows, but on 19 January 1915 German Zeppelin airships killed two people at Great Yarmouth, and two more at King's Lynn. The Germans had dropped bombs on Antwerp as early as August, killing six people in their beds, while since September, British aircraft had been bombing Zeppelin sheds, and on one occasion, had attacked Cologne railway station. Winston Churchill, then First Lord of the Admiralty, firmly believed it was best to destroy Zeppelins on the ground, rather than try to shoot them down as they cruised at more than 50 miles an hour at a height of up to 15,000ft.

On 12 February 1915, the Kaiser decided he wanted to step up the air war, and ordered raids to be carried out 'with the greatest energy'. He drew up a list of targets – military installations, petrol and oil stores, and the London docks. His imperial directive, however, forbade attacks on 'residential areas, and, above all royal palaces'. In an instruction that now looks rather quaint, he insisted that 'private property . . . be spared as much as possible'. When a bomb nearly hit the King's house at Sandringham, the Kaiser was furious, but sparing residential areas was easier said than done. Many of the places on the German target list were surrounded by houses, and bombing from high in the sky was simply not accurate enough to ensure they were not hit. The night of 31 May 1915 brought the first air raid on London, by a single Zeppelin that dropped ninety small incendiary bombs and thirty grenades, killing seven people, including one who jumped from the window of a burning house. Between April and October, there was a total of nineteen airship attacks. Most did little damage, though raids on Tyneside on 15 June and on London on 7 September each killed eighteen, and an attack on London on 8 September killed twenty-six. Then on 13 October, in the most destructive raid so far, five Zeppelins bombed London and the Home Counties, killing seventy-one people.

A limited blackout was enforced in built-up areas, and lights were set out on open land to try to confuse the bombers, but British aircraft could not be scrambled quickly enough to engage the enemy on their way in; they could only try to stop the airships getting back after their raids. The Midlands were attacked in January 1916, and then, in April, it was the turn of Sunderland and Edinburgh, while the attacks on East London continued. Anti-German feeling grew, and when inquests were held on victims, some juries brought in verdicts of 'wilful murder' by the Kaiser. During the summer of 1916, some improvements were made in air defences, with more powerful anti-aircraft guns, better searchlights, and training in night-flying for airmen, but it was not until the night of 2 September that defending aircraft scored their first success, when Lieutenant William Leefe Robinson used a new incendiary bullet to shoot down a Schutte-Lanz airship over Cuffley in Hertfordshire. People in the East End saw the fireball and climbed on to roof tops to watch the airship burning. Then they danced in the street and sang 'God Save the King'. Factory hooters and railway engine whistles were sounded and, over the next two days, 10,000 souvenir hunters flocked to the scene. Robertson was awarded the Victoria Cross, the only one given for an action in Britain. Over the next three months, the defenders brought down another four airships, but just as it looked as though we might be getting the better of the Zeppelin, the Germans started using aircraft in earnest.

From 1917, the Kaiser's 'England squadron' of Gotha biplane bombers began operations from captured Belgian airfields around Ghent. Because they had a shorter range than the airships, they had to concentrate on London and the south-east. On 25 May, they attacked Folkestone, where Canadians were waiting to embark for the Western Front. They killed sixteen soldiers at a military camp, but they also dropped bombs in the crowded town centre. One hit a greengrocer's shop, killing customers and staff. An eyewitness said, 'the whole street seemed to explode,' and another found the curly-haired head of a child on a doorstep. Seventy-one people were killed in Folkestone, including fifty-five women and children. The town sent a delegation to Lord French, then in charge of home defence, demanding to know why no warning was given. People also complained at the ineffectiveness of the anti-aircraft fire; 'they might just as well have been using pea-shooters,' said one. That seemed to be the view of the Germans too. One crewman dismissed the ground fire as 'cotton wool', while a pilot found the attacks exhilarating: 'in less time than it takes to tell, I have pushed the lever. I anxiously follow the flight of the released bombs. With a tremendous crash they strike the heart of England.'

On the morning of 13 June, a lone aeroplane headed for Margate and dropped five bombs, killing three people, including a boy and a baby. Defending aircraft were scrambled, but the attack was a diversion. Fourteen aircraft were heading for the Germans' number one target, London, with its docks packed with essential supplies and combustible materials, its munitions works supplying Britain's forces, and its railway stations crucial for getting men to the front. One bomb hit an office block, killing nineteen people. Three hit Liverpool Street station, killing sixteen. The soldier and poet Siegfried Sassoon saw it. He wrote: 'an invisible enemy sent destruction spinning down from a fine weather sky; poor old men bought a railway ticket and were trundled away again dead on a barrow; wounded women lay about in the station groaning.' But perhaps the most notorious bomb of the whole war was the one that made a huge crater in the infants' classroom at Upper North Street school in Poplar. It killed eighteen children and maimed another twenty-seven for life. The corridors were soon filled with shouting, screaming parents desperately looking for their boys and girls. The school caretaker found his own son dead in the rubble, but went on trying to rescue others. A man outside the school exclaimed: 'Fair fighting, man to man, one doesn't mind, but slaughtering babies is the work of the devil.' Altogether in the raid, the Germans dropped more than 100 bombs on the capital and killed 162 civilians, the highest death toll of the war.

Public feeling was so strong that Field Marshal Haig was told that he would have to release a couple of squadrons of aircraft from the Western Front for a week or two to make it look as though air defences were being improved; then they could be returned. And they were, in spite of Lord French's protests. On 7 July, the Germans killed another fifty-three people in London for the loss of one Gotha. *The Times* railed against 'the apparent ease with which the enemy airmen carried out their mission'. The government had always been ambivalent about air raid warnings, believing that: 'The occasions when air raids were threatened were many times more frequent than when air raids actually occurred. . . . If warnings were given on every occasion the result might be loss for a day of thousands of workmen.' Now, though, they had all fire stations linked by special telephone lines and arranged for them to be given warning of approaching aircraft so that they could set off loud fireworks, known as maroons. The authorities also deployed barrage balloons in great oblong box configurations, and observers spoke of aircraft flying around and around desperately trying to find a way out. In addition, a new unified command structure for the defence of London was introduced, and the better defences seemed to produce results. In an attack on 18 August, the Germans lost thirteen out of twenty-eight aircraft. Some crashed because of bad weather, but from September onwards, they restricted operations to night raids. On 29 September, the Kaiser introduced another new weapon, the four-engine Staaken R-39 Giant, the biggest aircraft to bomb Britain in either war.

Three of them joined three Gothas in a raid that killed forty people in London. On 6 December, the Germans tried systematic fire-raising on a major scale for the first time. Six aircraft dropped 276 incendiary bombs on London and started fifty-two fires, but firemen managed to contain casualties to two killed and six injured.

During a raid on 28 January 1918, a Giant dropped a 600lb bomb on the Odhams printing works at Covent Garden in London. Its basement was a designated public shelter where families took refuge during air raids. Firemen managed to dig nearly 100 people out of the rubble, but 38 died. Britain had been retaliating with raids on German cities, and on 18 May, thirty aircraft bombed Cologne, killing more than 100 civilians. The following night saw Britain's last raid of the war, when 49 people were killed in London, Essex and Kent, but six Gothas were destroyed. Altogether, during the war, there had been 103 raids, 51 by airships and 52 by aircraft, and they had killed more than 1,400 people, almost half of them in the London area. Many were shocked by the numbers at the time, but others foresaw worse to come. At the end of 1917, one observer commented perceptively that the most important event would turn out to have been 'not the Russian Revolution or even the stern intervention of the United States in a sacred course; but the appearance of a single German aeroplane flying at high noon over London.'

Just five years after the end of the First World War, the British Fire Prevention Committee picked up the theme: 'Take it for granted that in the next war, cities will be bombed without warning; what has been done in the past will be altogether eclipsed by the horrors of future aerial bombardments.' By then, the RAF had already attacked dissident Afghan tribesmen from the air, and bombed the grounds of the Amir of Afghanistan's palace. Then, in the thirties, the Japanese bombed the Chinese, Mussolini dropped poison gas on Abyssinian tribesmen and, during the Spanish Civil War, the Germans and Italians dive-bombed cities, while the newsreel cameras recorded the terror of a defenceless civilian population. Bertrand Russell predicted that air raids would turn London into 'one vast raving bedlam'. Aldous Huxley said the army would not be fighting the enemy, but trying to keep order among the panic-stricken population. Even Churchill believed that up to 4 million Londoners would flee from the city. Many shared the view of three-times Prime Minister Stanley Baldwin that 'the bomber will always get through.' It had led Baldwin to a chilling conclusion: 'The only defence is offence, which means that you have to kill more women and children more quickly than the enemy if you want to save yourselves.' It was calculated that during air raids on Barcelona each ton of high explosive caused fifty casualties. According to the most alarming official estimates, the British people had to expect 3,500 tons to fall on them in the first 24 hours, then 700 tons a day, leading to something like 2 million casualties in the first two months. These figures were not published.

During the crisis over Czechoslovakia in 1938, many mothers left London for the country with their children. They returned when Hitler and Prime Minister Neville Chamberlain signed the Munich agreement, but the respite was short, and by 1939 Hitler was demanding Danzig from Poland, whose safety Britain was pledged to guarantee. That summer, the government handed out more than 50 million gas masks (the Germans were expected to launch poison gas attacks), and Londoners were given corrugated iron sheets to make primitive 'Anderson' air raid shelters in their back gardens. Then, on 1 September, Hitler invaded Poland. Railway stations filled with children being evacuated, air raid precautions began, the new Auxiliary Fire Service was mobilised, and at eleven o'clock on the morning of Sunday 3 September, Chamberlain announced that Britain was at war with Germany. Twenty-eight minutes later, London heard its first air raid siren of the war. After another half-hour, the 'all clear' sounded. The alert had been caused by a civil aircraft that had not filed a flight plan. Many false alarms punctuated the first weeks of the war, but gradually they became a rarity. What actually happened was not the dreaded air raids, but the so-called Phoney War. For months people dutifully carried their gas masks around in cardboard boxes, but, for the moment, Hitler needed his air force to attack Poland. Anyway, he assumed that once he had conquered it, Britain and France would give up, so there seemed no point in antagonising them with air raids. In fact, the first bombs of the Second World War in London came not from the Germans, but from the IRA (see Chapter 5), and the main increase in civilian deaths resulted from the blackout, which brought a sevenfold increase in fatal road accidents.

Nearly one and a half million women and children left Greater London in September 1939, and people were also evacuated from Manchester, Merseyside, Tyneside, Birmingham, industrial Yorkshire, Southampton and Portsmouth. Some soon got miserable in unwelcoming billets, others were bored by life away from the city, and many were not convinced that the places they had gone to would be any safer than those they had left. So by January

1940, about a million children had returned home. Some unhappy East End youngsters even made their way back from Dorset on foot. The first civilian casualties from enemy action in Britain came on 30 April 1940, when a German aeroplane that had been laying mines crashed, killing two people at Clacton-on-Sea. It was soon plain, though, that the Nazis had no qualms about bombing civilians. They killed up to 800 when they bombed Rotterdam, and they also bombed and strafed refugee columns in France. In response, on 15 May, the RAF bombed the Ruhr, the first of a long series of raids. Hitler then ordered the Luftwaffe to attack Britain in retaliation. The first bombs fell on Kent. On 25 May, German bombers attacked Middlesbrough. There were a number of raids in June, and the Luftwaffe came on twenty-seven nights in July. The targets were airfields, ports, railways and factories, and they did hamper the war effort, with one raid on Vickers at Weybridge, for example, causing damage equivalent to the loss of 125 Wellington bombers. However, although the Germans used radio beams to guide in their bombs, launching air raids from thousands of feet up while being harassed by fighters and anti-aircraft fire was never an exact science, and churches, schools and houses were also hit. In August, the attacks became more intense. Birmingham, Liverpool, Coventry, Plymouth, Bristol and Swansea were all hit, and more than 1,000 civilians were killed.

On the night of 24 August, two German raiders dropped bombs on the City of London, almost destroying the ancient church of St Giles-without-Cripplegate, where Shakespeare had worshipped, Cromwell had married, and Milton was buried. They also killed nine people. It seems likely the bombers were trying to find the oil storage depot at Thames Haven and got lost, but in retaliation, Churchill ordered a series of raids on Berlin. Most did little damage, but one killed ten civilians near a railway station. On 4 September, Hitler made a speech threatening terrible revenge. Goering had promised the Führer that if he ordered a determined attack on the capital, Londoners would flee in terror, government would collapse, and Britain would sue for peace. The sirens went at four o'clock on the beautiful afternoon of 7 September 1940. London was the biggest target on earth, spread out over 80 square miles, and to attack it, Germany had assembled the most powerful force ever directed against a single target – nearly 350 bombers escorted by more than 600 fighters. As they flew towards London, some observers could not help admiring their 'majestic orderliness'. By day, or even on the darkest night, the Thames was always a wonderful aid to navigation, and high explosives and incendiaries rained down on the docks, and on road and railway links. Inevitably, the terraced houses and blocks of flats among them were hit too. The Luftwaffe attacked with 50-gallon oil bombs that could throw burning liquid over an area of 1,500 square feet, starting enormous fires, and with small magnesium incendiaries that slid into every nook and cranny. Half a mile of the Surrey shore was soon ablaze 'like a lake in hell', as A.P. Herbert put it.

The 'all clear' sounded at ten past six, but two hours later, more bombers flew in and, guided in by the flames, continued the attack for another eight hours. One firefighter described 'a raging inferno against which were silhouetted groups of pigmy firemen directing their futile jets against the wall of flame'. The Germans claimed they had dropped nearly 1,000 tons of bombs on the capital during the raids, and the fires in the docklands were so fierce that for the Dean on the roof of St Paul's Cathedral: 'The whole of that night was almost as bright as a sunny day.' It became known as 'Black Saturday'; 430 people were killed and 1,600 injured, while the Germans lost thirty-three aircraft against twenty-eight British fighters. One East Ender, seeing the destruction the bombers brought, exclaimed: 'Blimey, we've lost the war.' The next day, though, Churchill visited Bethnal Green, and when he roared, 'Are we downhearted?' the crowd shouted back 'No!' with 'astonishing gusto', according to an official accompanying him. People also shouted 'We can take it – but give it them back'. Churchill promised 'repayment with compound interest', but the next night, the Luftwaffe was back, finding its targets easily because of the fires that were still raging, and killing another 400 people. In two days, the Germans had killed more Londoners than in the whole of the First World War, and for the next seventy-six nights, with the exception of one when the weather was too bad, London was bombed.

During that first week of attacks the most devastating single bomb of the war came down on a school at Canning Town in East London, where hundreds of families were awaiting evacuation, though the intended target may well have been the docks or a nearby power station. Four hundred people died in the rubble. The King and Queen were quick to visit the areas that had been bombed. When she was asked whether they were going to be evacuated, Queen Elizabeth replied: 'The children won't leave without me. I won't leave without the King, and the King will never leave.' Buckingham Palace was hit twice in the next few days, and the Queen famously remarked: 'I am glad we've been bombed. It makes me feel I can look the East End in the face.' In the East End, though, the situation was grave. After three weeks of bombing, it was estimated that half the population of Stepney had moved out. Many East Enders drifted to West London, hoping it was safer, and then when they found it was not immune from attack, they got on trains at Paddington and ended up wandering the streets of Oxford or Reading. Oxford was said to have taken in 22,000 evacuees, and the quadrangles of Christ Church were turned over to drying nappies. During the First World War, tens of thousands had sheltered on the tube network, but now the government did not want them let in, fearing the development of a 'shelter mentality'; once people had gone down they would be reluctant to come up again. So Londoners took matters into their own hands. According to one account: 'Thousands upon thousands . . . pushed their way into Liverpool Street Station and demanded to be let down to shelter.' At first the authorities got soldiers to bar the way, but the crowd would not give up. It is not clear who exactly took the momentous decision, but eventually 'a great yell went up and the gates were opened.' The tube became a vital refuge, and on one night when a census was taken, 177,000 were found to be sheltering there, but more than half of all Londoners continued to sleep in their own beds during raids.

One of the attractions of the tube was that in the deeper stations, you could not hear the bombs, but it did not guarantee safety. A direct hit on Balham station sent a torrent of sludge and water from a burst main on to the platform, burying sixty-five people alive, while a bomb bounced down the escalator at Bank and exploded on the platform, killing more than 100, some of whom were blown on to the line in front of an oncoming train. Fortunately, the Germans did not have a heavy bomber, and so were not able to deliver the tonnage of bombs that had been feared, and in addition, the average of twenty casualties per ton was also lower than expected. What the authorities had underestimated, though, was the strain on relief services. For every civilian killed, thirty-five were made homeless. During the first fifty-seven nights of the London Blitz, a quarter of a million people were without a roof over their heads for a time. Unfortunately, planning had been based on the assumption that they would stay in the rest centres for only a few hours, and facilities were basic or worse. At Stepney, 300 people had to sleep on the floor. There were ten pails and coal scuttles as lavatories, seven wash basins with cold water, and the only lighting was from hurricane lamps, while the stock of cutlery at Bethnal Green amounted to two spoons and a blunt knife. By the end of September, 14,000 people were said to be living in London rest centres in 'desperately overcrowded' conditions.

These first raids were, according to one German pilot, 'quite routine, like running a bus service', with planes taking off at 2-minute intervals, but by the end of September, the Luftwaffe was suffering a casualty rate of two-thirds on some daylight raids, and by mid-October it was generally restricted to night operations. Over the course of the war, anti-aircraft fire killed many more Londoners than it did German pilots, through shrapnel or unexploded shells falling back to earth, but the government noted that morale improved when the guns kept up a steady barrage, and, besides, they soon became more effective. In September 1940, it had taken 30,000 shells to destroy a single enemy aircraft, but by January 1941, the ratio had come down to 4,000. Unfortunately, improving defences meant enemy aircraft had to fly higher and thus became less accurate, meaning they were even less likely to be able to hit particular targets, putting people's homes at greater risk. Everywhere in London, though, the 'Business as Usual' attitude was being demonstrated. When John Lewis's store in Oxford Street was destroyed, the shop girls set up counters on the pavement outside to sell lingerie. A sign on another bombed shop read 'More open than usual'; a barber declared, 'We've had a close shave. Come and get one', while at a bombed police station, the notice read: 'Be good – we're still open.' Parliament and the law courts met, the banks and the stock exchange did business, newspapers came out more or less on time, while the bombing also broke down traditional British reserve. The Blitz, said H.E. Bates, 'smashed the silence of the railway carriage'.

While the bombs rained down on London, it did not mean that other places were spared. In Cardiff in September, bombers set fire to the Admiralty's fuel oil storage depot at Pembroke Dock. It burned for seventeen days, and five auxiliary firemen died trying to put out the flames. Birmingham was raided on 14 October and sustained nearly 200 casualties, and from November onwards, Hitler concentrated more and more on provincial cities. On the night of 14 November, lit by a 'bomber's moon', 400 aircraft attacked Coventry in a raid that lasted 11 hours. The Germans code-named the operation 'Moonlight Sonata', and it followed a tried and trusted formula. The first wave of aircraft pinpointed the town centre with flares and incendiary bombs, creating a conspicuous target for the next wave to attack with high explosive and parachute mines. Coventry was a crucial centre for engineering and arms manufacturing, and twenty-one factories were damaged, but so were 100 acres of the historic city centre, including the cathedral. Nearly 2,300 buildings were destroyed, including seven hospitals, while 50,000 were damaged and 554 people were killed. Fire engines came to fight the flames from as far away as Wigan. The next day, the air was so dense with soot particles that it was dark till noon, and the city was in a dreadful state. All the biggest water mains were blocked, the central fire station had been hit, the telephone system was knocked out so that fire service units had no way of communicating with each other, and they had no petrol either. It brought a new word into the language – 'Coventrated'. If the Germans had returned the following night, some feared Coventry could be damaged beyond repair; but instead they attacked London again.

The raid did disrupt the war effort, but Coventry's workers showed themselves extremely resourceful. The Morris engine works had lost its roof, but the workers carried on in the open air, and in six weeks, production was back to normal. Other factories brought in coke braziers for heating, and replaced damaged roofs with tarpaulin. By now, Britain was also getting its act together on feeding those bombed out of their homes. Coventry saw the first appearance of Queen's Messengers – mobile feeding convoys, organised by the Americans in London, with lorries that could carry 6,000 meals at a time. When they made their next appearance in Swansea, they were cheered through the streets. On 19 November, the Germans attacked another major industrial centre, Birmingham, where even parts of Cadbury's chocolate factory had been turned over to war production. Three nights of raids left nearly 800 dead, including fifty workers at the BSA factory. By now around 15,000 British people had been killed, compared to fewer than 1,000 from RAF raids in Germany. Indeed, until September 1942, you were more likely to die if you were a British civilian than if you were in the British armed forces. No wonder one woman in a blitzed city remarked: 'I'm only glad my Jim is in the army and out of all this.'

Bristol was an important centre for aircraft manufacture, and 1,100 people were killed there in attacks that continued from December through to April. Churchill arrived to collect an honorary degree from the university after one heavy raid. People cooking breakfast in half-demolished houses shouted 'Good Old Winnie' as he passed. At the university, buildings were still burning, and many of those attending the ceremony simply put on academic gowns over the clothes they had worn all night for firefighting. In Southampton, with its port, shipyards and Spitfire factory, a series of raids left 500 people dead by the end of 1940, and it was said that most of the population was trekking out into the countryside or surrounding towns every night. Sheffield, the centre of steel-making, was hit in December. The bombs did little damage to the steelworks, but they killed more than 600 people, and made 36,000 homeless. It was a similar story in Manchester, which made Lancaster bombers, tanks and guns. Raids on 22 and 23 December wrought most destruction in residential areas, killing 1,000 people, and making 37,000 homeless for Christmas.

December 29 looked a great night for an air raid. It was the Sunday between Christmas and New Year, and offices, warehouses and churches in the City of London were locked up and deserted, fire-watchers were at home, and the water in the Thames was very low. What better time could there be to start the second Great Fire of London? So the Luftwaffe hurled down 100,000 incendiaries in what became known as the 'Great Fire Raid'. Six huge conflagrations consumed much of the historic City, including the Guildhall, the Old Bailey, the Temple and eight of Sir Christopher Wren's churches. Churchill gave the order that St Paul's must be saved at all costs, and, as twenty-eight incendiaries struck it, 300 volunteers patrolled the building, searching out fire in every corner. This was the night when the famous picture was taken of the great dome rising above the smoke and flames. One observer, watching from a hill in south-east London, said: 'at times it was engulfed and we thought it had gone; then the fiery tide lowered and the cathedral was above the capital as ever.' At one point, the verger said: 'All we can do now is pray.' 'Then pray standing up, with your stirrup pump handy', replied the Dean. American reporters even cabled that the cathedral had been lost, but at midnight fog rolled across the Channel, preventing any more bombers crossing, and at four in the morning, the tide turned in the Thames, allowing firemen finally to get a decent supply of water. As ever they had braved bombs, flying embers and falling masonry to fight the flames. A dozen paid with their lives, and another 160 people were killed.

The New Year began with a major raid on Cardiff, which killed 160 people and ripped the roof off Llandaff Cathedral. On 10 January, Old Portsmouth was virtually destroyed – the Guildhall, the early nineteenth-century residential squares, churches, as well as the shopping centres of Portsmouth and Southsea. In Portsmouth, as in many other places, people were in the habit of seeking refuge outside the city – a favourite place was Portsdown Hill, where big shelters had been tunnelled into the chalk and equipped with bunks and canteens. The problem was that in the empty houses left behind, undetected small fires could soon develop into big ones. On 20 and 21

March, the ancient centre of Plymouth was also turned into a desert, with the Old Guildhall and a whole collection of medieval buildings destroyed. Altogether, 18,000 houses were destroyed, as local people trekked out of the city to shelter in barns, churches, cowsheds, ditches and quarries. The Royal Navy dockyard, though, never stopped working. Lady Astor, the Mayor, walked the streets during raids in a steel helmet and did cartwheels to cheer people up, then, when the bombers had gone, organised dances on Plymouth Hoe. The raids in March were followed by another five in April which brought the number of people killed to 1,000. The sustained bombing obliterated whole districts, and one trader said he could stand in the central shopping area of Plymouth and Devonport 'without being able to see an inhabited building'.

After London, the Luftwaffe's most important target was probably Liverpool, the main port for goods from the United States. By the end of 1940, hundreds had already been killed there, and now over two nights in March, Merseyside suffered another 1,300 deaths. The area was attacked again for the first seven nights of May. In one raid, an ammunition ship was hit, sending flames 1,600ft up in the air, and flinging metal plates 2 miles. Altogether, more than fifty vessels were sunk or destroyed. The whole dock area had to be evacuated, and half the shipping berths were knocked out of action, though if a consignment was urgent, dockers often continued to unload it as the bombs fell. Another 1,900 people were killed, and 70,000 left homeless, and in Bootle near the docks, only one house in ten was left undamaged. Clydeside was a crucial centre for shipbuilding and engineering, and Glasgow was the second biggest city in Britain. Inevitably, it too attracted heavy bombing. Rolls-Royce's aero engine works at Hillington was struck, while a parachute mine scored a direct hit on a tenement, killing eighty-three people. Clydebank suffered proportionately more than any other town in Britain. Its 47,000 people were clustered around the John Brown shipyard, and just eight of its 12,000 houses escaped damage. In one street, eighty people were killed, while one family lost fifteen members. By the second night of the attack, 35,000 of Clydebank's population were homeless. At night, the population sank to just 2,000, but people still turned up to work in the morning, and only two weeks after the attack, production was back to normal. Altogether along the Clyde, more than 1,000 people were killed in raids on consecutive nights, but most of the shipyards, docks and factories that lined the river continued to operate.

Belfast was another important shipbuilding and aerospace centre, and was the only place in Northern Ireland to face major bombing raids. On 15 April 1941, Easter Tuesday, 180 bombers attacked for seven hours, but perhaps the Luftwaffe pilots were confused by a smokescreen hastily flung up to protect the shipyards, because the bombs landed not on the city's industrial heartland, but on the residential areas to the north, with terrible carnage in the New Lodge, Lower Shankill and Antrim Road. The raiders started more than 140 fires. One woman watching said: 'You would have thought that someone had set fire to the world.' The War Office despatched pumps and firemen from Glasgow, Liverpool and Preston, while the Northern Ireland government sent a telegram to the President of the Irish Republic, Eamon de Valera. Awoken in the middle of the night, he immediately agreed to help, and thirteen engines and seventy men volunteered to go north. Up to 900 people were killed, the biggest number in any single raid outside London, and the Falls Road public baths had to be emptied so that 150 corpses could be laid out. Another raid on Sunday 4 May devastated Harland and Wolff's shipyard, destroying three warships that were nearing completion and reducing its capacity for six months. A large part of the High Street also burned down, and nearly 200 people were killed. By the end of May, it was reckoned that around half the population had left – the biggest proportion in any British city. Streams of people pushed prams and handcarts with mattresses and bedclothes strapped to them. A newspaper said scenes 'were like the pictures of American pioneers'.

On two separate nights in April, the Luftwaffe killed more than 1,000 people in London, then on 5 May came what was to be the worst raid of the war. Bombs pounded the capital for five hours, destroying the debating chamber of the House of Commons, and damaging Westminster Abbey, St Paul's, Scotland Yard, the Law Courts, the British Museum, the Mansion House, St James's Palace and the Tower of London. Fourteen hospitals were hit, as well as thirty factories. Five thousand houses were destroyed, and more than 1,400 people were killed. Like London, Hull was an easy place to spot, perched conspicuously on a bend in the river Humber. Often it was also the last major city that German air crews passed on their way home, so they would unload what was left of their bombs there rather than carry them back. This had already happened about fifty times, but on 8 and 9 May, Hull became the last big town in Britain to be blitzed. The shopping centre was destroyed, 1,000 people were killed, and the fires could be seen 50 miles away. An anti-aircraft gunner said: 'I never knew what All Hell Let Loose meant until I looked at the bombing of Hull . . . I thought "Hell's bells, nobody will live in this."' The authorities in Hull, though, showed themselves very efficient. Even though twenty-four rest centres were damaged in the raid, the city still managed to billet all the homeless within two days.

Hard as it might be for those on the receiving end to believe, defensive measures had improved dramatically. Ways were found of jamming the Luftwaffe's radio beam bomb guidance system, and simple deception was used, with dummy towns set up on open land, featuring lights that dimmed as the raiders approached, or special effects, like virtual blast furnaces. They were known as 'Starfish'. The one for London was in Richmond Park, but there were another thirty for places like Bristol, Swansea and Cardiff. Often the Luftwaffe was not deceived, but the most successful, at Sinach Common near Portsmouth, attracted 200 high-explosive bombs and parachute mines as well as 5,000 incendiaries meant for the city. On 8 May 1941, though, a successful decoy operation that had protected Rolls Royce and other key factories in Derby had tragic consequences for Nottingham. The Luftwaffe was misled by a Starfish near Cropwell Butler to the south-east of Nottingham, and more than 430 people were killed or injured in the city and the surrounding area.

From late 1940 radar began to transform air defence, and there were more guns, more searchlights, and more fighters specialising in night operations, so that the cost of the Blitz for Germany got higher all the time. In March 1941, the fighters claimed twenty-two kills, and in May, ninety-six, while the total number of German aircraft brought down through all causes from March to May was said to be 271. During the first ten days of May 1941, seventy German aircraft were shot down, the same number as in the first four months of the Blitz. Besides, the Fuehrer now needed his aircraft for other things. In June, he invaded Russia, and though there were heavy attacks on Hull in June and July, most of the rest of Britain was left alone. The Blitz had lasted for eight months with scarcely a night's break. Now it was over, and bizarrely, it may have been Britain's salvation. In late August and early September 1940, the Luftwaffe had conducted a ruthless campaign against fighter bases in south-east England, and had destroyed RAF aircraft at an alarming rate. Hitler's decision to divert his aircraft to bombing civilians may have let us off a very dangerous hook. Devastating though the Blitz was, it appeared to have no clear objective, with the Luftwaffe targeting in turn London, then the great industrial centres, then the major ports, without knocking any of them out of action, or breaking Britain's spirit.

Improvements to living conditions had helped to keep up that spirit. From early 1941, there was a determined campaign to upgrade public shelters. Stronger buildings were provided, made of concrete and steel rods, and by the end of April, 600,000 wooden bunks had been provided in the London region alone. For those sheltering at home, the government devised the Morrison shelter, a steel table with sides of wire mesh that could be put up indoors, and was stronger than the Anderson. It cost £7 12s 6d, but it was free to any family with an income of less than £350 a year. There was self-help too. At Swiss Cottage underground station in London, shelterers produced their own newspaper. Bethnal Green's public shelter boasted a library, while the Chislehurst Caves, to which 8,000 Londoners commuted nightly, had a church. Many, though, preferred to shelter in a cinema or a pub where they would sing to drown out the noise of the bombs. In many ways, the Blitz disrupted public services less than might have been expected. Portsmouth once lost electricity for two and a half days, and Plymouth for a day, but generally supplies were rarely interrupted for more than a few hours, nor were water supplies, though even that could be a severe handicap for firefighters. Oil installations were a key target, but only 3 per cent of supplies was lost, and the government protected industry by building new plants on the outskirts of towns or away from centres of population. Seventy thousand tons of food were destroyed, but from May 1941, American lend-lease supplies began to pour in. The British got used to eating more bread and potatoes, and many 'dug for victory', growing vegetables on allotments. The government also opened 'British Restaurants', providing good quality food at affordable prices. Indeed, many working people ate better than they had during the slump of the 1930s.

For the first few months of the Blitz, the RAF had continued trying to hit specific targets rather than bombing less discriminately, but from December 1940, it did start area raids, though on a much smaller scale than those perpetrated by the Luftwaffe. In March 1942, 'Bomber' Harris mounted attacks on the medieval Hanseatic ports of Lubeck and Rostock. Being built largely of wood, they blazed fiercely. Hitler was incensed, and launched what a German Foreign Office official described as the 'Baedeker raids'. The idea was to attack every English city to which the famous guide book had awarded three stars for cultural interest. The Nazi propaganda chief Josef Goebbels wrote of 'razing English cultural shrines to the ground'. The bombers attacked Exeter, Bath, Norwich and York. They were not 'razed'. York's fifteenth-century Guildhall was destroyed, but Bath's Georgian centre was largely untouched and all the cathedrals escaped terminal damage. Again, it was civilian bodies that suffered worst, with the Luftwaffe killing 400 at Bath, where they machine-gunned the streets, and another 500 in the other cities. After the RAF mounted a 1,000-bomber raid on Cologne, the Germans bombed Canterbury three times. During one attack the Dean stood on the cathedral roof in his gaiters, supervising firemen who were hurling incendiaries by the dozen down on to the lawns below. The building trembled 'like a ship buffeted by waves', but it survived.

Right up until the last days of the war, the Germans continued to mount raids, often using hit and run tactics, with fast fighter bombers. The first three months of 1944 saw the 'Little Blitz', with thirteen attacks on London, Bristol and Hull. There were rarely many more than 100 aircraft, and the crews were often poorly trained. Faced with improved defences, on some nights no more than twenty would reach their target. The main weapon was the 'Molotov Breadbasket', a canister of up to fifty incendiaries designed to burst about 100ft above the ground and scatter the bombs. Then, a week after D-day in June, with the end seemingly in sight, a huge explosion destroyed a railway bridge at Bow in East London. The official story was that a German bomber had crashed, but actually this was a V1, a 'doodlebug'. The V stood for *Vergeltungswaffe*, weapon of vengeance, while the '1' was meant to suggest that this was the first of a whole series of fearsome devices. V1s were pilotless aircraft, forerunners of the cruise missile. They flew at 400 miles an hour, carrying a warhead of nearly 1,900lb, as big as all but the biggest bombs, with an engine mounted on the tail. In the final phase of their journey, the engine cut out, and then those within earshot had 12 seconds to find cover before a fearful explosion that could damage buildings and shatter glass up to a quarter of a mile away. A total of 10,500 was launched from sites in France, of which 7,000 reached Britain. Half of them were brought down by guns or aircraft, while the new Gloster Meteor jet fighter could tip a V1's wing and cause it to crash, but 2,340 landed on London, killing 5,475 people. In the capital, the government opened three new deep shelters below the level of tube stations, but in the later stages of the war, another 750 V1s were launched from aircraft over the North Sea, striking targets as far north as Manchester (which was hit by eighteen), Oldham and Yorkshire.

The most destructive single V1 hit the Guards' Chapel in London on the sunny Sunday morning of 20 June just as the congregation of servicemen and women, their relatives and other civilians were getting to their feet after the first lesson. The explosion destroyed the building and killed 119 people. Other V1s damaged the Law Courts and demolished Carey Street bankruptcy court. The doodle bugs brought horrifying new sights. Trees had their leaves blown off, but were left with shreds of human flesh hanging from them. After one explosion, a man stepped out from the doorway where he had been sheltering, and a sheet of plate glass falling from above promptly cut him in half. By August, a million people had once again left London. Croydon was the place hit most often – 141 times. (This was partly because of a deliberate deception plan mounted by the government to make the Germans believe the V1s were landing 2 or 3 miles beyond the point where they actually exploded. The Germans then 'corrected' their targeting so that most fell short of central London, and landed south of the Thames.) Two hundred and eleven people were killed, and 54,000 homes were damaged. The authorities converted furniture vans into mobile bath houses, to cater for those who had been bombed out of their homes.

On 5 September, eighty days after the attacks began, allied troops overran the launch sites, and two days later, Duncan Sandys, the junior minister responsible for coordinating defences against the V1s, felt able to announce that 'except possibly for a few last shots', London's ordeal was over. The last shots proved to be the loudest. At a quarter to seven the following evening, two thunderous explosions were heard at each end of London, one at Chiswick and one at Epping. The first official explanation was that gas mains had blown up. In fact, these were V2s, ballistic missiles, weighing 14 tons and carrying a 1-ton warhead. They were launched from mobile sites in Holland, travelled at twice the speed of sound, and could reach London in 4 minutes. When they landed they could knock down a whole row of houses. 'I thought the end of the world had come', said one man who saw their destructive power. 'The earth trembled, the very air seemed to vibrate.' Radar could pick them up, but there was no way of intercepting them, and no useful warning could be given. Most V2s landed in the East End or the suburbs to the east and north. The place worst hit was Ilford, struck by thirty-five. The most devastating individual strike happened just before Christmas 1944, when a V2 struck Woolworth's in New Cross while it was packed with shoppers, killing 168 people. A thousand men worked for 48 hours to free survivors.

Some found the V2s less terrifying than the V1s, because the rockets came without warning, and people did not fear they would have to spend the last few seconds of life in a frantic, undignified search for safety, but the government was alarmed. At one point, it considered evacuating 85,000 civil servants from London, and hospitals were emptied to free up 25,000 beds for the expected casualties.

Finally, in March, the launch sites in Holland were captured and the rockets stopped, with the last V2 hitting Orpington on 28 March 1945. They had killed more than 2,500 people. Overall during the war, 60,595 British civilians were killed, nearly 30,000 of them in London. In addition, 86,182 were seriously injured, including more than 50,000 in London, while 220,000 houses were destroyed, 133,000 in the capital. Britain was the only country to fight through the whole of the Second World War, from the first day to the last, and for a long time, it had stood alone against the forces of Nazism and Fascism. British civilians had been in the front line of that war in a way that had never happened before. The US ambassador was impressed by 'the effort to maintain the appearance of normal life in the face of danger, and . . . the patient acceptance of hardships and hazards by ordinary people', but perhaps the most telling tribute came from an unexpected quarter. When the tide began to turn in 1943, and Germany started to face the kind of bombing raids that had killed and maimed British people and flattened British buildings for so long, Goebbels, who in 1940 had expected such tactics to bring Britain to its knees, now called on the German people to follow the example of fortitude shown by the British.

# CHAPTER FIVE

# TERRORISM

The first enemy bombs of the Second World War in Britain were detonated not by the Germans, but by the Irish Republican Army. On 22 February 1940, under cover of the blackout, they planted two devices in the centre of London. One in Oxford Street tore off a woman's leg as the bomb exploded in a waste bin. Days before war broke out, on 25 August 1939, an IRA bomb had killed five people and injured more than fifty in Coventry. There had already been more than 130 IRA explosions that year in cities such as London, Manchester and Birmingham. These blasts, though, were just the latest episode in a conflict that had continued for centuries, and had first scarred Britain's streets more than seventy years before.

Back in November 1867, following the killing of a police sergeant in Manchester by Fenians, a group dedicated to the liberation of Ireland from British rule, two of its members were arrested in London; the armaments organiser, Richard Burke, and his colleague Theobald Casey. While they were being held in Clerkenwell House of Detention, they smuggled out messages in invisible ink about what they thought was a weak point in the prison walls to comrades in the capital, who agreed to blow a hole there while the prisoners were at exercise. The first time they tried, they could not get the gunpowder to go off. On 13 December they had another go, but the authorities had got wind of the plot, and kept the prisoners in their cells. This time the gunpowder went off, and blew a 20ft gap in the wall, but it did much more than that. When the dust settled, it was clear that most of the houses in Corporation Lane, opposite the prison, lay in ruins, and fourteen other streets were damaged. Firemen had a dreadful task trying to free people from their wrecked homes. One woman had been killed instantly, and three more people died as they reached hospital. Over the next few days the death toll reached fifteen, including two girls aged 7 and 11, with forty seriously injured. A 27-year-old stevedore named Michael Barrett was convicted of lighting the fuse, though he stoutly maintained his innocence, and on 26 May 1868, he became the last man to be hanged publicly in Britain, meeting his fate outside the gates of Newgate prison. Burke was sentenced to fifteen years for treason, but was released under an amnesty and allowed to go to the United States, where he became assistant city engineer of Chicago.

The Fenian attacks went on. In 1881, they were believed to have started a huge fire at the Royal Victoria dock that caused £500,000 worth of damage, and altogether between 1883 and 1885, they planted thirteen bombs in London, but like most Fenian devices, these caused few serious injuries. The parliamentary battle over Irish independence was to go on for another forty years, and as it was nearing its conclusion, in 1920 two young Irishmen started fourteen fires in timber yards and cotton warehouses in Liverpool, causing the then colossal figure of nearly £1 million worth of damage. In 1922, Ireland secured its independence, but six counties in the North remained British. For Republicans, that meant Ireland was only 'half-free', and the IRA remained determined to overturn the settlement.

Just as the Easter rebels had risen during the First World War, with the Second World War looming the IRA wanted once again to turn England's difficulty into Ireland's opportunity. On 12 January 1939 it sent an ultimatum, demanding British withdrawal. Five days later, at six o'clock in the morning, eight bombs went off simultaneously in London and other cities, some causing extensive damage. The attacks continued into 1940, but a number of the bombers were caught and gaoled, and two who had been involved in the Coventry bombing were sentenced to death. The Irish President, Eamon de Valera, grew more and more worried about extreme Republicans, and alarmed that their flirtation with the Nazis might jeopardise Ireland's neutrality, so he brought in a series of measures which culminated in internment without trial. The IRA's campaign in England petered out for the moment, though they continued attacks in Northern Ireland, shooting dead three police officers during 1942.

In the 1950s, the IRA attacked a BBC transmitter and police and army buildings in Northern Ireland, and killed a policeman in an ambush. The authorities north and south of the border introduced internment and, after a total of eighteen people had been killed, the organisation called off its campaign, admitting that the people it intended to 'liberate' did not support it. In the mid-sixties, though, inter-communal tensions revived, and in 1964, Belfast had its first major sectarian riots for thirty years. Catholics in the

North faced electoral gerrymandering and discrimination in housing and jobs, and a civil rights movement began to attract formidable support, while loyalists began killing Catholics. In the late sixties, the civil rights movement began a series of marches which Protestants, and sometimes police, attacked brutally, allowing them increasingly to be hijacked by extremists who were looking for confrontation with the police. Though many Protestants simply regarded the civil rights movement as a Republican front organisation, it appeared in reality to have caught the IRA on the hop. The Republicans were very short of weapons for any 'armed struggle', although members often acted as stewards at marches and demonstrations.

March 1969 saw a bombing campaign launched against water mains and electricity substations. At the time, this was thought to be the work of the IRA, but the explosions had, in fact, been set off by Loyalist terrorists. Now relations between Protestants and Catholics deteriorated further, and August 1969 saw fifty hours of vicious sectarian fighting in Londonderry in the 'Battle of the Bogside'. The British Prime Minister, James Callaghan, sent in the army for a 'limited operation', and Catholics at first saw the soldiers as protectors, welcoming them with cups of tea. During a riot in Belfast on 14 August, the B Specials part-time police killed a man when they fired into a crowd, making him the first victim of what became known as 'the Troubles'. Later that evening, they also killed a 9-year-old boy sheltering from the gunfire in a back room of the Divis Flats, while the IRA fired its first shots and killed a Protestant. Altogether five other people were killed, while more than 100 mainly Catholic houses were wrecked by petrol bombs. Over the next two months, another ten people were killed, with 900 injured. In October, a Loyalist mob opened fire on the police and killed Constable Victor Arbuckle, the first victim of the Troubles from the security services.

Well into 1970, the British army experienced more hostility from the Protestants than from the Catholics. Then, in July, soldiers found an arms cache, and imposed a curfew for thirty-five hot summer hours in the Catholic Lower Falls, mounting rigorous house-to-house searches, sometimes damaging property in the process. It had a disastrous effect on relations with the Catholic community. The Official IRA started shooting, and killed three people, but it was the breakaway, hardline Provisional IRA, formed the previous December, that was now preparing to exploit and foment the discord. During that summer, they began threatening or beating up any Catholics who fraternised with the soldiers, and they exploded about 100 small bombs, attacking targets like bus depots, telephone exchanges and pubs. On 6 February 1971, the first British soldier to die in the Troubles was killed by IRA machine-gun fire in the New Lodge Road. Meanwhile, the bombing campaign grew more vicious; a suitcase full of gelignite flung into the reception area of a police station injured twenty-two people. An army sergeant was killed trying to protect a 2-year-old child. As the marching season stoked up the temperature, explosions began averaging two a day, and in August, the government introduced internment once again.

The authorities made no attempt to arrest Loyalist terrorists – only Catholics were picked up, more than 300 in the first sweep, of whom nearly a third were released after two days. Intelligence was poor; most IRA men had already slipped away, and often IRA members would anonymously give false information to the security forces, so that they arrested innocent Catholics, helping to give another twist to the downward spiral in relations. By the end of 1971, 1,500 people had been interned. Two in every three were released, but not before some had been deprived of food, sleep and sanitation, and had been kicked and beaten. In the four months before internment, 8 people were killed; in the four months after, the figure was 114. The Home Secretary Reginald Maudling was to remark prophetically: 'I don't think one can speak of defeating the IRA, of eliminating them completely, but it is the design of the security services to reduce their level of violence to something like an acceptable level.' Among the victims of the last four months of 1971 were fifteen killed in one of the worst individual incidents of the Troubles. On 4 December, an 8-year-old boy selling newspapers saw a car with a Union Jack sticker stop in Belfast's North Queen Street. A passenger got out and placed a 50lb bomb in the doorway of McGurk's Catholic bar, then got back into the car as it drove off. The explosion brought the building crashing down. Almost at once, fighting broke out between Catholic and Protestant mobs, and police and soldiers were injured by gunfire, hampering the rescue effort. Among the dead bodies found in the rubble were two women and three children. Although many believed at the time that it was an IRA device that went off by mistake, the bomb had actually been planted by the Loyalist Ulster Volunteer Force.

Meanwhile, the IRA was developing its own arsenal. Some weapons they made themselves, but many came from abroad, with the United States a key source; in those days, the Americans had not yet discovered the 'War on Terror'. (In fact, just three weeks before the Provisionals killed eighteen

British soldiers in August 1979, the US government had refused to allow the sale of guns to Britain's security forces.) Other weapons came from Libya, a country America later saw as part of the 'axis of evil'. In the last two weeks of January 1972, the IRA killed two soldiers and wounded two others. For months the army had been fighting rioters every night; since August, in Londonderry alone, soldiers had been shot at more than 2,600 times. On Sunday 30 January, the Northern Ireland Civil Rights Association planned to hold a march in the city. It had been banned by the authorities, and soldiers of the 1st Battalion, the Parachute Regiment, arguably the toughest in Northern Ireland, were brought in from Belfast especially for the occasion. The organisers planned to march up to the army barrier, then withdraw. Thousands did precisely that, but a small group stayed behind throwing stones, fire grates, metal rods or any other missiles they could lay their hands on. The soldiers replied with rubber bullets. Shortly after four o'clock, one army commander decided to try to arrest trouble makers, and ordered the paratroopers to move out from behind their barriers. The question of what happened next has been one of the most bitterly disputed of the entire Troubles. The Paras insisted they had come under fire (and some independent witnesses supported them) or that they had fired only at nail bombers. During the course of twenty minutes, they fired more than 100 bullets and killed thirteen people, but there was no convincing evidence that any of the victims had been handling guns or bombs. The coroner called the soldiers' action 'sheer, unadulterated murder', while even the official government report, widely condemned as a whitewash, conceded that some of the Paras' shooting 'had bordered on the reckless.' For the army and the British government, whatever may have been the rights and wrongs of the soldiers' actions, 'Bloody Sunday' was undeniably a public relations disaster.

Less than a month later, the Official IRA bombed the Parachute Regiment's officers' mess at Aldershot, killing five women who worked at the camp and a Catholic padre. In May, the Officials called a ceasefire, but by now they had been eclipsed by the Provisionals, and their action was of little relevance. The British government tried imposing direct rule from Westminster in place of a Northern Ireland administration seen by many Catholics as blatantly sectarian, but nothing seemed to slow the violence, and 1972 turned out to be the worst year of the Troubles. In an hour and a quarter of the afternoon of 27 July, 'Bloody Friday', the Provisionals detonated twenty-six bombs in the centre of Belfast, killing two soldiers and seven other people, and injuring

130. The Loyalist paramilitaries, meanwhile, were responding with a systematic campaign of sectarian killings, and the death toll for the year reached 467, including 103 soldiers and 41 police. The figure also included more than 30 IRA men killed by their own bombs.

The death toll for 1973 was lower, at 250, and towards the end of the year, the British government established a power-sharing executive in Northern Ireland in which Protestant and Catholic politicians could cooperate, but 1974 saw the Provisional IRA extending its terrorist campaign. There had been bombs in England already, with IRA woman Dolours Price, for example, arguing that: 'an incursion into the mainland would be more effective than twenty car bombs in any part of the North.' She had helped to plot a bombing campaign in London in 1973, with explosions at the Old Bailey and in Whitehall. Late at night on Sunday 3 February 1974, soldiers, airmen and their families boarded a coach at Manchester's Chorlton Street bus station to return from weekend leave to bases at Catterick and Leeming. At about two o'clock in the morning, as they sped along the M62 south of Leeds, a 50lb bomb went off in the luggage compartment. The windscreen shattered and fell on the head of the coach driver, but as the blood poured down his face, he managed to pull the coach on to the side of the motorway and bring it to a stop, preventing an even worse disaster. He said: 'I'm told I held on for 200 yards, but I don't know. I just gripped the wheel.' Then he scrambled from the wrecked cab with a torch and found 'bodies all over the place.' A 17-year-old girl on the coach said, 'The floor just opened up and I fell through.' A corporal from Manchester and his wife, both aged 23, and their children aged 5 and 2 were all killed, along with seven other soldiers in their teens and twenties. An Englishwoman, Judith Ward, was later gaoled for life for the bombing, but after she had spent eighteen years in prison, the Court of Appeal declared her conviction unsafe, and she was released.

Back in Northern Ireland, by May the power-sharing executive had been brought down by a widespread strike of Protestant workers, many of them conscripted through liberal doses of intimidation by Loyalist paramilitaries, but worse was to come on Thursday 21 November. One of Birmingham's main landmarks was the Rotunda, a high-rise round glass building in the city centre which housed, among other things, the local Inland Revenue. That evening, a man with an Irish accent called the *Birmingham Post and Mail* using a recognised code word to say there was a bomb in the tax office. The IRA had already bombed the Rotunda twice, and the police began to clear it, but just six minutes after the bomb warning, there was a violent explosion in the Mulberry Bush pub at the bottom of the building. A 15lb bomb had blown a hole through 9in-thick reinforced concrete and had brought down the roof, sending lumps crashing down on drinkers in a haze of brick dust and smoke. The blast was heard clearly in a basement bar just around the corner, the Tavern in the Town, and moments later, another bomb exploded there. The pubs were very popular with young people, and a 16-year-old police cadet who was one of the first people on the scene said: 'Whoever put the bomb in there knew they would only be getting kids.' An 18-year-old who had been in the Tavern remembered: 'I was going to put a record on the juke box when all hell was let loose. There was a massive explosion with bodies everywhere and I had to climb over them to get out. The screaming and groaning of the injured was terrible.' A teenage girl who had been drinking in the Tavern said: 'The ceiling came down and the lights went out. I remember my boyfriend holding my face to his chest. If he hadn't it would have been blown to bits.' Taxi drivers piled casualties into their cabs to ferry them to hospital, along with every available ambulance in the city.

Twenty-one people were killed; ten at the Mulberry Bush and eleven at the Tavern, and 162 were injured. Twelve of the dead were in their teens or early twenties. 'Worse Than Ulster', screamed the headline in the *Birmingham Evening Mail* the next day. Parliament immediately rushed through the Prevention of Terrorism Act, banning the IRA and allowing police to detain suspects for longer. In 1975, six men were convicted of the killings and sentenced to life imprisonment, but after they had served sixteen years in gaol, their sentences were quashed by the Court of Appeal, and they received large sums in compensation. It was many years before the IRA admitted carrying out the attacks, and the real bombers have never been brought to justice.

In Northern Ireland, the melancholy catalogue of violence and suffering continued, punctuated every so often by an act so appalling that it provoked more than routine horror outside the immediate circle of those affected by it. One such came in July 1975, when Loyalist terrorists wearing uniforms of the part-time Ulster Defence Regiment halted the Miami Showband near Newry on its way home from a concert, and killed three of its members. The following January, the IRA stopped a bus carrying twelve workmen near Whitecross. One of them was a Catholic. He was allowed to leave. The terrorists then mowed down the other eleven with automatic fire. Ten died.

The youngest victim of the Troubles was 6-week-old Andrew Maguire, who was hit by a car driven by an IRA man who had fired on the army and then tried to flee on 10 August 1976. His mother Anne Maguire was badly injured, and two of her other children were also killed. The next day, with two other women, she formed the Peace People. For a time, in spite of violence and intimidation from Republican and Loyalist terrorists, they won support from tens of thousands. The Peace People were awarded the Nobel Peace Prize, but like many others they found the hatreds of Northern Ireland too deep and intractable for the solutions they offered. A new hardline approach by the security forces brought the death toll down to eighty-one in 1978, though there were loud allegations that the police and army were pursuing a 'shoot to kill' policy, and the fall in deaths did not mean an end to horrific outrages. In February 1978, the Provisionals used a new kind of petrochemical bomb to attack the La Mon House Hotel near Comber, County Down, in the heart of Unionist territory, killing twelve people and inflicting dreadful burns on another twenty-three.

The following year, on 27 August 1979, the IRA launched its most devastating attack on the British army. That morning, in the Irish Republic, they had blown up the Queen's cousin, 79-year-old Earl Mountbatten, his 14-year-old grandson, and two other people. In the afternoon, a convoy of vehicles from the 2nd Parachute Regiment was driving along a dual carriageway on the north side of Carlingford Lough between Warrenpoint and Newry. The other side of the water was in the Irish Republic, and there the IRA waited. They had hidden a bomb in a hay wagon by the side of the road. As the last army truck passed, the Provisionals used a model aircraft radio control device to detonate it. Burning hay was scattered all over the road, and the last truck was left a twisted, blackened hulk with the bodies of six dead soldiers – but this was just the first phase of the operation. The IRA had observed army procedure carefully; they knew the other trucks would go on. Now they opened fire from across the water, and, as they had expected, the soldiers withdrew to a strong defensive position by the stone gateway to a derelict lodge a quarter of a mile away and returned fire. Reinforcements arrived from a helicopter, which also took away some of the wounded, but just as it was taking off, there was another huge explosion. A few days before, the IRA had hidden 500lb of explosives underneath the gateway. The helicopter managed to make off, but another twelve soldiers on the ground were killed. When the Provisionals opened fire across the water again, the army fired back, but were not able to kill any of their assailants. Their only victim was one of the Queen's coachmen who was on holiday on the south side of the lough. One of the patrol bitterly conceded: 'Any soldier would admit that as an operation, it was very well done.' A month later, the Pope came to Ireland, and pleaded for peace: 'On my knees I beg you to turn away from the paths of violence.' It had no discernible effect.

In the early eighties, tension was given a further twist by the hunger strikes in which Bobby Sands and another nine Republican prisoners died. Sands and his family had been burned out of their home in north Belfast in 1972. In the seven months following his refusal to eat on 1 March 1981, there was frequent rioting and more than sixty people were killed, including thirty members of the security forces. Before his death, Bobby Sands had been elected a Westminster MP, and in November the political wing of the IRA, Sinn Fein, unveiled a new strategy, as its director of publicity Danny Morrison asked: 'will anyone here object if with a ballot box in this hand and an Armalite in this hand we take power in Ireland?' From then on, Sinn Fein began to develop a formidable political machine, but in line with Morrison's strategy, that did not mean an end to killing, and Republicans murdered 71 people out of the 100 who died in 1982. Seventeen of them were killed at a Monday night discotheque at the Droppin' Well pub at Ballykelly in County Londonderry, a popular haunt with soldiers. On the night of 6 December 1982, two couples had had a drink and left, after planting a holdall containing a time bomb, carefully placed to blow out a wall and bring the concrete roof down on the dancers. It exploded half an hour before closing time, when the disco was packed with about 150 young people. Rescue services had to search through the rubble in freezing cold for people trapped till dawn. Seventeen were killed, including twelve soldiers. A breakaway Republican terrorist group, the Irish National Liberation Army, said they had done it.

In the early hours of 12 October 1984, the Provisionals came very close to killing the Prime Minister, Margaret Thatcher, with an explosion at the Grand Hotel in Brighton during the Conservative Party Conference. She escaped, though five other people were killed. Just over a year later, the British and Irish governments tried yet another 'political solution', with the Anglo-Irish agreement giving a guarantee that there would be no change in the status of Northern Ireland without the consent of the majority of its people. Protestants, though, were suspicious of the cross-border organisations it established, and Loyalist terrorists began a systematic campaign of violence against the police, mounting 500 attacks in 1986 alone. The IRA carried on killing, too. Just before eleven o'clock on the morning of Remembrance Sunday in November 1987, as a crowd gathered by Enniskillen's war memorial, a Semtex bomb went off in the nearby community hall. It killed eleven people, including three couples in their sixties and seventies and Marie Wilson, a 20-year-old nurse. Sixty-three people were injured. Dr Robin Eames, the Church of Ireland Primate of All Ireland, said the memory of 'the faces of good, honest, decent people who have never done wrong to anyone else, who have lost a loved one, blown to bits by a terrorist bomb' would never leave him. One UDR man who was helping with the rescue realised that the person he was trying to dig out was his mother. She was dead. In Dublin, thousands signed a book of condolences, and when the Lord Mayor came to the town the following week to present the book, she broke down in tears. Loyalist paramilitaries later admitted that they had been planning fearful retaliation, but had abandoned their plans after Gordon Wilson, Marie's father, broadcast a plea that there should be no retribution. It was one of a number of moments during the Troubles when it seemed that revulsion was so heartfelt and so widespread that it might bring the terrorist campaigns to an end, but once again hopes were disappointed.

The Provisionals not only continued their campaign in Ulster; in 1989 they destroyed the recreation centre of the Royal Marines School of Music at Deal in Kent, killing eleven young bandsmen. Then, in April 1992, the day after Sinn Fein President Gerry Adams had lost his seat in the general election, they set off a huge explosion in the City of London that destroyed the world's leading shipping market, the Baltic Exchange, and gutted Commercial Union's 23-storey headquarters, as well as damaging other buildings. Three people were killed and seventy-five injured, and the damage was estimated at £800 million, more than all the compensation that had been paid out for all the bomb explosions in Northern Ireland over the previous twenty-three years.

By now, deaths in Northern Ireland were running at 50 to 100 a year. Perhaps this was an 'acceptable level of violence', but what was changing was who was doing the killing. Loyalist terrorists had always gone in for sectarian murder. In the mid-seventies the so-called Shankill Butchers had murdered at least seventeen people, often with revolting sadism, but before 1985, Loyalists had been responsible for only about one in fourteen deaths in the Province, while in 1993 they killed virtually as many as the IRA and, during the following eight months, murdered about fifteen leading

Republicans. In turn, the IRA tried to hit leading Loyalists. On 23 October 1993 it was a lovely, warm Saturday in the Shankill Road, the heartland of the Loyalist paramilitaries, where the biggest organisation, the Ulster Defence Association, had an office above a fish shop. Two IRA men dressed as fishmongers in white coats and hats carried a box into the shop. As one of them put it down, it exploded prematurely. He was blown to pieces and the building collapsed in a heap of rubble. Local people, firemen and ambulancemen tore at the debris with axes, crowbars and bare hands. By evening they had found nine bodies in addition to that of the bomber – including two girls, aged 7 and 13. Fifty-seven people were injured. One of the bereaved said the local hospital was 'like the waiting room of hell – families in every corner. They were waiting in line to be told their loved ones had died.' The IRA claimed the target had been a UDA meeting going on upstairs. There was no meeting, and there were no UDA men in the office. Republicans gave the bomber a hero's funeral with a great procession of men, women (some pushing babies in prams) and children. During the next eight days, Loyalist gunmen shot dead fourteen people.

In December 1993, the British and Irish governments made another attempt to halt the bloodshed with the Downing Street Declaration, which stated that it was for 'the people of the island of Ireland alone . . . to exercise their right of self-determination on the basis of consent.' After a few months of requesting 'clarifications', the IRA declared a 'complete cessation' of violence in August 1994. It soon became clear, though, that beating up and killing joy-riders, burglars and drugs dealers did not count as violence. Loyalists also announced a ceasefire, but not before they had killed the oldest victim of the Troubles, 87-year-old Barney Green, one of six people they murdered in a bar at Loughinisland in County Down. The atmosphere was also poisoned by a wrangle over whether the IRA was required to decommission its weapons, and by the terrorists' practice of continuing to stalk potential targets. Then, on 9 February 1996, the IRA announced the end of its ceasefire with a bomb weighing half a ton in London's Docklands that killed two newsagents, injured 100 people, and caused damage estimated at £85 million. However, the following year, the IRA restored its ceasefire, and in 1998, the Good Friday agreement sought to draw Republicans and Loyalists into the mainstream political process.

There were some on the Republican side who felt this was a betrayal, and that the 'armed struggle' should continue, so just four months later, dissident

Republicans perpetrated Northern Ireland's worst ever terrorist outrage. At about half past two on the Saturday afternoon of 15 August 1998, Ulster Television received a telephone warning that there was a bomb in Omagh, the busy county town of County Tyrone. Many people had come in from the surrounding villages to shop, or to watch a carnival. Omagh had a Catholic majority, though about 40 per cent of the population was Protestant. The first warning said the bomb was outside the courthouse on 'Main Street', and that it would go off in half an hour. The town has no Main Street, but there is a courthouse that stands at the top of its main thoroughfare, Market Street. Two minutes after the first bomb warning came a second. This time the man sounded agitated and incoherent, and said the bomb was going to go off in fifteen minutes. Police began clearing the apparent danger area, but what they did not know was that the bomb would explode 400yds from the courthouse outside a school outfitter's, an area into which many people had been cleared. A devout Catholic family lost a 65-year-old grandmother, her 30-year-old daughter who was expecting twins and her 20-month-old granddaughter. Also blown up were a 60-year-old man and his 26-year-old son, both Presbyterians, while a group of Spanish tourists lost a teacher and a pupil. The total death toll was twenty-nine, including ten children, with 220 injured.

In the outcry that followed, a dissident Republican organisation, the 'Real IRA', admitted that it had planted the bomb, and immediately announced a ceasefire, offering apologies to the 'civilians' who had been hurt. In 2002, a man was convicted for the Omagh bombing and sentenced to fourteen years in gaol for playing a 'back-up' role in the atrocity, but after he had served three years, his conviction was declared unsafe. Altogether, during the Troubles to that point, there had been more than 3,600 deaths out of a Northern Ireland population of around 1.5 million. If that rate had been repeated over Britain as a whole, something like 140,000 would have been killed. Of the 3,600 killed, nearly 700 were from the British army, and more than 280 were police. Nearly 60 per cent were killed by Republican paramilitaries, and 28 per cent died at the hands of Loyalist paramilitaries.

The worst terrorist atrocity in British history, however, would have nothing to do with the Troubles in Ireland. Four days before Christmas Day 1988, Pan Am Flight 103 was on its way from Heathrow to New York, carrying 246 passengers and 13 crew. Just after seven o'clock the aircraft had been cleared for its transatlantic crossing. It was flying at 31,000ft, and the flight crew were preparing to serve dinner, when suddenly air traffic controllers at

Prestwick saw something strange and terrible on their screens. The one box that had represented the aircraft dissolved into five and each sweep of the radar showed them moving further and further apart. At that point, the aircraft was above Lockerbie, a town of 3,000 people, 15 miles north of the English border. The wings and central section of the fuselage containing 50,000 gallons of aviation fuel fell on Sherwood Crescent, close to the A74 London to Glasgow road, and a great fireball rose 300ft into the night sky. As the wreckage left a blazing crater 30yds long and 40ft deep, houses had their roofs ripped off, and one resident talked of a 'whirlwind' taking hold of a bed and flinging it through a third-floor window on to the ground. Seventeen-year-old Ian Hamilton had gone out for a walk 'when the world seemed to explode'. As the wreckage fell, he started to run, through 'bits of metal flying through the air at incredible speed.' He escaped with a gash to his face. On the main road, at least five cars were set on fire. In Rosewood Crescent, fifty bodies, some still strapped into their seats, fell into a back garden, while part of the economy cabin crashed into the home of a widow, but she survived. Sixty corpses fell on the golf course, while others were found on the A74, and one was left hanging from a tree.

The cockpit and forward first-class cabin section was found lying on its side intact, with many of its windows unbroken, while one engine came down near a housing estate half a mile away. Altogether eleven people died on the ground, while debris, including Christmas cards, was found up to 35 miles away. Scores of local people evacuated from their homes were put up in community centres, schools and hotels. It soon became clear that a bomb had gone off on the aircraft, killing everyone on board in what was not only Britain's worst terrorist outrage, but also its worst ever air disaster. The flight had started from Frankfurt, where about seventy items of luggage had been transferred to it from connecting Pan Am flights. Two weeks before, the US embassy in Helsinki had received an anonymous warning that Flight 103 would be bombed before Christmas, but bomb warnings were flooding in the whole time. Initially, a group called the Guardians of the Islamic Revolution claimed it had brought down the aircraft in revenge for a US Navy attack on an Iran Air flight over the Persian Gulf the previous July in which 290 people had died, but later Libya began to be blamed – perhaps this was revenge for the American bombing of Tripoli in 1986?

Twelve years after Lockerbie, following tortuous negotiations with President Gaddafi, two Libyans, Abdelbaset Ali Mohmed al-Megrahi, aged 48, and Al

Amin Khalifa Fhimah, aged 44, were handed over to stand trial for planting the bomb. The President's decision to give them up was part of a complex process that saw Libya agreeing to pay compensation to the families of those killed, while trade sanctions against it were lifted. This was followed by a promise from Gaddafi to halt Libya's weapons of mass destruction programme, which helped to end the country's diplomatic isolation. The court in the Netherlands was told that Flight 103 was blown up by 400gm of Semtex plastic explosive that had been concealed along with a timer and detonator inside a radio-cassette player. Prosecution lawyers said al-Megrahi had been a high-ranking Libyan intelligence officer, and that he had got the bomb on board Flight 103 from a connecting flight from Malta, though they admitted they did not know how. The two accused denied the charges and said that Palestinians were responsible for the bombing, naming names and organisations. The Palestinians denied any involvement. After a trial lasting nearly nine months, Fhimah was acquitted, but al-Megrahi was sentenced to twenty-seven years in prison. He appealed against his conviction, and the appeal heard new evidence that there had been a break-in at a baggage store at Heathrow eighteen hours before Flight 103 departed, and that it would have been possible for someone to have smuggled a bag on to the flight by getting it into this area. Al-Megrahi's appeal was rejected, but some of the victims' families did not believe the Libyan was the real killer. They raised questions about who exactly had been aware of the bomb warnings that had been given, and why Flight 103 had been the only transatlantic flight during the holiday period which had empty seats. Many remain convinced that the whole truth has not been told.

It was nearly 17 years after Lockerbie that Britain suffered its first suicide bombing. In the two years following the government's fiercely contested decision to join the United States' bombing, invasion and occupation of Iraq in 2003, Britons had frequently been warned that terrorist attacks were inevitable. On 6 July 2005 London was chosen to host the 2012 Olympic Games amid great national celebration, and at 7.20 the following morning the Metropolitan Police Commissioner, Sir Ian Blair, was asked on BBC radio about potential security threats to the event. He reassured listeners that his force was considered 'the envy of the policing world in relation to counter-terrorism'. Only the previous month, Britain's terrorism alert status had been downgraded one notch, and that day, hundreds of London police officers were away in Scotland, guarding the G8 international conference, being chaired by Prime Minister Tony Blair. It might be true that Britain's police were highly regarded, but just an hour and a half after Sir Ian's interview, a bomb exploded on a London tube train near Aldgate. Within a minute, another two had gone off on trains near Edgware Road and King's Cross. Then, less than an hour later, a bus was blown apart outside the British Medical Association's headquarters in Bloomsbury. No warnings had been given.

On the Aldgate train, a coffee shop manager travelling in the third carriage heard 'a bang louder than you can imagine, a noise so big that it felt like a punch in the face . . . then came blackness, followed by the smell of flesh, gunpowder and burning rubber. . . My ears were ringing so hard that I found it difficult to open my eyes.' When he was able to look, he could see through the dust that a bomb had ripped a hole in the side of the carriage. Wires and metal hung down from the ceiling, windows had been blown away. On the floor were lifeless bodies. At first he did not want to move towards the doors because it would mean stepping on them. People were holding things to their mouths to try to filter the choking dust. Another man wondered: 'Am I dead?' Then he reflected that if he was still thinking, he must be alive. Moments later, there was an explosion in the second carriage of the Edgware Road train. A passenger in the next car saw it had been 'ripped apart like it had been done with a can opener'. At the same time, about 700 passengers were packed aboard a Piccadilly Line train as it left King's Cross on its journey towards Russell Square. It was negotiating one of the deepest sections of the underground system 100ft below the pavements when there was a huge explosion in the first carriage. A 26-year-old woman said: 'There was 4 or 5 seconds and then everyone was going "oh my God, we can't breathe."' Someone started to pray. A lawyer commented: 'We were trapped like sardines waiting to die.' As they waited to be rescued, not knowing whether there were more bombs or whether the tunnel might collapse, the woman closed her eyes and kept 'thinking of outside'.

The emergency services began the perilous and horrifying descent into the tunnels, while on the surface supermarkets handed over water and clingfilm to dress burns, and lorries and shopping trolleys were commandeered to deliver medical supplies. Hotels, town halls and burger bars were pressed into service as emergency treatment centres, as victims started to appear, covered 'head to toe in blood'. Then the bomb went off on the number 30 bus, carrying some passengers who had been turned away from tube stations closed in the wake of the earlier explosions. The driver said he heard a bang, 'then turned around and realised the whole of the back of the bus was gone'. He suffered only cuts and bruises and helped to drag survivors from the wreckage. A man standing at the bus stop saw 'the top of the bus peeled off like a sardine tin. About five or six people were thrown out.' A passenger on another bus said the roof 'flew five feet in the air then seemed to slowly float down to the road'. The explosion left the BMA building spattered with blood as its courtyard was quickly turned into a field hospital. Motorists approaching London on the M4 motorway were greeted by the extraordinary, alarming sign: 'Avoid London. Area closed.'

The rescue operation on the underground was fearfully difficult, especially on the Piccadilly Line, where the tunnel was only a few inches higher than the train, and temperatures were said at times to reach 60°C. For days after the explosions, people put up posters or showed photographs to passers-by in a desperate search for their loved ones. Altogether 56 people were killed including the four suicide bombers who had carried their explosives in rucksacks. Most of the victims – 27 – were on the train from King's Cross, where the narrowness of the tunnel had concentrated the blast, making it more lethal. Fourteen people were killed on the bus. Three of the bombers were young men of Asian descent from West Yorkshire, the fourth a Jamaican who lived in Buckinghamshire. An al-Qaeda website announced that: 'The time of revenge against the Zionist crusader British government has come.' Attacking a well-guarded government minister, though, would be difficult. The million people on the move in the London rush hour every day were a much more tempting target. One expert defined the terrorists' strategy as: 'Why attack a tiger when there are so many sheep?' In the words of the Mayor of London, Ken Livingstone: 'This was not a terrorist attack against the mighty. It was aimed at ordinary working-class Londoners – black and white, Muslim and Christian, Hindu and Jew, young and old.' The names of the dead perfectly illustrated their diversity – Adams, Yuen, Ciaccia, Gunoral, Ikeagwu, Islam, Matsushita, Mozakka, Parathasangary, Rosenberg, Sharifi, Suchocka. After the disaster, hundreds of London police who had been removed to guard the G8 were brought back to the capital, but their presence might have made little difference. Every day in Iraq, the British and American occupying forces were being given a demonstration of the impossibility of stopping suicide bombers, which seemed the favourite mode of attack of Islamist terrorists. It gave an uncomfortable new resonance to Stanley Baldwin's 70-year-old warning that 'the bomber will always get through'.

 PART TWO

# ACCIDENTS

CHAPTER SIX

# FIRES WAITING TO HAPPEN

The first records of serious fires that we have date from Roman times, and at some point between AD 122 and 130, one or perhaps a number of fires caused terrible destruction to Roman London, devastating more than 100 acres in the present-day City of London. Some major stone buildings survived, but many of those constructed from wattle and daub, with timber frames, were destroyed. At that time, as they would be for the next millennium and a half, London and other British towns were fires waiting to happen. In about AD 155, there was a disastrous fire at Verulamium, modern-day St Albans, which destroyed more than 50 acres of buildings. We know that at about the same time there was also a very destructive fire in the forum at Wroxeter in Shropshire.

The era following the departure of the Romans is known as the Dark Ages because of the paucity of information that has survived about it, but we do know that there were several serious fires in London, including one that destroyed the original, wooden St Paul's Cathedral in the seventh century. After Duke William of Normandy conquered England in 1066, he introduced the *couvre feu* or curfew (though it is possible that something similar existed in Saxon times), which required householders to put out their fires when a bell rang at eight o'clock. How strictly the rules were observed, we do not know, but the Anglo-Saxon Chronicle records that 1077 was a 'dry summer; and wild fire came upon many shires, and burned many towns; and also many cities were ruined thereby.' Ten years later, London was struck again when St Paul's Cathedral was burned down once more, along with 'the largest and fairest part of the whole city'.

On Friday 4 August 1116, Peterborough was almost completely destroyed by a fire that spared only the dormitory and chapter house of the cathedral. The story goes that a servant in the monastery bakehouse was having trouble lighting a fire, and used the devil's name to curse it. The flames immediately went berserk, 'and burned all the houses and the whole of the monastery, and in the town no house remained entire'. Among other disastrous fires of the twelfth century was one in 1137 which was said to have destroyed the whole of York, including the cathedral and thirty-nine churches, and one in 1189 that burned down Carlisle. Twenty-three, or possibly twenty-four, years later, depending which historians you believe, came what until 1666 was known as the 'Great Fire of London'. If the sixteenth-century historian John Stow is right, it was the worst fire Britain has ever seen in terms of loss of life. Starting in Southwark on 11 July, it spread rapidly, destroying many buildings, including the church of St Mary Overie, which stood on the site of Southwark Cathedral. As it reached the houses at the southern end of London Bridge, people rushed on to the bridge, some to try to put out the flames, others just to watch, but then the wind fanned the flames on to the houses at the north end too, and the crowds were trapped. Boats appeared below and many tried to clamber down to them, but it was a perilous descent because of the treacherous rapids and currents produced by the narrow arches of the bridge, and many slipped and drowned. Stow claimed that 3,000 people were killed. It is hard to accept this figure, but this still may have been one of Britain's most disastrous fires.

In 1272, the burghers of Norwich quarrelled with the abbey and burned it to the ground; then the fire spread into the town, doing more damage there. Edward I had thirty-five of the rioters put to death. In the fifteenth century, major fires in Scotland devastated Stirling in 1408, Linlithgow in 1411 and 1424, and Aberdeen in 1423. In December 1583 at Nantwich in Cheshire, a man named Nicholas Brown was brewing ale when he set his kitchen on fire. Fanned by a strong westerly wind, the flames spread quickly along the High Street. Women ran to and fro to the river with pitiful amounts of water in leather buckets, but even this rudimentary firefighting was interrupted when the local publican released the bears he kept for baiting and the women ran for their lives. In some places, the flames did not burn out till they reached open fields, having destroyed 150 buildings, including thirty shops and seven inns. In the sixteenth century, there were also bad fires at Darlington in 1585, at Wolverhampton in 1590, and at Stratford-upon-Avon in 1594 and 1595. As the century drew to its close, on 3 April 1598 a major blaze badly damaged Tiverton in Devon. It started in the thatched house of 'a poor needy woman' who was baking pancakes over a straw fire; 'suddenly the fire got into the frying pan' and spread to the roof, setting alight a 'hay house' nearby and then the town mills. There was plenty of water available from the river Exe and, as it was market day, plenty of people around to fight the flames, but they had no buckets, and so were unable to halt the fire 'to their great sorrow and cost'. Altogether, 400 houses were destroyed and fifty people were killed, including some of 'the best men in all that town who did hazard themselves so far into the hot fire that they were most pitifully burned to death'. Just fourteen years later, the town burned again; this time the fire started in the workshop of a dyer, who lit his furnace to dry some clothes. He left a boy in charge, but the boy wanted to go off and play, so to dry the clothes quicker, he made the flames burn more fiercely, which set the house on fire. Then the flames spread so rapidly that the whole town was destroyed, apart from the schoolhouse and a few cottages.

In 1643, a fire at Wrexham destroyed a quarter of the town, while the following year, a blaze that began near Oxford's North Gate cut a swathe all the way to the Isis, burning down 300 houses. In 1652, a fire in Glasgow's High Street was spread by the wind, and engulfed the Saltmarket, the Trongate and the Gallowgate, spreading as far as the Bridgegate. It took 18 hours before the flames began to die down, and by then a third of the city had been destroyed. Oliver Cromwell asked people to give generously to alleviate Glasgow's distress, and Parliament itself allocated £100,000. The Lord Protector stepped in again the following year, when a 'fearful and most violent fire' hit Marlborough, the main weaving town in Wiltshire, destroying more than 200 houses and a church within 4 hours. Cromwell authorised a collection throughout England and Wales to help the stricken citizens, and set the ball rolling himself with a handsome gift of £2,000.

Around this time, London housed a tenth of Britain's population, and Londoners owned half of the country's wealth. England's capital, though, was still a fire trap, full of little streets, packed with oak-framed houses, their fronts filled in with lath and plaster or covered with pitch-smeared weatherboards. Pudding Lane, just to the north-east of London Bridge, was so narrow that 'a cart could scarcely pass'. As it does today, it led into Thames Street, where there were wharfingers' premises stocked with timber, tallow oil, spirits, hemp, fodder and all manner of inflammable goods. Close to the junction was the bakehouse of Thomas Farriner, who made ship's biscuit for the navy. At about midnight on Saturday 1 September 1666 he went downstairs to see if there were any red embers in his oven to light a candle. He later said there were none; the fire had completely gone out, so he went back to bed. An hour or so later, the household was woken by smoke; the downstairs rooms were already blazing.

When questioned later, Farriner would say that he noticed the flames were nowhere near his oven, before he realised the only escape for him and his family was through the window and across the roof to a neighbour's house. The Farriners crawled, choking, to safety, but the maid was too frightened, and stayed behind to become the first victim of the Great Fire of London. At first the fire spread slowly, and the next-door neighbour had time to remove his goods before his house burned down, but across the lane was the Star Inn with a yard full of straw and fodder. With few people around at that time of the morning to fight the flames, sure enough, it too caught light. At three o'clock, Samuel Pepys, who lived more than a quarter of a mile away in Seething Lane, was roused by his cook, Jane, to see the fire. 'I rose', he wrote, 'and slipped on my nightgown and went to her window . . . I thought it far enough off, and so went to bed again and to sleep.'

At about this time, people living around Pudding Lane called out the Lord Mayor, Sir Thomas Bludworth. He took one look at it, declared 'a woman could piss it out', and went back to bed. When asked to authorise the creation of a firebreak by pulling down a shop and four houses, the Mayor said he could not because of the uncertainty over who would pay for rebuilding. When Pepys got up at about seven o'clock, he records that he 'looked out at the window and saw the fire not so much as it was, and further off', but his relief was short-lived. By eight o'clock the flames had spread to Thames Street's warehouses and were being driven westwards by a strong wind. St Magnus Church at the northern end of London Bridge was now alight, and embers were flying from its high roof, spreading the blaze further. Pepys' cook now told him that more than 300 houses had been burned down. The diarist walked to high ground by the Tower of London and saw 'all the houses at that end of the bridge all on fire, and an infinite great fire on this and the other side of the bridge'.

Underneath London Bridge were great wooden wheels that could pump up emergency water supplies, but as the flames took hold of the buildings above, burning beams fell, destroying them before they could play any part in the firefighting. Fortunately, there was a natural firebreak on the bridge, a gap left by an earlier fire in 1633, and this helped to prevent the fire spreading south of the Thames. On the north bank, though, the intense heat meant that people could not get close enough to fight the fire, while the wind continued to fan the flames. As one witness put it, 'God with his great bellows blows upon it!' The weather had been very dry, 'everything, after so long a drought, proving combustible,' wrote Pepys, 'even the very stones of the churches'. What the diarist found most disturbing was the absence of any coordinated effort to halt the blaze. The fire was raging 'every way, and nobody to my sight endeavouring to quench it'. So he raced off to what was then the King's main residence, the Palace of Whitehall, to find Charles II and his brother, the Duke of York (the future King James II); 'people came about me and I did give them an account dismayed them all; and word was carried in to the King, so I was called for and did tell the King and Duke of York what I saw, and that unless his Majesty did command houses to be pulled down, nothing could stop the fire.' The King then sent Pepys with instructions to the Lord Mayor 'to spare no houses but to pull down before the fire every way'.

After going back to bed, the Lord Mayor had soon been roused again, and Pepys went off to look for him, encountering 'every creature coming away loaden with goods to save – and here and there sick people carried away in beds'. Eventually, he found Bludworth: 'to the King's message, he cried like a fainting woman, "Lord, what can I do? I am spent. People will not obey me. I have been pulling down houses. But the fire overtakes us faster than we can do it."' That was the end of the encounter, and Pepys went home, 'seeing people all almost distracted and no manner of means used to quench the fire'. Fortunately, Charles II himself was interested in firefighting, and would often row along the Thames looking for a good blaze at which he could direct operations. By afternoon, he and the Duke of York had arrived on the scene. They ordered houses to be pulled down, but by the time men had laboriously dragged them down with fire hooks, the wind was already blowing the flames across the narrow gaps, and there was no time to move the fallen timber and thatch or the inflammable materials with which many of the buildings were packed. After all the dry weather, the Thames was very low, and desperate firefighters were simply cutting pipes where they needed water, which meant that there would be none further away from the river.

Now burning debris carried on the wind was spreading the fire at an alarming speed, with, it was said, 100 houses an hour being consumed. The Secretary of Queen Christina of Sweden, on a visit to London, had lunch at Covent Garden with a 'fine company', some of whom got back home to find 'their houses gone up in fire and smoke', while a Nonconformist minister, the Revd Thomas Vincent, lamented that: 'London, so famous for wisdom and dexterity, can now find neither brains nor hands to prevent its ruin.' There were few fire engines, and anyway firefighters could not get them along the narrow alleyways in the face of the crowds trying to escape with their belongings. By now, the spire of St Laurence Pountney, one of the tallest in London, was ablaze, and Londoners were increasingly desperate to get their possessions to safety. Pepys found 'the streets full of nothing but people and horses and carts loaden with goods, ready to run over one another'.

On Sunday evening, the diarist crossed the river to the cool of an alehouse, and saw many people's goods bobbing in the Thames. Those who could got their possessions into lighters, but with no quay along the north bank of the Thames, this was often easier said than done, so the alternative was just 'flinging them into the river'. Facing the wind, said Pepys, 'you were almost burned with a shower of firedrops', and as darkness fell, the fire 'appeared more and more, and in corners and upon steeples and between churches and houses, as far as we could see up the hill of the City, in a most horrid malicious bloody flame, not like the fine flame of an ordinary fire'. The north bank was framed in an arch of fire. 'It made me weep to see it,' wrote Pepys. 'The churches, houses, and all on fire and flaming at once, and a horrid noise the flames made, and the cracking of houses at their ruin.' By the end of that first day, the fire had burned half a mile of the riverfront.

Pepys returned home 'with a sad heart'; it was clear now that his own house was in danger, 'so we were forced to pack up our own goods and prepare for their removal'. He spent the night shifting furniture into the garden, and at four o'clock in the morning a cart appeared to take away his most treasured possessions – money, plate and his famous diary – to a friend's house in Bethnal Green, 'riding myself in my nightgown in the cart; and Lord, to see how the streets and highways are crowded with people, running and riding and getting of carts at any rate to fetch away things'. Many cart owners were charging astonishing sums of up to £30 to carry people's goods to the fields of Bethnal Green or Soho. The fire blazed on through the night. On Monday, it would make devastating progress, destroying perhaps twenty churches. By now, the King had put the Duke of York in charge of the firefighting, but at first he had little success. The fire was not only advancing westwards, driven by the wind, it was also making progress to the north. Cornhill was one of the widest streets in the city, and should have presented one of the best chances to halt the flames. Firefighters pulled down houses on the south side, but they were not able to clear the debris fast enough, so the flames fastened on to timber left in the street and continued unchecked.

Pepys managed to find a lighter by Tower dock for the rest of his possessions, 'and we did carry them (myself some) over Tower Hill, which was by this time full of people's goods'. To try to prevent looting, the authorities called out the militia to guard the possessions lying around so invitingly. By now the initial shock of the fire had dissipated, and people began to wonder who or what had caused it. Anyone Dutch or French was immediately in the frame, because England was at war with the Netherlands and France. A Dutch baker heating his oven to make bread was accused of trying to set the city on fire, dragged out and beaten within an inch of his life, while a Frenchman was felled by a blow from an iron bar, but any foreigner was under suspicion, and a member of the Swedish ambassador's retinue was saved from being hanged only by the chance appearance of a troop of the Duke of York's bodyguard.

By Monday night, there was precious little water anywhere, while the flames were so fierce they were even making progress against the wind. The halls of the Cutlers', Vintners' and Salters' companies had all been gutted, and among the churches destroyed was St Michael Paternoster Royal, where Dick Whittington was buried. London also lost one of its most imposing secular buildings, the Royal Exchange, which was filled with valuable goods. The firefighters did manage one notable success, when they managed to stop the blaze at the high stone walls of Leadenhall, but by midnight on Monday, the fire was four times as big as it had been 24 hours earlier.

Tuesday dawned hot and cloudless, and the fire continued its remorseless advance. The Duke of York ordered houses to be demolished along the line of the Fleet River, which is now buried under Faringdon Road, to make a broader firebreak, but by mid-day, the flames had got across. Both the Duke and the King were always to be found in the thick of the action. They could be seen up to their ankles in water, carrying buckets and using fire engines for hours on end, or climbing on to the roof of a building to assess the situation. The King's fine costume was soaked and bedraggled with mud, and now and then he would pause to toss gold coins to reward the efforts of those fighting the fire, while on at least one occasion the Duke had to run for his life as flames nearly reached him.

This was perhaps the darkest hour. Water was still scarce, the wind was still blowing strongly, and the firefighters were getting exhausted. The updraught of hot air tore flaming debris from burning buildings and started new fires in streets that had until then been untouched. One of the King's leading ministers, the Earl of Arlington, commented despairingly: 'The fire has burnt far into the body of the city with such violence that no art or pains can meddle with it.' Now the Guildhall was under threat, and amid fears that the flames might even reach Whitehall Palace, the King's treasures were being shipped away. Then, at eight o'clock that night, the roof of St Paul's, which was covered in wooden scaffolding because of restoration work, caught fire. The churchyard, by far the biggest open space in the city, was crammed with goods, as was the building itself, many believing it to be a safe haven, while beneath the cathedral was a huge store of books. The cathedral burned for hours, until the famous choir roof fell in and crashed through the floor, destroying the books beneath. It was said to be the biggest loss since the burning of the great library at Alexandria more than 1,000 years before. Molten lead poured from St Paul's roof and ran down the streets 'like snow before the sun'. The diarist John Evelyn wrote of stones flying from the building like grenades and the pavements around it glowing red, and prayed 'God grant my eyes may never behold the like'.

It was beginning to look as though the next major task might be to save the Tower of London. If the flames reached the gunpowder store in the White Tower, the consequences would be catastrophic. Sailors were brought in to blow up buildings nearby and to drag debris away from the advancing flames. Mercifully, their efforts checked the fire. However, during Tuesday it had destroyed twice the area it had devastated the previous day and, in addition to St Paul's, the toll included thirty-five churches and many company halls, as well as much of the Guildhall. At about two o'clock on Wednesday morning, Pepys was once again woken in the middle of the night. 'My wife calls me up and tells us of new cries of "Fire" – it being come to Barking Church, which is the bottom of our lane.' He took his wife, his maid and his gold by boat to Woolwich, but when he got back at about seven o'clock, he found to his surprise that his house was not on fire, and that the church had been saved too. Pepys took the opportunity to climb to the top of the steeple, 'and there saw the saddest sight of desolation that I ever saw. Everywhere great fires. Oil cellars and brimstone and other things burning.' What Pepys may not have realised, though, is that there had been a crucial development; the wind had dropped.

Now the firefighters began to get the upper hand, halting the flames at Fetter Lane and Shoe Lane and then dousing them, and by evening nearly all the fires to the west of the city had been extinguished. Although there was a further outbreak at the Temple, by Thursday morning the worst was over, and the firefighters were able to close in on the remaining pockets and put them out. In five days, more than 436 acres had been devastated. More than 13,000 houses, one in every three, were burned down, as well as eighty-seven churches and fifty-two livery halls. Astonishingly, the death toll was only half a dozen, but something like 70,000 people were left homeless. For months after the fire, many Londoners had to camp in the fields around the city, and in the winter that followed, far more died from the hardships of living outside than perished in the inferno. Evelyn said London was like a city 'laid waste by a cruel enemy', and much of the rest of Europe was convinced that it was finished as a great centre of trade and commerce. On London Bridge, though, shopkeepers quickly set up in the ruins, and markets reopened within a week. On the very day the flames were finally extinguished, Charles II was informed that some people were already preparing to start rebuilding, and he had to issue a proclamation that no work should be done before new regulations had been drawn up. A special tax on coal was levied to raise money for the rebuilding of fifty-two churches, including St Paul's Cathedral, all designed by Sir Christopher Wren. The Guildhall and nearly all of the livery halls that had been destroyed were rebuilt, as was the Royal Exchange.

An official inquiry decided that the fire had been caused by 'the hand of God, a great wind and a dry season'. That did not prevent the execution of a French watchmaker, named Robert Hubert, who claimed that he had started it. Hubert was 'a poor, distracted wretch, weary of this life', and scarcely anyone in authority believed he was guilty. The monument to the fire that stands to this day was built close to the site of Thomas Farriner's house, with an inscription saying it was 'in perpetual remembrance of the most dreadful burning of this Protestant City began and carried on by treachery and malice of the Popish faction'. One of the Duke of York's attendants said of his role in fighting the fire: 'Had not the Duke been present, and forced all people to submit to his command, I am confident there had not been a house standing. The citizens of the first rank minded only their own preservation; the middle sort so distracted that they did not know what they did; the poorer minded nothing but pilfering.' Seven years later, though, the Duke converted to Roman Catholicism; thereafter his efforts were forgotten, and the popular imagination put him down as one of the Papist conspirators who had started the Great Fire of London.

Nine years after the Great Fire of London came the Great Fire of Northampton. An 'infamous and common woman' left a pot boiling while she popped in to her next-door neighbour's. When she came out again, her house was on fire, so 'she took up her bastard and ran away crying "I shall be hanged"'. Meanwhile, the fire spread remorselessly, and soon the bells of All-Hallows Church 'sounded their last and doleful knell'. Some of the citizens tried to save their houses by covering them with wet blankets, but to no avail. Even when the authorities blew up buildings, it did not halt the flames; 'had it been a leisurely fire, proceeding in order of houses and streets,' lamented a contemporary, 'then buckets might have quenched it . . . but this fire would have scorned an engine.' It burned for 30 hours, and the town was said to be 'almost all consumed'.

The 'infamous and common woman' seems to have been guilty only of carelessness, but deliberate mischief was the cause of a major fire in Glasgow in November 1677. A blacksmith at the corner of the Saltmarket and the Trongate gave his apprentice a beating. To get his revenge, the young man set fire to his master's premises, but also inadvertently destroyed another 130 houses as the blaze burned out of control. Edinburgh also had many disastrous fires, which were often hard to fight because of the number of skyscrapers; fourteen-storey buildings were common in the city as early as the sixteenth century. On 3 February 1700 'these Babels' were brought to the ground, and their fall was 'very terrible', according to one witness of a fire that devastated Scotland's capital. The blaze, he wrote, 'burned with the greatest fervour and vehemency that ever I saw a fire do, notwithstanding that I saw London burn'. It started in the Mealmarket, spread up the hill to Parliament Close and attacked the High Street. Up to 400 families were made homeless, 'most of the lords, lawyers and clerks were burnt besides many poor', and 'all the pride of Edinburgh is sunk'.

Meanwhile, London was soon burning again after the Great Fire of 1666. In 1698, a careless servant lit a fire to dry some linen, then wandered off, allowing it to start a blaze that almost completely destroyed the Palace of Whitehall, once the greatest in Europe. In 1715, urged on by a high wind, a great fire at Wapping was said to have killed fifty people and destroyed 150 houses. A Dutch merchant described it as 'a terrible calamity', lamenting that in London, it was hard to get people to put out a fire, because most preferred to 'only look on'. Another great fire of the eighteenth century devastated Blandford Forum in Dorset on Friday 4 June 1731. It started at a soap-boiler's house in the middle of the town, then – feasting on the thatched roofs and urged on by a strong wind – spread with such speed and fury that it left 'not a piece of timber but what was burnt to a coal. The pewter in many houses was not only melted but reduced to ashes.' People dragged their goods out into the street, but the fire soon caught and destroyed them, and they 'were now thankful they could escape with their own lives! . . . they scarce had time to look back on what they had left behind them.' Three fire engines were brought out, but within half an hour, all were burned or destroyed, and by seven o'clock in the evening, there were only about thirty houses left. Some of the citizens tried to shelter themselves and their belongings in the church, but at two in the morning, it too caught fire; 'the lead melted, the stones spit and flew; so fervent and irresistible was the heat, that the bells themselves dissolved and ran down in streams.' Altogether, thirteen people were killed and 3,000 made homeless, so that many 'who were never inured to hardship were obliged to lie, some in barns and outhouses, others under the arches of a large bridge, and more under hedges and in the open air'. Unfortunately, there was a smallpox epidemic raging in the town, and a night out in the open proved the death of some. Three hundred houses and shops were gone, along with the church and the Guildhall, but after the fire, Blandford Forum was rebuilt as the elegant Georgian town we see today.

Sparks carried on the wind from Blandford had spread the flames to the neighbouring village of St Mary Blandford, in which only three houses survived. It was quite common in those days for villages to be obliterated by fire; this was a fate met by Shipwash in Devon in 1742, and by Offord Cluny in Huntingdonshire in 1763. One particularly disastrous village fire occurred at Barnwell in Cambridgeshire in September 1727. A travelling troupe of puppeteers had run out of money and found themselves stranded, so they hired a barn to put on a show. Perhaps it was a while since anything so exciting had happened at Barnwell; anyway, the villagers crowded in to watch. When the improvised venue was absolutely crammed, the doors were locked to stop anyone else getting in. The audience was evidently getting its money's worth, because when one person smelt smoke and tried to raise the alarm, the rest were so engrossed that they told him to be quiet. On this occasion, there was no smoke without fire, but by the time the crowd realised it, they were trapped in the blazing barn. Seventy-eight died, and it was said that their screams could be heard 2 miles away. In the same year, Gravesend saw 'the largest and best half of the town destroyed, so that all that remains are naked walls'. There had apparently been only one fire engine in the town, and that was unfit for action. The Kent town seems to have been particularly unlucky, as further conflagrations engulfed it in 1731, 1748, 1779 and 1801.

# CHAPTER SEVEN

# FETCH THE ENGINES

In October 1824, Edinburgh became the first city in the world to establish a municipal fire brigade. The 26-year-old James Braidwood was put in charge as 'Master of Fire-Engines'. Within three weeks, he had to deal with a huge fire that burned down a number of tenement blocks, the steeple of the Tron Kirk and the offices of the *Evening Courant* newspaper. With firemen exhausted and water in short supply, another fire broke out the following evening on the top floor of an 11-storey tenement block in Parliament Square. It was too high for the fire engines to reach, and, according to the *Courant*, 'the fire spread resistlessly' and soon 'the whole horizon was completely enveloped in lurid flame'. Only the steeple of St Giles' Cathedral seemed to rise above the conflagration 'like a spectre awakened to behold the fall and ruin of the devoted city'. The fire raged on through the night, until there were fears that the whole town would be destroyed, but then around daybreak, mercifully, heavy rain began to fall.

By then, though, Parliament Square, the Cowgate and the High Street had been devastated. Four hundred people were homeless, 10 had been killed and many more injured. Echoing the words of John Evelyn on the Great Fire of London, one contemporary writer recorded: 'It gives an impression of a city sacked and burnt by an enemy.' The new fire chief had worked tirelessly through the day and night, and had almost been killed by a collapsing wall. The firefighting, though, had proved something of a shambles. Braidwood lacked a proper infrastructure of experienced officers beneath him, and all manner of people – magistrates, sheriffs, army officers and 'gentlemen in authority' – had been merrily issuing orders and counter-orders without apparent reference to him. But the city fathers did not blame him for the disaster, and the following January they doubled his pay and agreed to his suggestions for making the brigade more efficient. Braidwood went on to become one of the great firefighters, inventing one of the first forms of breathing apparatus, and writing a highly influential firefighting manual. After nine years in Edinburgh, he was poached by London's new fire brigade to become its first chief. In the capital, he fought fires at the Houses of Parliament, the Tower of London, the Royal Exchange and Windsor Castle, before losing his life at a fearful warehouse conflagration in 1861.

Liverpool, too, was often prey to serious warehouse fires. In 1802, the Goree warehouse, containing grain, sugar, coffee and cotton, was burned down, and the ruins smouldered for three months. Over the next four decades, there were another four major fires. Then, in 1842, what became known as 'the great Formby Street fire' started in a wooden shed used as an oil store in Paisley Street. The city's new fire brigade got fourteen engines to the scene, but the blaze soon spread into Formby Street, Neptune Street and Compton Street, which were virtually wall-to-wall cotton warehouses. One after another they collapsed, leaving 'burning mountains of cotton 70 feet high sending up flames as high again.' The flames did their worst for three days, destroying 48,000 bales. There were so many bad warehouse fires in the port that year that insurance companies jacked up their premiums to more than five times the previous level, while a contemporary complained that it was no wonder the city's warehouses caught fire, because they were 'frequently in proximity or immediate contact with the active sources of ignition, such as smithies, cooperages, mills, steam-engines etc'.

Another great port, Newcastle upon Tyne, was devastated in a fire that also engulfed Gateshead, where it began just after midnight on the morning of Friday 6 October 1854. From the opposite bank of the Tyne, a Newcastle policeman spotted flames on the upper floors of a worsted mill in Hillgate, and ran over the bridge to alert the Gateshead police, who forced their way into the building. This unfortunately had the effect of providing great gulps of fresh air on which the flames could feed. Two insurance companies' fire engines arrived, but within 2 hours the flames had spread to a 6-storey warehouse next door. It was said to be a 'double fireproof structure most strongly built', but unfortunately it contained more than 4,000 tons of sulphur, as well as other goods including coal tar and rags, all excellent nourishment for the flames. In one vault there were 45 tons of highly explosive sodium nitrate. About three o'clock in the morning, the whole building went up in a violent explosion that flung lumps of masonry and burning beams into the air. These crashed through people's roofs, killing them in their beds. Six people died on the opposite bank of the river. Burning debris set fire to ships on the river, and to offices and warehouses on the quay at Newcastle, and soon, in the words of *The Times*, 'houses and buildings on both sides of the river were one sheet of fire'. Some people fled 'as if from an earthquake'; others could not, because they had fainted, overcome by the fumes from the burning sulphur. The explosion was heard in Sunderland, 11 miles away, where miners came rushing to the surface of the pit in alarm.

The fires that had started on the Newcastle side now coalesced into one great conflagration that spread from Butcher's Bank to Pilgrim Street. Fire engines were wrecked, and even though help arrived by special trains from Sunderland, Durham and Morpeth, the flames burned all day. Spectators gathered on the best vantage point, the high-level bridge, and soldiers and police had to be called in to keep order. Watching from here took a fair bit of nerve; when the explosion went off, the bridge began to shake alarmingly, and it seemed it might collapse into the river. *The Times*'s reporter was also there, noting that: 'Every now and then the ear was appalled by an explosion, as the fire reached gunpowder or kindred substances, and thus the flames were fed and the conflagration extended.' The next morning, nearly every street in Gateshead was strewn with debris, and with the firefighters tiring, the Mayor of Newcastle ordered corporation workmen to the pumps with promises of special overtime payments and other rewards. Every available policeman was drafted in, along with soldiers who could blow up buildings to create firebreaks. Also deployed was a floating fire engine that sprayed a ton and a half of water every minute, so that by Saturday evening, the major outbreaks had been brought under control, though small fires kept appearing among the ruins. By this time, though, according to the *Newcastle Chronicle*, the quayside had been reduced to 'entire desolation'. In Gateshead, the fires burned for longer, and it was not until the following Thursday morning that the main streets of the two towns were reopened. Many houses, particularly those owned by the poor, 'fell like they were made of cards', and there were 'many poor persons continually passing through the throng, bearing with them their humble possessions saved from the wreck, and seeking places in which to lay their heads'. Soup kitchens were opened for the destitute, and a relief fund organised, while to the indignation of local people, the railway company ran excursions for those who wanted to come and gawp at the devastation. Even Queen Victoria got her train to stop on the high-level bridge so that she and her family could view the ruins as they passed through Tyneside soon after. She then made a gift of £100 to the relief fund.

Altogether, fifty-three people died. The body of one man caught up in the explosion on the Gateshead side was found on the quayside in Newcastle. An 18-year-old ensign was one of a number of soldiers and police who were killed. His father, a London magistrate, philosophised: 'Should the loss of so many valuable lives on this melancholy occasion lead to the making provisions for protecting from similar catastrophes in future . . . I shall then endeavour to draw further consolation from thinking that my beloved son and those that fell with him, have not fallen in vain.'

One place that took a fairly relaxed attitude to making such provisions was the Theatre Royal in Exeter, both predecessors of which had burned down. The new building had taken just five months to complete from the laying of the foundation stone, and at the opening night, the manager delivered a prologue containing the prophetic words:

> If faults there are, and faults there are no doubt
> We'll rectify them as we find them out.

The architect had promised that the theatre would comply with all the latest safety regulations, but in fact, it did not. For example, there was no safety curtain and no proper division of the stage from the auditorium, while the scene dock, the carpenters' shop and the dressing rooms backstage were not separated from the stage by fire-resistant walls. Exits from the auditorium were too few, tight, and difficult to negotiate, but the local magistrates had passed the building. On 5 September 1887, less than a year after the theatre had opened, there was a good, though mercifully not a full, house of about 800 for the first night of the melodrama *Romany Rye*. There were a few technical hitches. A street scene was lowered instead of an office interior, and a desk and chairs appeared in the middle of the road, but this only seemed to add to the audience's appreciation. Then, in Act IV, Scene iii, during a speech by the chief villain, Scragger, the curtain suddenly came down, almost hitting him. The audience laughed, believing it was another hitch. Rather puzzled, the orchestra leader thought he had better get his musicians to play, but they had completed only a few bars when suddenly, in the words of *The Times*, the curtain 'puffed out like the sail of a ship'. Then it rose a little, and the audience was horrified to see smoke and flames on stage. As cries of 'Fire!' went up and people began to rush for the exits, the curtain shrivelled up and 'at once revealed the scene in all its terrors'.

There were nearly 200 people in the gallery, and because the roof was very low, they were soon choking in suffocating fumes. At the one tortuous exit from this part of the theatre, 'a fearful panic occurred. Women shrieked and swooned; men half mad with excitement rushed and stumbled over the prostrate bodies, while in the only means of exit a block ensued.' One woman said the house was plunged into darkness, then fire burst right around the upper part. She scrambled to the back of the gallery, but had no idea where she was going, and found herself in a refreshment room; 'the room was in darkness and I gave myself up for lost', but at that moment, she saw a gleam of light from a small window, and scrambled on to a parapet outside. Along with three other people she was rescued by ladder. The stage manager grabbed a hose and tried to spray water on to the flames, but he said the whole theatre seemed to be burning in a matter of seconds. One patron in the dress circle said that at first the audience moved out in a fairly leisurely way, thinking it only a case of 'a little something alight', but almost immediately, the place became a mass of flames and smoke, and 'the rapidity with which the fire spread astounded and appalled everybody'. In fact, lamented *The Times*, the theatre caught fire with such speed that 'persons in the better parts of the house scarcely had time to reach the main entrance hall before the interior was converted into a furnace'. The city and neighbouring fire brigades were on the scene very quickly, but there was little they could do. Everywhere on steps and in passages in the theatre were crushed, charred and bleeding bodies. In desperation, some of the audience jumped 40ft from windows to the street, often with fatal consequences. One of the actors' company was trying to save its costumes from destruction when he was carried into the street by the throng of people. When he fought his way back inside, he found a little girl cowering in one of the smoke-filled passages, and managed to carry her to safety. A bombardier and an able seaman who had been in the audience made a number of daring rescues. Sadly, the bombardier attempted one sally too many into the burning building, and this time did not return.

The many bystanders outside were horrified by the gas explosions, the sound of crashing glass, and the roar of the flames as they got higher and higher. One witness said: 'I never saw anything burn so quickly in my life. It burnt like oil.' The fire seems to have started up in the flies, high above the stage, when a piece of scenery came into contact with one of the naked gas jets used for stage lighting. As soon as it was spotted, the company brought down the curtain and the flymen and props men tried to put it out with a hose, but the blaze spread alarmingly quickly, and they were driven back by burning scenery falling on to the stage. Then there was a gas explosion. Most of the company managed to escape through the great double stage doors leading on to the street, but when they were opened, it created a draught that sent the flames straight into the audience. Altogether, 188 people died. It is thought that at least 140 of them had been in the gallery, with most of the remainder from the upper circle, plus two who had been working backstage. At the inquest, the jury castigated the architect over the design of the theatre and the magistrates for licensing it. They demanded tougher laws on safety in theatres and public buildings. The Home Secretary asked Sir Eyre Massey Shaw, chief officer of London's fire brigade, to report on the fire, and Shaw's rather disturbing conclusion was that while the building was clearly 'unfit to be licensed as a theatre', it was probably no worse than many others. Three years later, Parliament did toughen up the law, insisting that all public buildings must have 'ample safe and convenient' exits and entrances.

At the beginning of the twentieth century, the lunatic asylum at Colney Hatch in Hertfordshire was probably one of the most pleasant in the country. It sounds almost idyllic; set in its 165 acres with gardens, a cricket field, and arable and pastoral farmland. The foundation stone had been laid by Queen Victoria's husband Prince Albert back in 1849, and it housed about 2,500 inmates. In the last years of the nineteenth century, the county council had taken it over and had erected some new temporary buildings of Norwegian pine, containing dormitories for women, day rooms and staff accommodation, linked to the main building by a covered corridor. At about half past five on the morning of 27 January 1903, a duty nurse saw flames and raised the alarm, but the wards were all locked, and only select members of staff held keys. With the fire fanned by a stiff breeze, the corridor soon became a blazing funnel, and no one could escape through it.

The medical officer in charge quickly began running around unlocking doors. The superintendent, a specialist named Dr Seward who was known throughout Europe, risked his life to rescue inmates, some of whom were highly agitated and had to be carried out. The asylum's own fire brigade attacked the flames, but found them too fierce. A siren sounded in what was then the village of New Southgate, where many of the staff lived, to call them to come and help, but by the time they arrived, two wards had already burned down. The local fire brigades turned out and dammed a stream to get water, but day broke to reveal there was nothing left of the annexe except brick foundations and the twisted remains of the roof. In the ward where the alarm was first raised, seven or eight bodies were found huddled together, and others had died still lying on their bedsteads. Altogether the fire claimed fifty-one victims, mainly through suffocation by smoke. Investigations revealed that it had started in a clothes store. The new structure had been approved by the London County Council, the Lunacy Commissioners and the Home Office, but the inquest jury was highly critical, saying 'the authorities named are greatly to blame for sanctioning such plans'.

Strong liquor is highly inflammable and has to be stored in conditions of strict security – a potentially lethal cocktail. In 1960, a bonded warehouse in Anderston, Glasgow, holding more than a million gallons of whisky and rum, caught fire. The narrow, congested streets made it hard for firemen to get enough water on to the flames, and vapours given off by the spirits exploded, bringing the building crashing down. Fourteen firemen and five men from the Glasgow Salvage Corps were killed. Eight years later, in the same area, there was another serious fire in a bonded warehouse that had been converted to an upholstery factory. The old barred windows and other security precautions remained, though, and hampered the attempts of workers to escape. Twenty-two were killed.

On the Isle of Man, the afternoon of 2 August 1973 had been cold and miserable, but it was for just such weather that the Summerland entertainment complex at Douglas had been built. This was a place, boasted the publicity, 'where it never rains, the wind never blows and the temperature never gets chilly'. It offered 'total entertainment' in what was said to be the biggest complex under one roof in the world. The seven-storey building housed a funfair, a discotheque, a sundeck, a solarium, restaurants and bars, as well as amusement arcades and stages. Parents could drink or dance on the top floors while children played in other areas under constant supervision. Summerland had been opened the previous year, and was already pulling in one-eighth of the island's tourist revenue. That drizzly afternoon, 3,000 holidaymakers had crowded inside. At about half past seven in the evening, as some of the visitors were listening to the centre's organist, stories began to circulate that there was a fire, but the audience was reassured when he joked that he had been asked to play 'The Blue Danube' to put it out. Some who had been planning to leave returned to their seats, but a few minutes later, flames burst into the room. Now the organist changed his tune, screaming: 'My God, it's burning! Get out.'

The reason why Summerland had been able to promise constant good weather was that it was 'cocooned in a protective sheath of transparent acrylic sheeting'. The structure was rather like a giant greenhouse, but now the fire transformed the 'cocoon' into a major hazard, as the roof turned molten and red-hot droplets began to fall on those below. An inflammable material had been used to line the inner walls, and, as there were no fireproof compartments, the flames spread alarmingly quickly. With so many parents in different parts of the building from their children, there was panic as they now rushed to find them, and that took priority over trying to escape. The fire brigade was called not by the centre itself, but by a taxi driver on the promenade. When it first arrived, one fireman said the blaze was spreading 'quicker than I could walk down the building. Soon the flames were engulfing the whole thing from one end to another. It looked awesome. We thought, "What the hell are we going to do with this?"' Eventually, every available fireman was drafted in to fight the blaze, using water pumped from the sea.

A pall of black smoke rose hundreds of feet into the air, and flames climbed higher than the cliff behind the centre. Ambulances ran a shuttle service to get the injured to hospital, and holidaymakers' cars were also commandeered, while plasma and blood had to be flown in from Liverpool. One man said he was just about to go inside with his family when he saw people trying to put water on a fire: 'The next thing it seemed to go up the front of the building in a great sheet of flame.' Another man said visitors 'were screaming and trying to get out through the main doors. People were unable to get the emergency doors open.' He escaped by putting his foot through a window. Another account spoke of people sobbing as they searched for their loved ones. According to firemen, most of the bodies were found by burnt-out staircases on the upper floors. They had often been overcome by heat or smoke. Some had been crushed to death. A Liverpool woman said: 'Inside there was complete panic. Many fell at the exits and were crushed. When I fell there were children underneath me.' All seven floors were gutted, and the next day all that was left was a couple of concrete stairways balanced precariously inside the blackened steel-mesh shell of the building. Altogether, fifty-one people died, including seven married couples. Eighty were seriously injured.

Although many voices declared that such a building would not have been allowed on the mainland, the official report into the fire concluded that there were 'no villains', and commented that 'not every failure which is obvious now would be obvious before the disaster put the structure and people to the test', but the authorities, the architects and the suppliers of some of the building materials were all criticised for not being sufficiently alive to the risks. Trust House Forte, which leased the centre from Douglas Corporation and the Isle of Man government, was also castigated for the failure of its staff to call the fire brigade until more than 20 minutes after the blaze was discovered. 'The members of the staff who tried to extinguish the fire were individually zealous,' said the report, 'but their efforts were useless and no one thought of calling the fire brigade in time.' A number of emergency exits were locked, which constituted 'a particularly grave disregard of safety precautions', and this in spite of previous complaints from the fire brigade.

As early as the day after the blaze, police were looking for three youths who had been seen behaving suspiciously near a kiosk which had caught fire and then fallen against the outside of the building. In September 1973, a juvenile court at Douglas was told that three Liverpool schoolboys, two aged 12 and one aged 14, had shared an illicit cigarette in the kiosk at about seven thirty. One had initially denied being there, and then broke down under questioning, saying that after they had smoked their cigarette, he had stood on it to put it out. Then they had gone outside. 'I smelled burning and saw the hut was on fire. We tried to stamp it out but it got too hot and dangerous and I ran away. We ran as far as the promenade and then just watched as the fire spread from the kiosk to the whole of the Summerland building. We were too scared to admit this before.' They admitted wilful damage to the lock of the kiosk, and were each fined £3, and ordered to pay 33p compensation and 15p costs.

There were three major fires in the 1980s, all causing serious loss of life. The first happened in two illegal drinking clubs on the upper floors of a 3-storey building in London's Soho in the early hours of Saturday 16 August 1980. The clubs had been closed down on a number of occasions, but they always seemed to reopen under new management. Many of the patrons were illegal immigrants. The front door was of double thickness, lined with steel and secured with concealed locks on the inside. The windows had wooden shutters, while inside the building was a flight of wooden stairs leading up to a landing, off which was the entrance to the club on the first floor, and a wrought-iron fire escape enclosed with plywood that led up to the one on the second floor. There was a broken-down fire escape leading down to a door at the back of the building, but it was bolted and barred. The clubs were hot and steamy, with about 150 people inside, so the inside doors had been left open.

When firemen were called to the building just after half past three, they could see smoke starting to seep from the shuttered windows. Injured people were struggling off into the night, plainly not wanting to wait for treatment, and giving highly evasive answers when asked where they had come from. A fireman found the back exit from the fire escape, where people were trapped behind the locked door. He managed to break in and rescue six, many of whom were badly burned. At the front of the building, it took the fire brigade nearly 4 minutes to break down the door, then they had to battle against fierce flames on the staircase. Fortunately, the fire had been so strong it had burned the roof away, and much of the heat had escaped. Once the firemen began to get the flames under control, they started to find bodies. One fire officer said: 'People seem to have died on the spot without even having time to move an inch.' Some were slumped at tables. Seven were at the bar, and appeared to have fallen with drinks still in their hands. Of the survivors, some had smashed windows with their bare hands, and then jumped to the ground with their clothes on fire, breaking bones. The final death toll was thirty-seven. But how could the fire have spread so fast? The answer was simple. A few moments before the blaze began, a man had been spotted leaning against the door of the club. The streets were quiet, and the few people who saw him assumed he was urinating. In fact, he was a customer who had been thrown out about 50 minutes before, after getting involved in a fight. He had come back with a 2-gallon container full of petrol, poured it through the letter box, then lit a scrap of paper and pushed it in. The flames had shot straight up the wooden staircase, setting the whole building on fire within a matter of seconds.

Another fire that spread at alarming speed was the one that swept through Bradford City's Valley Parade football ground on 11 May 1985. This was the last match of a season in which Bradford had already won promotion to the Second Division of the Football League, and the home team's players had paraded the Third Division championship trophy before the 12,000 people there for the visit of Lincoln City; 2,500 of them were in the 77-year-old main stand. Promotion meant that the following season the club would come within the provisions of the Safety of Sports Grounds Act that was introduced after the Ibrox Park disaster of 1971 (see Chapter 8), and work on replacing the wood and felt roof of the stand was due to start the following Monday. There was a carnival atmosphere, and at first few spectators noticed the bright orange tongues of flame licking at the base of a row of seats in the stand a few minutes before half time. A water company worker sitting nearby said that at this point a bucket of water would have been enough to put them out, but soon people in the immediate vicinity began to move away, and a ripple of fire could be seen travelling under the seats of the wooden stand, feasting on the debris of years that had accumulated up to a foot deep. It spread faster than supporters could run away, and within 5 minutes had engulfed the whole structure. The temperature reached 1,000°C as the felt roof stopped the heat escaping upwards, instead forcing it out sideways, sending thick choking smoke pouring out in waves, and bringing burning timbers down on to the people below.

Quite legally, there were no fire extinguishers in the stand. At one time there had been, but unruly fans had set them off or used them as missiles. Turnstiles and doors at the back that would have allowed people to escape into the street behind were locked to make sure no one could get in without paying. A 46-year-old man said his life was saved by three 'burly' men who smashed open a padlock, but about fifteen charred bodies were found in a 4ft-wide walkway that ran along the back of the stand, and a dozen more were clustered around the six turnstile exits. A 58-year-old housewife, who was in intensive care for a time, said: 'everybody seemed to be trampling on everybody. My God, I trampled on old women and old men but I was just being dragged along.' She probably owed her life to a stranger who grabbed her and dragged her out, while all the time trying to douse her burning hair. A 76-year-old ex-firemen said he survived only because he had learned to fall to his knees and get below the smoke, though he added, 'I've never experienced anything like this in all my 30 years in the service.' Younger fans were able to climb over the 4ft wall at the front of the stand and escape on to the pitch. Some were on fire by the time they reached the grass, and police and spectators rolled them on the ground to smother the flames. The chairman of the supporters' club said: 'We just picked up kids and people and threw them on to the pitch.' The Conservative MP for Lincoln, Kenneth Carlisle, expressed his alarm about his government's plans to make football clubs put up fences around the pitch to prevent hooliganism, giving a warning that they would have made the disaster 'even more horrific'. Among the fifty-six dead were eleven children and nineteen pensioners. One family lost an 11-year-old boy, his father, his uncle and his grandfather. The oldest victim was 86-year-old Samuel Firth, a former chairman of the club. Two hundred people were injured.

The government set up a judicial inquiry into the fire under Mr Justice Popplewell, but it was also charged with examining the death of a 15-year-old youth during a fight at a match at Birmingham City the same day. Meanwhile, football clubs complained vociferously at what they saw as discrimination against their sport, saying that while the government took 42.5 per cent in betting tax from football, it took only 8 per cent off horse racing, and that money was ploughed back into improving racecourses. One football chairman complained that: 'Every racecourse in the country has improvements paid for by betting tax but we get nothing.' Evidence was now produced that in 1984, West Yorkshire County Council had written to Bradford City to point out the dangers arising from the accumulation of rubbish under the main stand, also pointing out that: 'A carelessly discarded cigarette could give rise to a fire risk.' However, the local authority had taken no steps to apply for restrictions on the ground, as it could have done. Ironically, steel for the new roof had been delivered back in March, but the club had decided it would be too disruptive to do the work until the end of the season. Popplewell said the fire had indeed been caused by rubbish under the stand catching fire, and that the disaster would not have happened if the Home Office's Green Code, issued in 1976, had been followed. This required the sealing of the area under stands and inspection of grounds after every event, as well as the provision of enough exits for orderly evacuation. The inquiry also had to consider the Heysel disaster, in which thirty-nine people had died after a riot by Liverpool fans two weeks after the Bradford fire. Among the recommendations Popplewell made in his interim report were that all fans should have to carry identification cards, that visiting supporters should be excluded, and that perimeter fences should be installed. There should be a smoking ban in stands that presented a fire risk, all exits should be manned at all times, and it should be possible to open them from the inside in an emergency, while the fire authorities should be authorised to close down any stand they considered unsafe. The government accepted the main recommendations, so that in future all grounds that held more than 10,000 spectators would come under the safety laws, though in his final report, Popplewell backed off from his idea of excluding away fans from matches.

After a court case brought by the 34-year-old woman who had lost her husband, her 11-year-old son, her father and her brother-in-law, Bradford City was held two-thirds responsible for the fire, and West Yorkshire County Council one-third. It was revealed that the Health and Safety Executive had written to the club back in 1980 to warn it about the build-up of litter under the seating, and that firemen searching the charred remains of the stand had found papers dating back to the 1960s. The judge criticised the club for keeping exits locked and for its failure to have any plan for emergency evacuation. The court also heard evidence that an officer of the County Council's engineers' department had been so concerned about the state of the stand that he had written to the council and the club, neither of whom appear to have been moved to act. The fire at Valley Parade was not the first to ravage a football ground. Stands at Brighton, Bristol Rovers, Brentford and Norwich City had all burned down, but because no one was in them at the time, there had been no real demand for action. Now, the Bradford City chairman, toy-maker Stafford Heginbotham, said he was sure that at every football club in the country they were saying 'there but for the grace of God go I'.

There were disturbing similarities between the Bradford City fire and the other great fire of the eighties, the King's Cross disaster. Each was caused by a stray cigarette or match igniting rubbish accumulated over years, and in each the response of those in charge proved inadequate. King's Cross was the busiest station on the London Underground, with five lines converging, and more than 30,000 commuters passing through a baffling maze of passageways and tunnels during the evening peak. At about half past seven on the evening of 18 November 1987, a passenger noticed a small fire beneath one of the escalators. He immediately reported it to the ticket office, and a member of staff went to investigate, but he had received no fire training, and did not tell the station manager or the line controller. A minute later, another passenger saw the fire, pressed the emergency stop button, and shouted to people to get off. A third passenger reported it to the booking office clerk, but he had had no training in evacuation procedures, and did not think it looked serious enough for him to leave the office. Fortunately, two British Transport police constables happened to be at the station, and they decided to alert the fire brigade.

A couple of minutes later, the station inspector went to the lower machine room of the escalator, but could not see any sign of fire. By now, though, smoke was clearly coming from escalator four, and London Underground staff blocked access to it. This time, the inspector went to the upper machine room, and saw smoke and flames. He tried to use a fire extinguisher but could not get close enough. There was also equipment available to throw a mist of water over the escalator, but he did not think to use it. It was revealed later that he had never used the equipment, nor had he ever seen it used. Now the police decided to evacuate the ticket hall. They also stopped the booking clerk selling tickets and allowing people to go down the escalators – which he had been doing quite happily until 7.41pm – and ordered the booking office staff to leave. Unfortunately, they did not know the station had a separate exit through the Midland City subway, so they believed that the only escape from the platforms was up the escalators.

The crew at the nearest fire station was out on a false alarm, so the first firemen did not arrive until 7.42. All they knew was that an escalator was on fire. Their leader, Station Officer Colin Townley, found himself at London's busiest and most complex Underground station, with no idea where the fire was, no prearranged rendezvous point with London Underground staff, and no sign of anyone in authority. He sent Temporary Sub-Officer Roger Bell down to stop people getting off trains while he organised things on the surface, and got a request sent for more engines. Roger Bell said that at first the fire was about the size of a large cardboard box, 'not a big fire at all', but soon it was raging right up to the top of the shaft. He knew there should be a hosepipe on the platform, but he could not find it.

In the concourse, a fireman was seen urging people to get out. This was probably the last sighting of SO Townley alive. Suddenly, there was a fearful flash, and the whole ticket hall was engulfed in intense heat followed by dense, hot, acrid, black smoke. Everything went dark, and the air was filled with the sound of people screaming and crying for help. Firemen had to run for their lives, dragging with them as many people as they could. In the escalator shaft, British Transport Policeman Stephen Hanson saw 'a jet of flame that shot up and then collected into a kind of ball', before hitting the ceiling of the ticket hall. It knocked him off balance and burned him severely. This was the flashover, rather like a giant blowtorch, the moment that turned the King's Cross fire into a disaster. It stopped the digital clock at 7.45, just three minutes after the fire brigade had arrived. Very few of the people who saw the flashover in the ticket office survived, and most of those who did were seriously injured. In the 15 minutes since the fire had first been reported to London Underground staff, they had done nothing to impede its progress, in spite of the fact that all platforms had fire hydrants and sand buckets, there were fire extinguishers at the top and bottom of each set of escalators, and the machine room had extinguishers and a hose reel. Trains were still stopping at the station and disgorging passengers into a death trap; as late as a quarter to nine, one Northern Line service had not received the order to drive through King's Cross and stopped to let off passengers, who were promptly put back on the train by police.

Underground, Roger Bell could see that the tops of all three Piccadilly Line escalators were now ablaze. With the help of a police constable, he found a hose in an unmarked cupboard, and began attacking the flames, tearing off wooden panels, but each time they seemed to have knocked them out, they took hold again. The burning escalator shaft behaved like a chimney, with draughts of air from the passing trains playing the part of a pair of bellows. One fireman said: 'every time a train came through the station it was like a blast furnace.' Upstairs, ticket machines exploded, the air was filled with the noise of metal panels banging and buckling in the heat, of tiles cracking and flying off walls, and of hoardings splitting. The thick smoke meant firemen had to stumble their way along using hoses as guidelines, while the searing heat made the air in their breathing apparatus run out quicker, and turned a jet of water to steam a few feet from the nozzle. One staff member did send passengers to the alternative escape route through the Midland City subway exit, but they found it was locked. It was only at a quarter past eight that the gates were finally opened, by a British Rail cleaner who had heard cries for help. Rescuers had been trying to get a badly burned passenger out that way for 20 minutes.

Up above, firemen were fighting their way back into the ticket hall. They found SO Townley face down 6ft from the bottom of a flight of stairs that would have taken him to safety. He was next to the body of a woman he had been trying to rescue. Nearly all of the dead were flat on their faces in the concourse and the subways around it, having suffocated during a desperate dash to escape in the first few seconds after the flashover. The fire, funnelled up the escalator shaft, had been highly concentrated, hardly charring the wooden panels on the walls of the concourse, while two staff who were rescued from a staff mess room had been saved by nothing more elaborate than a wooden door. For more than an hour, the only information firemen had about the layout of the station was a plan sketched by a British Rail manager. There were two sets of London Underground plans they should have been able to use, but one was in a box behind a builders' hoarding (which also concealed a fire hydrant and hose), while the other was in the station's perimeter subway and could not be reached because of the dense smoke. By the time the fire was finally contained at a quarter to two in the morning, more than 200 firemen had been involved in fighting it. Thirty-one people died, and more than 50 were injured. SO Townley was awarded the George Medal posthumously.

The official inquiry found that grease, dust, fibre and other debris had gathered under the escalator, providing an ideal place for the flames to take hold once a lighted match fell on to it. A maintenance manager said that, as far as he knew, the running tracks of the Piccadilly Line escalators at King's Cross had never been properly cleaned. It became clear that fires had started on many previous occasions, but had then gone out. The inquiry chairman, Desmond Fennel QC, said that on the whole London Underground operated a safe system, but that its management had 'a blind spot – a belief that fires were inevitable, coupled with a belief that any fire on a wooden escalator, and there have been many, would never develop in a way which would endanger passengers'. Much of his report is a scathing indictment of the management's unpreparedness. There should have been twenty-three staff on duty, but three were absent, and two others were not at their posts. These two, the ones rescued from the mess room, were taking a meal break of an hour and a half, even though they were only supposed to take half an hour, because it was 'accepted practice'. However, the inquiry concluded it would have made no difference if everyone had been at their posts, because they would not have known what to do, and commented: 'The response of the staff was uncoordinated, haphazard and untrained.'

Only four of those on duty said they had had any training in evacuation or fire drills. It was clear some did not know where to find hydrants or firefighting equipment. The most senior member of staff, the station manager, was stuck in a remote temporary office, and was not even told about the fire until twelve minutes after it was first reported. Even then, he made no attempt to contact the firemen, and it was another hour before any senior London Underground official offered them help. The public address system at the station was not used at any time during the fire, and the failure to turn on the water fog equipment in the first few minutes meant a vital chance was lost to slow its progress enough to enable the fire brigade to deal with it. The report concluded that 'there was no effective control of King's Cross station by London Underground supervisors or staff', and that, fortunately, the decision to evacuate passengers and order trains not to stop was taken by British Transport Police, 'who effectively assumed responsibility for station control'. Smoking had been banned on escalators since 1985, but the ban was not properly enforced, and it was common to see passengers 'lighting up' as they ascended – as presumably did the unknown person who discarded the fatal match.

## CHAPTER EIGHT

# CRUSHES AND COLLAPSES

Sometimes the fear of fire can be as deadly as fire itself. In February 1849 at the Theatre Royal in Glasgow, a small gas leak caught light. Someone shouted 'Fire!' and the audience rushed for the exits. The flames were quickly put out, but in the stampede for safety from the upper floors, sixty-five people were crushed to death on the stairs. Thirty-four years later in Sunderland, the cause of disaster was not the fear of fire, but the fear of not getting a free toy. On the afternoon of Saturday 16 June 1883, a Tynemouth ventriloquist and conjurer named Alexander Fay and his sister Annie had hired the Victoria Hall to put on a show for local children. It was an 'exceedingly handsome', big, modern building. The Fays had promoted the show energetically, giving out free tickets to teachers in order to get access to local schools. It was 1*d* each for children to get in, including a free toy, but 3*d* for each parent or nurse accompanying them. Perhaps because of this, when the curtain went up, there were very few adults in the audience, probably not many more than a score among more than 2,000 youngsters. Most of the children were upstairs in the gallery, and some amused themselves by spitting or throwing cockle shells on the ones below. As the performance neared its end around five o'clock, Fay began throwing toys to the children downstairs. A rumour spread through the gallery that those upstairs would not get their free gift, and some of the children raced for the exits to get down to the ground floor.

After leaving the gallery, they had to go down twenty-five steps in a poorly lit stairway, then there was a turn to the left past the entrance to the dress circle, then a further fourteen stairs led down to a landing where a door partly blocked the 7ft opening, leaving a gap of less than 2ft. A few of the leading children got through, but those behind got stuck in the doorway, and over the minutes that followed, up to 300 children piled up behind them. Few people outside or in the rest of the theatre could hear the shrieks and screams as the children tumbled head over heels, landing on top of each other, and those who were aware of anything put it down to the delight of children on an exciting afternoon out. In a scene that almost defies belief, the heap of desperately struggling humanity eventually reached 6ft, but so tight was the crush that the whole pile of bodies was crammed on to the landing and the first four steps leading up from it.

Knowing the show would soon be over, the manager, Frederick Graham, had set off on his round of the hall to make sure all the exits were clear. As he climbed up towards the gallery stairs, he heard 'fearful screams, groans, and noises of struggling'. He tried to force open the door, but he could not, because 'the opening was jammed up nearly as high as my head with the bodies of children'. Graham decided his first task must be to stop any more children rushing down from the gallery and recruited the few adults in the building to help. Then he fought his way down the stairs. At the fourth step, he found the pile of children. 'There seemed to be hundreds of them,' he said. 'At first I did not think that any were dead, but when we came to attempt releasing them I discovered my mistake.' With the help of a policeman and two other men, he concentrated on rescuing children who were groaning or showing other signs of life from near the top of the heap, where little bodies were wedged eight deep. Helped by his wife, he managed to revive about a dozen. Many of the dead children had faces horribly bruised, blackened and swollen. Some had had their clothes torn off in the melee. One of the people helping Graham told *The Times*'s reporter that some of the children were so terribly crushed, they were afraid they 'might pull the bodies to pieces'.

Soon the news began to spread around Sunderland, and the building was surrounded by parents terrified about what might have happened to their offspring. All the town's cabmen turned out to help take the dead to their homes, and it was said that one or two parents took home what they thought were the remains of their child – only to get home and find to their astonishment that their son or daughter was waiting for them there alive and well. Few experienced such relief, though, as 180 children, aged 4 to 12, were suffocated or crushed to death, and many more were injured.

It emerged later that one of Fay's assistants, named Charles Hesletine, had tried to get up to the gallery to hand out toys, but he had been almost overwhelmed by the rush of children, and had had to take refuge behind the bolted door, narrowly escaping serious injury. After the disaster, Fay found himself under attack, but he declared that he had often performed for big audiences of children and that he had 'always taken every care for their safety', while his sister said they invariably distributed toys systematically so there was no need for any panic among the children. At an inquest on the boys and girls from Bishopswearmouth, the jury wondered who had shot the bolt that locked the door with such fatal consequences, but decided there was not enough evidence to decide. It did, however, demand that the door should be removed immediately, and said that not enough staff had been on duty. At another inquest at Monkwearmouth on thirty-two of the dead children, a former secretary of the hall testified that the door had been fitted in 1876 to try to prevent crushing on the stairs, and to stop the draught when biting easterly winds were blowing. It had never before caused any problems. The inquest also heard that Hesletine had worked himself to exhaustion trying to rescue the victims. In addition to criticising the hall and Fay for not having enough people on duty, this jury also said that parents should not have let their children go to the show without knowing which adults would be in charge, and that teachers should not have allowed the distribution of tickets unless they were satisfied with the safety arrangements. They also called for a law insisting that exits should open outwards, and requiring the inspection of public buildings.

By the 1920s the cinema was taking over from the theatre as an attraction for young people, but the ease with which film could catch fire led to another disaster in which many small children died, at Paisley on 31 December 1929. About 750 boys and girls had crowded into a special Hogmanay matinee at the Glen cinema in the centre of town. After the first film had finished, a 15-year-old assistant operator took it to a room next to the projector enclosure to rewind it. After he had put it away, he saw smoke coming from the film can. He tried to carry it out of the building, but could only get as far as the foyer. The manager, Charles Dorward, rushed out of his office, grabbed the can, and flung it on to a piece of wasteland outside, but by now, the tragedy was already unfolding.

Smoke had begun to seep into the auditorium. Up went the shout of 'Fire!' and, not surprisingly, the children dashed for the two exits furthest from the projection area. Two doors on either side of the screen led into a passageway to a concertina lattice metal door that opened into the street. A 10-year-old named Jeanie Brown, who was in the cinema with her two younger sisters, said she smelt smoke coming from the projection room, and then 'all the folk began to run . . . I took May by one hand and Emily by the other and started to follow the crowd rushing to the door.' The fire brigade reached the scene within 2 minutes, and quickly dealt with the burning film, but the desperate crowd now gathered outside the cinema shouted to them that the cinema was full of children. Police climbed up on their ladders and smashed open windows to haul the children out, some unconscious, some weeping in terror. Once they got inside, though, they found the smoke was not as bad as they had feared. The manager was trying to persuade children it was safe to go out through the exit at the back of the cinema, but many were so maddened with fear that they would not listen. Even if, like Jeanie Brown, they followed the advice, it was not easy to escape: 'When I turned to go to the other door I lost Emily . . . there was a rush from behind and both of us were knocked down, and May began to cry.' In fact, all three children got out, and many others who had not joined the rush to the front exits escaped with nothing worse than discomfort, but up by the screen was a disaster area.

There, one senior fire officer said children were 'as tightly packed as a wall of cement bags. Some still moved, others were motionless. Legs and arms were intertwined in the most appalling tangle.' Another fireman said the bodies were piled up breast-high: 'Half a dozen terror-stricken youngsters grabbed hold of my coat and my belt, and I just turned and grabbed them all out into the fresh air . . . I saw what appeared to be a baby of about 18 months lying in the pile.' According to Jeanie Brown's mother, there was only one doctor at the scene of the disaster, but he showed mothers in the crowd how to perform artificial respiration, and many whose own children were still missing bravely tried to revive the casualties. In spite of all these efforts, though, 70 children, all under 15, were found crushed to death or suffocated. Nearly 40 were seriously injured, and more than 150 had to be taken to hospital, often in tramcars that were pressed into service as makeshift ambulances.

A relief fund was quickly launched, with *The Times* noting that: 'The cinema is patronized by some of the poorest people', many of whom would not be able to afford to bury their children. As the funerals began, all over Paisley, flags flew at half-mast, and the town council interred many victims without charge in the municipal cemetery. The hall had been passed as safe by the fire brigade on the morning of the fire, but five days later, the manager was charged with culpable homicide and taken to prison. At his trial, the indictment alleged that he had failed to keep the exits open, allowing the lattice metal gate to be locked. The jury heard that Dorward had been warned that the gate must be kept open, and a policeman said in evidence that the gate was padlocked and he had tried to break it open with his truncheon, while the Lord Advocate reminded them of 'that awful picture of a little girl walking with outstretched arms and staring eyes over the dead and dying children wedged so tightly that they formed a human floor'. A chocolate seller at the theatre, though, swore that the gate had not been locked; she had seen Dorward slide it back, and a fireman also testified that everything had seemed in order. The judge in his summing up said there was abundant evidence that the gate had been treated as if it had been locked. It had been violently wrenched open, and bent and twisted in the process, but during all these desperate struggles, might it really have been possible to just slide it open? After deliberating for 20 minutes, the jury decided the prosecution had not proved the gate had been locked, and returned a verdict of 'not guilty'. The following month, the chief inspector of explosives, Major T.H. Crozier, in his official report, said that if there had been more staff on duty, it might have been possible to calm the children, and stop the mad rush. He also noted that, although smoking was banned in the projection enclosure and the rewinding room, cigarette ends and empty cigarette and matchboxes were found there.

Coal mining has always been a dangerous job, and many miners have paid with their lives to keep the home fires burning and the wheels of industry turning (see Chapter 10), but at Aberfan in Glamorgan in 1966, it was the children of miners and their neighbours who died. At about a quarter past nine on Friday 21 October, the younger children at Pantglas Junior School had just gone to their classrooms after morning assembly to prepare for the first lesson. It was a sunny day on the hilltops, but at the school down in the valley, fog had reduced visibility to about 50yd. Some of the older children were still in the playground, and one said he saw a wave of slurry higher than a house coming over a railway embankment and heading towards him 'as fast as a car', while a 10-year-old boy peering through the fog saw his two friends engulfed. The heap 'looked like water pouring down the hillside. It uprooted a great tree on its way. . . . It just sucked them away. . . . It hit the school like a big wave, splattering all over the place, and crushing the buildings.' Nearby, a hairdresser heard a noise 'like a jet plane' and saw the windows and doors of houses crashing in 'like a pile of dominoes coming down'. He was saved by a piece of corrugated sheeting that protected him until council workmen could rescue him.

Inside the school, a 10-year-old girl said they were laughing and talking, waiting for the teacher to call the register, when 'we heard a noise and we saw stuff flying around. The desks were falling over and the children were shouting and screaming. We could not see anything but then the dust began to go away. My leg was caught in a desk and I could not move.' A boy, then aged 8, recalled later: 'It was a tremendous rumbling sound and all the school went dead. You could hear a pin drop. Everyone just froze in their seats.' The girl's teacher was also pinned to the floor at first, but managed to break free and smash the window in the classroom door with a stone, then help the children climb out.

A tip at Merthyr Vale colliery had slid half a mile, engulfing the school and twenty houses under 45ft of slag. One of the first rescuers on the scene said: 'We rushed up to the top of the street to find the school buried. It was little more than a mass of tangled wreckage.' A 27-year-old woman managed to climb in through a window. 'When I got inside,' she said, 'there were about a dozen children screaming in one classroom which had only half collapsed.' With the help of a nurse, she managed to get them out. 'Then we went to another classroom which was terribly damaged, and we could hear the voice of a girl, but we could not see her. We could not get at her because there were other children with her, and if we moved anything, everything would collapse on them.' Miners at two nearby collieries immediately stopped work, and joined the rescue. One found a boy alive. 'He was standing against the heater in the schoolroom and was crying because his leg had been caught in something. By his seat were three other children. They were dead.'

Two thousand men and women hacked at the slag with shovels, picks and their bare hands throughout the day, then at night by floodlight, setting up bucket chains to remove the slurry. Bulldozers and earth movers also worked on it, though if any faint cry was heard, they would stop. Just before midnight, the body of the deputy head was found clutching five children in his arms. From the houses near the school, a motor mechanic managed to rescue one woman who was lying under the rubble still in her bed. The army and navy were also called in, and eventually up to 5,000 people were involved in the clear-up. Those who had seen the disaster said there had been a rumbling noise, and then the tip had moved with terrifying suddenness. A maintenance man from the pit, who was near the top of the heap when it started to slide, said: 'Suddenly we could see the tip moving 300 yards away from us. We could hear the trees on the side of the tip being crushed.' He ran for a quarter of a mile to the colliery to try to raise the alarm. The slag heap had also moved in 1959 and 1964, when a councillor had warned that the school might be in danger. A local man said: 'It has been piling higher and higher and with a stream filtering through beneath it, it was always liable to shift.' The National Coal Board's chief geologist for South Wales maintained that water normally seeped away from the base of the tip, but said that this time, for some reason, it seemed to have built up inside, and some people living nearby said they had seen the slag beginning to slide on Thursday evening.

The disaster claimed the lives of 144 people, including 116 children, but there were many such heaps in Wales, and people remembered that in 1939, lower down the same valley, one had slid one-third of a mile, but was spotted in time to prevent any loss of life. Miners complained that safety rules on the surface were much less stringent than those underground, and in the week after the disaster, mothers at Cwm, near Ebbw Vale, kept eighty-eight children away from school because of fears about a slag heap right next to it, while the Bishop of Llandaff said: 'Never before have we paid for our coal with the lives of children and we must never do so again.' To try to prevent another Aberfan, the government announced a public inquiry under Lord Justice Edmund Davies, who had presided at the trial of the Great Train Robbers. He was a local man, born just 2 miles away at Mountain Ash, and he faced a formidable task. The coroner's inquest had been interrupted by shouts of 'Our children have been murdered' and 'Buried alive by the National Coal Board'.

A few days later, 10,000 people crowded into Aberfan's small hillside cemetery for the burial of eighty-one children and one woman. Wreaths sent from all over the world were made into a 100ft cross. *The Times* reported that a stern-faced police sergeant burst into tears when a relative threw teddy bears into one of the graves. In August of the following year, the official inquiry uncovered 'a terrifying tale of bungling ineptitude by many men charged with tasks for which they were totally unfitted', and declared that 'the disaster could and should have been prevented', but the Attorney General, Sir Elwyn Jones, did not institute any criminal proceedings because there were 'no villains'. Instead, 'decent men, led astray by foolishness or by ignorance or by both in combination, are responsible for what happened at Aberfan'. The inquiry's report said the Coal Board had no policy on the siting, maintenance and control of tips, and there had been no general inspection of those in the area since 1947. It was clear from earlier slides in the village 'that tips built on slopes can and do slip', and when Tip Number 7, the one that caused the disaster, was begun in 1958, there should have been a proper survey, but 'even without a survey, reference to the available geological map would have revealed a line of springs, the Ordnance Survey would have given warning of watercourses and the site would thus have been revealed as obviously unsuitable'.

As early as 1960, fears had been expressed to the board, and in 1963 there were several slides, one of which bore a disturbing resemblance to the one

A crucial incident in the Anglo-Saxon conquest. In AD 449, the British king Vortigern invites the Saxon brothers Hengest and Horsa to help him fight the Picts. Before long, though, Hengest would kill him in battle, and take over his kingdom. *(Mary Evans Picture Library)*

The Bayeux Tapestry's record of the moment when King Harold is hit in the eye by an arrow at the Battle of Hastings. Victory went to William the Conqueror, who blazed a savage trail of destruction through the Home Counties before taking the crown. *(Mary Evans Picture Library)*

As crusading fever swept the country at the beginning of Richard the Lionheart's reign, Jews were attacked all over England. In York in 1190 they took refuge in the castle, but Christians, some of whom owed them money, broke in. Many Jews killed themselves, but the mob slaughtered 150. *(Mary Evans Picture Library)*

How Foxe's *Book of Martyrs* portrayed the burning of six Protestants at Canterbury in 1555. Altogether Queen Mary burned 289 'heretics' in her five-year reign as she tried to restore England to Roman Catholicism. (*Mary Evans Picture Library*)

The BATTLE of EDGE-HILL

A rather genteel eighteenth-century view of the Battle of Edgehill of 1642, the first major encounter of the English Civil War. Altogether during the conflict, 85,000 people were killed, and at least 100,000 died from disease. About 150 towns were damaged. (*Mary Evans Picture Library*)

'Bring out your dead!' A victim is removed by night during the Great Plague of 1665. London lost perhaps 100,000 people to the disease, though in proportion to the capital's size, the outbreak was less devastating than the Black Death of 1348 that killed about a third of the population. (*Mary Evans Picture Library*)

The Great Fire of London of 1666 reaches St Paul's Cathedral. Stones are said to have flown from it like grenades while the pavements around glowed red. Altogether the fire destroyed 87 churches, and devastated more than 430 acres. (*Mary Evans Picture Library*)

After the defeat of the Duke of Monmouth's rebellion at Sedgmoor in 1685, Judge Jeffreys embarked on the 'Bloody Assizes' around the West Country, intimidating witnesses and raging at defendants. He had 320 hanged, and boasted that no one since the Norman Conquest had disposed of so many traitors. *(Mary Evans Picture Library)*

The most devastating storm in Britain's recorded history came on 27 November 1703. Hundreds lost their lives on land, but thousands were drowned around the coast, including 2,000 sailors as 13 men o' war went down. *(Mary Evans Picture Library)*

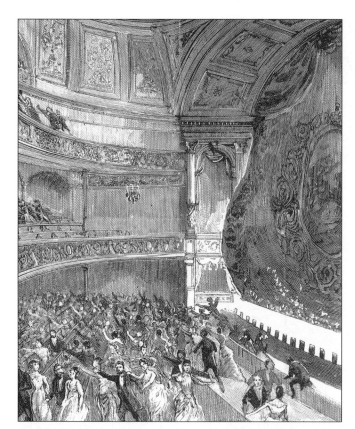

The curtain billows out at Exeter's Theatre Royal on 5 September 1887 to reveal a fire on stage. In the panic to escape through inadequate exits, 188 people were killed. *(Mary Evans Picture Library)*

The *Illustrated London News*'s impression of the fruitless search for survivors after the Tay Bridge disaster on the last Sunday of 1879. The bridge had collapsed during a storm taking all 75 passengers on the Dundee mail train to their deaths. *(Mary Evans Picture Library)*

A contemporary drawing of the scene at the pithead as an explosion rips through the underground workings at Senghenydd colliery, near Caerphilly in 1901, killing 82 miners. Twelve years later at the same pit, 440 would be killed in Britain's worst ever mining disaster. *(Mary Evans Picture Library)*

The First World War comes home. Just before Christmas 1914, German warships bombarded Hartlepool and other east coast towns, killing more than 70 people. Later in the war, more than 1,400 would be killed in air raids. *(Mary Evans Picture Library)*

The air raids of the Second World War killed more than 60,000 people in Britain. In November 1940, the Luftwaffe mounted a massive attack on Coventry destroying the cathedral and most of the city's historic centre. A new word was added to the language – 'coventrated'. *(EMPICS/PA)*

England's worst rail disaster came on the foggy morning of 8 October 1952, when three trains collided at Harrow and Wealdstone station on the outskirts of London. Rescuers worked for more than six hours to free the injured, but 112 people died. *(EMPICS/PA)*

Just a few months later, the east coast of England was hit by devastating floods in January 1953. From Lincolnshire to Essex, more than 300 people were drowned. One of the places worst hit was Canvey Island, shown here, where 58 people died. *(EMPICS/PA)*

Flood waters pour down the main street of Lynmouth in Devon in August 1952 after the Lyn rivers burst their banks. 34 people were killed, including 11 holidaymakers. *(EMPICS/PA)*

Rescue workers dig with their bare hands to try to reach children trapped under pit slurry at Pantglas Junior School at Aberfan. In October 1966, a slag heap slid half a mile, burying 116 children and 28 adults alive. *(EMPICS/PA)*

At Hillsborough on 15 April 1989, 95 football fans were crushed to death before the disbelieving eyes of 54,000 spectators at the FA Cup semi-final between Liverpool and Nottingham Forest. *(EMPICS/PA)*

The funeral cortege of a father and son killed in the Omagh bombing of 15 August 1998. Twenty-nine people died in the worst terrorist outrage of the Troubles in Ireland, committed by dissident Republicans after the Good Friday Agreement. *(EMPICS/PA)*

that caused the accident, but the NCB still exhibited a 'remarkable' lack of concern. After a slide on Tip Number 4 in 1944, tipping had been stopped, but no such action was taken after the slides at Tip Number 7. The judge declared that the board's behaviour had been tainted by 'subterfuge and arrogance', and also criticised its failure to admit liability until almost the end of the hearings, complaining that it had 'stubbornly resisted every attempt to lay the blame where it so clearly must rest – at its door'. There were harsh comments about the chairman, Lord Robens. He had made statements about the disaster when he did not know the full facts, and his evidence under cross-examination had been inconsistent. Robens offered his resignation, but the government persuaded him to stay on. In contrast, the report praised the 'heroic absence of panic' shown by teachers and children at the school. Many local people felt that the Coal Board officials shown to have been wanting should have been sacked, and that the local council should have been castigated for its failure to protect the children in its schools. A year after the disaster, it was said that on rainy nights, parents in the village would not go to bed, but instead would sit awake fully clothed by their children's beds.

For more than a century, few forms of mass entertainment have rivalled football, with crowds numbering tens of thousands turning up at matches every week during the season. On 2 January 1971, Ibrox Park, Glasgow – the home of Glasgow Rangers – was filled to capacity with 80,000 supporters for the traditional New Year 'derby' match with local rivals Celtic. Rangers were Protestant; Celtic were Catholic, and there was little love lost between the rival fans, but, on this occasion, even though a fair amount of drink was being consumed, the atmosphere on the terraces was fairly good-humoured, and the match came to an exciting climax with Celtic scoring just 2 minutes from time, and then Rangers equalising in the dying seconds. A senior police officer said that after Rangers' goal, their fans 'were singing, shouting, jumping up and down, waving their arms. The terracing was in uproar. I would say it was football mania at its highest.' Just after the home side scored, though, something terrible happened on the steep steps of Staircase 13 in the north-east corner of the ground as the crowd was leaving.

A 33-year-old woman who lived in the tenement block opposite the ground said, 'the people on the staircase began to fall like a pack of cards . . . it was as if they were all disappearing down a big hole'. To another eyewitness in the block, a 62-year-old man, it was 'like a river that burst its banks'. He said some people were so excited at Rangers' equaliser that they began running down the steps. Then he saw a young man lose his balance and fall. One man caught up in the crush said he felt himself being lifted off his feet and carried down the stairs by the weight of humanity. His arms were pinned to his sides, leaving him helpless, and he blacked out. When he came round, he saw his brother, who seemed to have died standing up. A 13½-stone man said that he too was lifted bodily off the steps; 'the next minute there was a bang and a banister to my left went. Everyone flew forward. I seemed to fly through the air and I landed on top of the bodies.' For 40 minutes, he lay pinned down by the dead and injured. When he was freed, he tried to help a sandy-haired youth, but there was 'not a blink from his eyes'. The steps were covered with the bodies of the dead and injured, and with shoes torn off during the mêlée, while steel barriers were left crushed and twisted.

At the subsequent fatal accident inquiry, a 22-year-old man said he had seen two boys throw an anorak and a Rangers scarf into the air, and that when they bent down to pick them up, the crowd began to fall on top of them, precipitating the disaster, though the general view was that it was hard to pinpoint the precise cause. Another supporter said that a young boy fell in front of him; 'his father said: "Stop, my son is being trampled on," but the father was carried away.' When it became clear what was happening, some supporters ran up the embankment on either side of the stairway and tried to pull down the wooden fences that enclosed it to relieve the crush. Altogether sixty-six people were killed; among them was one woman, a 19-year-old Rangers supporter who at Christmas had made a doll for the baby of Rangers' centre forward Colin Stein, the man who scored the fateful equaliser. Another 140 were injured in what was – at the time – the worst disaster at a British football ground.

A police superintendent told the inquiry that 'if you look at that stairway, there is nothing one can really do to control a very large mass of people coming down . . . any obstacle on that stairway would probably cause an accident'. There had been a serious disaster at Ibrox in 1902 when part of a stand collapsed at an international between Scotland and England, killing twenty-five people, and two people had been killed on Staircase 13 at a Rangers–Celtic match in 1961 when crush barriers collapsed. At that time, the steps were wooden, but after the accident they had been concreted, and new railings had been fitted. There were two further incidents on the staircase during the sixties, though, and in 1969 the police and the club had discussed whether it could be 'fanned out' to make it safer, but they had not reached any definite conclusion. Football grounds were not then licensed by local authorities and were exempt from the kind of safety regulations that applied to places like bingo halls and dance halls, but Glasgow's master of works said that Ibrox was inspected at the start of each season, and he was not aware of any problems. The ground also met the standards required by the club's insurers. The jury, though, decided that 'deaths or injuries will always be liable to occur on this stairway in its present state if a densely packed mass of people is allowed to descend'.

After the disaster, Rangers undertook one of the most ambitious rebuilding projects in the history of British football, demolishing three-quarters of the ground, and turning it into an all-seater stadium that today holds just 50,000 people. The disaster also prompted the government to introduce a Green Guide to Safety at Sports Grounds and the Safety of Sports Grounds Act, which required football grounds to be licensed by local authorities. Sadly, though, this attempt to make stadiums less dangerous was followed by an even worse football disaster.

During the years that followed Ibrox, the authorities tended to see hooliganism as a much more serious problem for football than crowd safety. The government passed laws to restrict drinking by spectators and to stop known troublemakers from getting into grounds, while perimeter fences were put up to prevent fans invading the pitch. The Heysel disaster seemed to confirm this view. British clubs were banned from Europe, and the government decided to bring in another law saying that anyone who wanted to go to a football match would have to carry an identity card. This bill was making its way through Parliament when Liverpool met Nottingham Forest in the FA Cup semi-final, one of the biggest matches of the year, on 15 April 1989. The clubs had met at the same stage in the competition the previous season, and the game had been played at Sheffield Wednesday's ground, Hillsborough. There had been no major problems, but Liverpool had been unhappy that – even though they had twice as many regular fans as Forest – their supporters had been allocated the smaller Leppings Lane end of the ground. The other end was nearer to the Forest fans' route from the M1, and police believed this would make it easier to keep the two groups of supporters apart as they travelled to and from the match. The Liverpool chief executive, Peter Robinson, said that when he knew they had once again been drawn against Forest, he had telephoned the Football Association to ask them not to play the game at Hillsborough, but that 'they came back to me one hour later to tell me they had chosen to play the game at Sheffield Wednesday and the police were insisting on the same allocation'. Still, the Sheffield ground was regarded as one of the best in Britain. It had often been used for semi-finals, and its pre-war capacity of 74,000 had been reduced to 54,000.

On the day of the match, there were roadworks on the M62 motorway, meaning that much of the Liverpool contingent was delayed. Twenty minutes before the kick-off at three o'clock, most Forest supporters were in their seats, but the area outside the Leppings Lane turnstiles was getting more and more crowded with Liverpool fans afraid they were going to miss the start. One supporter described it as 'bedlam. We were crushed and pushed against the walls and there were people fighting to get into the turnstiles with tickets for the wrong areas – or no tickets at all. People were climbing over the walls and there were no policemen whatsoever doing anything about it.' Some complained police were sitting in parked cars and vans apparently ignoring the growing chaos. At about five to three, a police superintendent ordered a gate to the side of the turnstiles to be opened. Fans rushed in 'like a train', making it impossible to check tickets. Inside the gate, the terraces were divided into eight pens, and supporters could climb up to the higher sections where there were spaces, but the quickest and easiest thing to do was to go straight through a tunnel to the two pens directly behind the goal. In any case, as they came in, the supporters had no way of telling how busy each pen was, nor, unless they were familiar with the ground, would they know into which pen their route was leading them.

Inside, things were getting worse by the minute. Stephen Hendry, aged 19, said there was a severe crush outside the turnstiles, but when they got into the stadium, 'the problem seemed much worse, there was lots of pushing and jostling, which we thought would settle down after about ten minutes. It didn't.' Once the teams came out, it was 'a nightmare. More and more people started to come into the ground and the crushing got worse. We got pushed to the front of the ground . . . people were screaming to push back the crowd.' Some fell and were trampled 'by fans helpless in the surge'. At the front of the terrace was the perimeter fence, its only exit a small, locked gate.

A 42-year-old company director named Trevor Hicks had gone to the match with his two teenage daughters. They had got into the ground at two o'clock, and so were right at the front. As the overcrowding got worse, Mr Hicks could see what was happening to his daughters. 'I shouted to one of the police officers that people were being crushed,' he said. 'I didn't get a very polite answer.' Helpless, he saw one of his daughters being passed over the heads of the crowd. When he finally managed to get out of the crush, he would find both his girls on the pitch, but attempts to revive them failed, and they died, all before the eyes of Mrs Hicks, who was in the stand. Stephen Hendry, meanwhile, was 'now unable to breathe as more and more fans streamed into the terrace. The gate still wasn't open and people were dying.' His heart stopped beating, but other supporters managed to get him on to the pitch and ambulancemen saved his life. By now, fans were climbing over the fences, while others at the back of the pens were grabbing outstretched arms that pulled them into the stand above. Those nearest the disaster area could see supporters crushed up against the fences, their faces horribly distorted. From other parts of the ground, though, while it was obvious that something was wrong, it was not clear what – hooliganism? A riot? Those who could shouted to the nearest player, the Liverpool goalkeeper, Bruce Grobbelaar, pleading with him to get the match stopped. As a judge put it later, the struggle to escape 'caused a horrendous blockage of bodies. The dead, the dying and the desperate became interwoven in the sump at the front of the pens, especially by the gates. Those with strength clambered over others submerged in the human heap and tried to climb out over the fence.' Six minutes into the game, a lone policeman ran up to the referee and got him to stop the match. After the players left, the dead and injured were gradually brought out and laid on the pitch. A senior St John Ambulance man tried to help the supporters behind the goal. 'They were vomiting and could not get the vomit out of their mouths,' he said. 'We tried to free the airways with our hands and give them oxygen. It was a terrible experience.' The death toll would be ninety-five; the youngest victim a boy of 10.

The first reaction was incredulity. *The Times*'s correspondent wrote: 'With disbelieving eyes, we sat in the grandstand and watched almost 100 people die in front of us at an FA Cup semi-final.' Soon, though, blame was being handed out in all directions. A senior lecturer in public health from Liverpool University who was at the game said that more than half an hour after the disaster began, 'there were no medical personnel apart from one or two St John Ambulance men. There was no equipment and there was only one ambulance. There was nobody in charge.' A doctor said, 'it was over an hour after the tragedy before I tracked down the barest medical supplies'. Most of the immediate criticism was laid on the police. The superintendent who got the gate by the turnstiles opened said he did it because he was afraid a wall would collapse on top of the milling supporters. He added that he had requested the main control room to ask the referee to delay the kick-off, to give Liverpool supporters more time to get into the ground. It was a request to which the referee would almost certainly have acceded, but it never reached him. Some police officers, meanwhile, blamed the Liverpool supporters, saying the crush had happened because many of them had arrived late after drinking in pubs near the ground. A Police Federation official claimed: 'Some arrived tanked up and the situation for officers trying to control them was terrifying.' A publican and a local MP backed up the claims, and a senior ambulance officer said one of his men had been attacked while he was tending the injured, while an unnamed senior police officer said: 'As we struggled in appalling conditions to save lives, fans standing further up the terraces were openly urinating on us and the bodies of the dead. As policemen on the pitch tried to save the injured they were hampered by other Liverpool fans running up, kicking and punching them.' These unruly elements, it was alleged, had even picked the pockets of the dead.

The secretary of the Merseyside Police Federation, though, was incensed at the allegations, saying they were 'ill-informed . . . television showed no evidence of supporters urinating on police or of hundreds of drunken hooligans', while the reaction of the secretary of the Liverpool supporters' club was that 'sadly it appears the police are now anxiously trying to divert blame from where it really rests – with them'. A Liverpool MP accused police of a cover-up. In Parliament, the government got the blame. There were demands for the removal of perimeter fences. Labour peer Lord Mason accused clubs of treating supporters like caged prisoners, while the party's home affairs spokesman, Roy Hattersley, complained: 'Perimeter fencing has been the product of an obsession with hooliganism as distinct from a concern with safety.'

The man given the task of sifting the truth from this mountain of accusation and counter-accusation was Lord Justice Taylor. He produced a devastating critique of those responsible for ensuring the safety of football supporters, concluding: 'It is a depressing and chastening fact that mine is the ninth official report covering crowd safety and control at football grounds.' He put the immediate blame for the disaster squarely on senior police officers. While commending many young constables who had behaved 'heroically', his comment on the performance of those in charge was that: 'ther their handling of the problems on the day nor their account of it in 'e showed the qualities of leadership to be expected of their rank.'

Before the inquiry, 'with some notable exceptions, the senior officers in command were defensive and evasive witnesses'. The chief superintendent in charge had only taken over the division three weeks before, and had made no proper arrangements for dealing with the crowd outside the Leppings Lane turnstiles. When one of his superintendents had asked for the gates to be opened, the chief superintendent's 'capacity to take decisions and give orders seemed to collapse'. After some delay, he had agreed to the request, but then failed to take action to control the inevitable inrush of fans and direct them to areas of the ground where there was still space. This was the key failure that had produced the disaster. He had now been moved to a desk job, but Lord Justice Taylor expressed concern over whether the police had really learned the necessary lessons, because of their reluctance to admit that they had been at fault: 'it would have been more seemly and encouraging for the future if responsibility had been faced.' There was evidence that 'an unruly minority who had drunk too much aggravated the problem', but not one witness had substantiated allegations that drunken supporters urinated on police officers, or urinated on the bodies of the dead, or stole their belongings. After the report appeared, the Chief Constable of South Yorkshire, Peter Wright, offered his resignation, but the Police Authority declined to accept it.

Sheffield City Council was also castigated as 'inefficient and dilatory' for allowing breaches of the Green Guide and for not inspecting the ground properly. The arrival of a large number of fans close to kick-off was 'foreseeable', but the turnstile area was not equipped to deal with it, while the small size and number of exit gates from the terracing on to the pitch made the rescue effort much more difficult. Football clubs were also condemned for 'chilling complacency', and Lord Justice Taylor insisted: 'The years of patching up grounds, of having periodic disasters and narrowly avoiding many others by muddling through on a wing and a prayer must be over.' He made seventy-six recommendations, including a requirement for major clubs to end standing on the terraces and to provide seats for all spectators. Perimeter fences should have patrolled emergency exits, police planning should be improved, and there should be better medical provision at grounds, but the identity card system, on which the government had been so keen, should be shelved. Lord Justice Taylor said it would make congestion outside grounds worse, and would increase the dangers of disorder. His report brought about the changes it demanded. Supporters now watch in all-seater stadiums, perimeter fences have gone, and there has not been another Hillsborough or Ibrox.

# CHAPTER NINE

# EXPLOSIONS

In 1796, with Britain enmeshed in a twenty-year war with revolutionary France, the 32-gun warship *Amphion* was on patrol, looking for any signs of the invasion the French were believed to be preparing, when her foremast was damaged in a gale. On 19 September, she put into Plymouth for repairs. Three days later, she was ready to set sail again, and many visitors came aboard to say goodbye to friends and loved ones at a farewell party. Unfortunately, the ship's gunner had been stealing gunpowder to sell, and spilt some. After a few drinks, he dropped a light. The forward magazine exploded and blew the front of the vessel to smithereens. The aft section sank to the bottom close to the dockyard jetty. Bodies and lumps of wreckage were flung as high as the masts, and four guns ended up on a hulk lying alongside, as did the commanding officer, Captain Israel Pellew, who escaped with head and chest injuries. A sailor's wife was flung into the air with her baby in her arms. She was killed, but when her body was found, the child was still clutched in her arms and still alive. Few others survived. Of 312 people on board, it is estimated that 300 were killed, including the gunner. When the remains of the vessel were raised, shipwrights found a biscuit bag that contained not only bread, but also 30lb of gunpowder, from which, in the words of the *Bath Chronicle*, 'it is inferred, that an illicit traffic of the ammunition of the ship had been on foot at the time of the disaster; and that to it, and it alone, is to be attributed the dreadful catastrophe.' Captain Pellew went on to serve at Trafalgar and had a distinguished naval career, becoming Admiral Sir Israel Pellew.

During the First World War, there was an even more disastrous explosion a warship. On the morning of Thursday 26 November 1914, the 15,000-battleship HMS *Bulwark* was moored to Number 17 Buoy in Kethole n the River Medway, almost opposite Sheerness, along with other ome of the crew had been given leave the previous day, and had returned aboard just a few minutes earlier. A band was practising, some of the 750 officers and men were drilling, and some were having breakfast. Others were below decks, clearing up in the ship's eleven magazines and re-stowing ammunition and cordite charges. The *Bulwark* had once been captained by Scott of the Antarctic, but now the commander was Captain Guy Lutley Slater. He was in his cabin, drinking the early morning tea his servant had brought him, when a series of explosions ripped through the ship, tearing her apart. She was lifted out of the water and fell back in a thick cloud of grey smoke, as further explosions followed. When the smoke eventually cleared, the *Bulwark* was gone. Debris crashed on to the other ships nearby, and on to Sheerness, while the explosion could be heard 15 miles away at Whitstable, and at Southend, where it shook the pier. Fortunately, few people lived near Kethole Reach, but buildings over a wide area sustained structural damage. After the explosion, there was an uncanny silence. Then shouts began to go up from vessels nearby, ordering 'away all boats'. What had happened? Was this an audacious strike by a German submarine or maybe a Zeppelin? The coxswain of a boat from another warship believed he had seen a periscope, but it was later identified as a spar from *Bulwark*'s mainmast moving almost upright through the water.

An eyewitness on another ship nearby told a local newspaper that at first he thought one of the ships had fired a salute, but when he got on deck, he saw 'something awful had happened. The water and sky were obscured by dense volumes of smoke. We were at once ordered to the scene of the disaster to render what assistance we could.' All the ships around launched boats to try to rescue any survivors, but they were hampered by the furniture, boxes and hundreds of mutilated bodies floating in the water. Fourteen sailors were rescued alive, but two died before reaching hospital, and three more perished over the next few days. One able seaman had been on the deck of the *Bulwark* when the explosion occurred. He was blown into the air, but fell clear of the debris and managed to swim to the wreckage and keep himself afloat until he was rescued. His injuries were only slight. That afternoon, Winston Churchill, then First Lord of the Admiralty, told the House of Commons he had some bad news: 'The *Bulwark* battleship, which was lying in Sheerness this morning, blew up at 7.35 o'clock. The Vice and Rear Admiral, who were present, have reported their conviction that it was an internal magazine explosion which rent the ship asunder.' He said an inquiry would be launched. The loss of the ship did not 'sensibly affect the military position, but I regret to say the loss of life is very severe'. Churchill then offered his sympathies to the relatives of those killed, but Sheerness was awash with rumours that German spies were behind the disaster, and the townspeople kept constant watch for suspicious characters.

It being wartime, the court of inquiry was held behind closed doors in Chatham Barracks, while an inquest also wrestled with the puzzle of what had happened. Divers went down to look for clues in the remains of the vessel, which were scattered for hundreds of yards along the bed of the Medway. Some of the handful of survivors had been interviewed in hospital, but most were too shocked and injured to throw any light on the disaster. A sergeant in the Royal Marines, suffering from a broken leg and burns, said he had just been finishing his breakfast when he saw a sudden flash, and at that instant the deck seemed to open up, and he fell. He remembered coming up to the surface of the water with great force and seeing that the battleship had disappeared. Then he was picked up by a boat. The Sheerness coaling officer gave evidence that he had been passing in his pinnace when he saw flames shoot up from just forward of the after gun turret, followed by a series of explosions. He testified that he saw no disturbance in the water, which would have been expected if the ship had been torpedoed. He had turned his boat back and had been able to pick up a couple of survivors. The president of the court of inquiry, Rear-Admiral Ernest Grant, said the evidence pointed to an explosion having taken place inside the ship. There was no evidence of treachery, and he was satisfied that it was an accident, though it was not clear exactly what had happened. For months after, bodies were washed up along the Kent shoreline, but many could not be identified. The cause of the accident remains a mystery.

Less than six months later, Sheerness would be shaking again. On the morning of 27 May 1915, the 5,900-ton minelayer HMS *Princess Irene* was on Number 28 Buoy about 3 miles from the town centre. She had been built at Dumbarton the previous year for the Canadian Pacific Railway Company, but was requisitioned and converted for naval use before she could sail to join her owners. On board were 222 officers and men plus a party of about 80 petty officers from Chatham, and 76 dockyard workers getting the vessel ready for her planned departure on 29 May. One of the tasks was to prime the 500 mines she was carrying. At about a quarter past eleven, there was a fearful explosion. Flames seemed to rise miles into the sky before settling down into a dense cloud of white smoke. Windows were shattered as far away as Sittingbourne, as debris once again rained down on the surrounding towns. Of all those on board, there was only one survivor – one of the Chatham dockyard workers. The usual rumours circulated of dastardly and ingenious enemy action. Particularly suspiciously, a dinghy was said to have left the vessel just before the explosion. In fact, the Royal Navy's official inquiry decided that the cause was a faulty primer, but it also became clear that the priming had been done hurriedly by untrained men.

Astonishingly, within a year Kent would be rocked by yet another huge explosion. Gunpowder had been produced in the Faversham area since the seventeenth century, and the Cotton Powder Company had a factory on a greenfield site at the Uplees marshes next to the Swale, 3 miles from the town centre. It covered 500 acres, and produced guncotton, detonators, cordite, gelignite and dynamite. In 1912, the Explosives Loading Company had established a plant immediately to the west of the Cotton Powder site, to compress TNT into charges for shells, torpedoes and mines. Workers came in from all over the area, some attracted, no doubt, by the extra two shillings a week 'danger money' they were paid, and, as the First World War began, by exemption from military service. TNT, though, was expensive to produce, and as demand rose, manufacturers began to mix it with cheaper ammonium nitrate to make mixtures known as 'amatols', which were used to fill shells and bombs.

The ELC's factory consisted of about thirty lightly constructed wooden buildings, well spread out but without any artificial mounds to screen them, and because of the salt soil, it was impossible to grow the shrubs and trees that were normally planted at explosives works to offer some protection in the event of an accident. The CPC had its own well-equipped fire brigade, but the ELC had only a single manual pump, and there were no fire hydrants. On 30 March 1916, the chief inspector of explosives looked at the fire precautions and described them in a secret report as 'totally inadequate'. With the company trying to meet the demands of the armed forces, the site was awash with explosives. One building, Number 833, contained 15 tons of TNT and 150 tons of ammonium nitrate, even though it was not licensed to hold ammonium nitrate. More cases of TNT were lying around outside, and empty TNT bags were left on the ground or resting against the matchwood walls. On the night of 1 April, a small fire broke out between the boiler house and building 833, but civilian patrolmen put it out without any difficulty. Just after noon the next day, some of the empty TNT bags next to Number 833 caught fire. The assistant manager called out the manual fire engine, and the CPC brigade turned out too. One of their number was a man named Steve Epps, who had moved from a brewery to get higher pay. He said that by the time the works firemen got there, 'the stuff inside the shed was already alight', and there were 'tons and tons' of TNT lying around in boxes. Soon there were 200 men fighting the flames, drawn from the workforces of both factories and from the 128 soldiers guarding the plant, but as there were no hydrants, they could only get water by a bucket chain from the dykes. Three local fire brigades were also called out, but it was a slow and difficult journey along rutted country lanes.

Finally, at about twenty past one, the CPC fire brigade managed to find enough hose to cover the 500yd to the nearest CPC hydrant, but at the moment they managed to play water on the flames, in the words of Epps, 'up she went'. A worker running to help with the firefighting suddenly found himself flung across a dyke with all his clothes blown off apart from his shoes and socks. He escaped with a broken arm, though he would be partially deaf for the rest of his life. The first explosion triggered two more in buildings 120yd away on the CPC site, each containing tons of nitro-glycerine. One eyewitness spoke of a 'tremendous burst of flame, followed by, at what seemed ages long, an appalling report'. Next, up went a building used by the ELC for moulding amatol charges, then flying debris set on fire a fifth building containing filled primers for mines. The ELC site manager had been knocked unconscious by the first explosion. When he came to, he saw his office on fire, and rushed in to try to save his papers. The roof fell in on him, but he managed to escape and, with the help of the CPC works manager, put out a fire in another building containing 25 tons of TNT. Eventually every lightly constructed building within a 200yd radius of the first explosion was destroyed, though the reinforced concrete partitions that strengthened one building were not even cracked. Beyond the inner circle of destruction, up to 200 of the CPC's sheds suffered some damage.

As explosions continued around them, the firemen toiled on bravely. One rolled hot shells into a dyke. The six men working with Steve Epps were all killed, while he was blown into a dyke and left for dead. Eventually, rescuers saw signs of life and took him off to hospital, but he was so badly injured that for days his wife and sister could not recognise him. More than thirty of those engaged in firefighting and rescue work were given bravery awards. An 'awful procession' of injured men was brought in to a variety of local hospitals; some on trolleys, some carried, some helped along. Some were bleeding, some had clothes torn or burnt off, some were soaking wet after being flung into a dyke. Bizarrely, while some men 100yd away from the explosions were blown to pieces, others who had been much closer survived. People came running up from the town with beds, bedding and hot water bottles, while doctors rushed to the disaster from as far away as Margate, Ramsgate and Maidstone. One ambulanceman was said to have been so horrified by what he saw that he hanged himself. It had been the worst accident in the history of the British explosives industry; 108 people aged between 17 and 61 were killed. Windows were shattered as far away as Southend, while the explosion was said to have been heard 90 miles away in Norwich, and in France.

The government confined itself to a coy statement (made three days later) that 'a serious fire broke out in a powder factory in Kent which led to a series of explosions at the works'. The British people were assured that it had been 'purely accidental'. The inquest jury agreed, but added that the cause was 'unknown'. The government's chief inspector of explosives, Major A. Cooper-Key, quickly conducted an inquiry, the findings of which were at the time kept secret. He identified a number of ways in which the initial fire involving the TNT bags could have happened; spontaneous combustion, someone throwing a lighted cigarette or match on to them, a spark from the nearby boiler house, or arson. The Major rejected the idea of spontaneous combustion because the flames were first seen 'low down at one corner'. As for the idea of a match or cigarette end, workers were not allowed to bring matches on to the premises and could only smoke in mess rooms, though some had been fined for disobeying the rule. He ruled out arson, because the premises were guarded by 128 military and 28 civilian patrolmen and it would have been very hard for any intruder to have got in, and because 'no one could have foreseen that the ignition of these bags would have had such serious consequences'. On the other hand, the patrolmen reported that sparks from the boiler house had started the small fire the night before, and this was 'by far the most probable explanation' of the disaster. His report made eight recommendations, including improving firefighting facilities and training works firemen better, keeping boiler houses away from potentially dangerous buildings, preventing accumulation of dangerous refuse, and ensuring that TNT and ammonium nitrate were not stored together. Meanwhile, the devastated ELC factory was quickly repaired and brought back into full production.

The fact that the appalling consequences of the fire could not have been foreseen did not, of course, actually rule out foul play; an earlier explosion at Faversham in 1880 had been caused deliberately. Naturally, there were suspicions that a German spy had caused the blaze, while some workers blamed it on a big grass fire that had broken out that morning. The government supported Cooper-Key's conclusion, while adding that 'when the maximum output of every factory is essential, when there is a shortage of labour, and when the labour there is not in every case efficient, it is very difficult to carry on work in the same careful and methodical manner as in normal times'. Certainly, during the First World War, accidents were frequent in explosives factories, with 485 in 1915 and 641 in 1916, and awareness of the hazards did not stop them. In 1917, seventy-three people were killed in an explosion at a TNT purifying plant in London, while another forty died in a similar accident in Lancashire. In 1918, a TNT purification plant at Rainham was destroyed, while there was another explosion at the CPC.

By the Second World War, weapons of mass destruction had progressed considerably. At Fauld, between Uttoxeter and Burton upon Trent, the RAF was storing nearly 15,000 tons of bombs in a former gypsum mine requisitioned from Peter Ford and Son in 1937. Gypsum mines were thought to be fairly safe from enemy attack; the one at Fauld was shielded by 90ft of rock. It was easy to keep them dry, and they rarely suffered from rock falls. At Fauld, the RAF had strengthened the underground walls and the ceiling with 2½ft of concrete, then built a mile of light railway to the main line from Derby to Crewe. Working in the store were more than 500 RAF personnel, 445 civilians and nearly 200 Italian prisoners of war, now dubbed 'co-operators', as Italy had officially switched to the Allied side, but skilled technicians were in short supply. The temperature was kept at a constant 58°F, and massive galleries led off the main roadway where there were narrow gauge railway tracks. An unnamed officer from the store told the *Derby Evening Telegraph*: 'It looked like an Aladdin's cave . . . in dark corners you could see eventually the tiers of enormous HE bombs. In other sections were piles of incendiaries . . . there were enough for hundreds of major raids on Germany.'

Confidence in the safety of gypsum mines, though, could be misplaced. In May 1940, a fall cut off 9,000 bombs at Fauld, while in March 1944, the roof collapsed on one of the roadways, which had to be barricaded off. Bombs could go wrong, too. In January 1942 a defective fuse caused a 25lb incendiary bomb to go off. An armourer remarked that if it had happened in the main mine, 'goodness knows what would have happened to Burton'. The *Evening Telegraph*'s unknown informant also wondered, if there was an explosion in one cavern, 'whether the resultant fall of earth would damp it down before the blast reached other parts'.

On the dull, cold morning of Monday 27 November 1944, an explosion ripped through the store. The first thought of many was that a German bomber had dropped a land mine. An airman who was underground labelling ammunition boxes felt 'a massive gush of air. There was no actual bang. A sort of whoosh and a thud. I was lifted off my feet and pinned against the roof, and it must have been a second or two but it seemed an eternity before I was released from the roof, and I fell.' He escaped with a few bruises. An armourer working with two others and six Italian prisoners in a side cavern saw the blast surge along the main avenue. Then the mine was plunged into complete darkness. He managed to work out which way they should be going from the alignment of the tracks. 'We kept walking and eventually saw a pinhole of light which was the main entrance and which had collapsed completely except for a foot and a half diameter.' It must have been a terrifying walk; 'there was all sorts going off, incendiary bombs, small incendiaries, all over the place.' They found an Air Ministry policeman lying with his head blown off. Another armourer was three-quarters of a mile inside the mine. 'It knocked me flat,' he said, 'and all these ammunition boxes were just flying about like feathers.' A sergeant next to him was 'smashed to bits', but he heard someone shouting to him, then crawled along on hands and knees using the rail to guide him, picking up another four men on the way. He reckoned it took him an hour to reach the entrance, where soil had fallen, but there was just enough of a gap to get out. Those who survived the blast faced poisoning by fumes, and the armourer thought that hardly anyone deeper into the mine than him had escaped alive.

When he heard the explosion, the policeman on duty at the gate began to run, believing that there were bound to be more. The blast lifted him into the air, 'and I have thought since many, many a time: how lovely to be a bird, because I floated in the air and next minute I hit the top of a fence.' The impact broke his ribs. Now black smoke was pouring out of the mine, boxes of incendiary bombs were burning, and all around, there were fires. The population of 500 at the nearby town of Hanbury saw the day turn dark as a great mushroom cloud rose, then objects as big as trees and boulders began to fall out of the sky. At Peter Ford's plaster works, roofs collapsed and workers had to shelter from flying debris, while two cottages in the yard simply disappeared. A huge boiler was flung 60yd 'as if it was a cork'. The blast burst a nearby reservoir and, according to one workman, 'the water came down just like a sea', bringing sludge rolling like cold volcanic lava through the works. It turned the area into a sea of mud, severely hampering the rescue effort. American servicemen from a camp nearby helped by laying down planks, trees and debris, but in some places it took a dozen men to carry a stretcher.

Upper Castle Hayes Farm, which stood directly above the dump, disappeared into a huge crater 800ft long by 300ft wide and up to 120ft deep. The farmer, his wife and sister and three workers were all killed, though the two children, who were at school, survived. At another farm, the family escaped because they were away at Lichfield market, but two labourers were killed. A witness said the explosion left a scene similar to No Man's Land in First World War battles, with incendiaries burning fiercely, small arms ammunition going off, and mud and filth everywhere. A local vicar said, 'shells, stone and rock were flying in all directions. Then there was a falling of fine earth, which covered me from head to foot . . . the whole landscape was changed in about 50 seconds. Where there had been trees and grass, there was nothing but bare earth and craters.' He went into a school to find the children sheltering under their desks, with the teacher urging them to sing 'There'll always be an England'. Another witness saw a cow hanging in a tree, one of more than 100 that were killed. Nearly every house in Hanbury was damaged, while 6 miles away at Burton, more than 140 buildings suffered, and the spire of Christ Church was so badly weakened that eventually it had to be demolished.

Three fire engines turned out from Burton. Said fireman Charlie Elliott, 'we looked at each other and we knew that what we had feared for years had finally happened'. The temporary commander of Fauld, Acting Wing Commander Kings, had tried to get inside the mine, but had been beaten back by the fumes. Now he took in Elliott and two other firemen. According to Elliott, it was pitch dark: 'the lighting had gone and the main tunnel was full of cordite fumes and alabaster dust and you could see very, very little with the light of small breathing apparatus lamps.' They struggled on to the main tunnel roadway until they found their way blocked. 'You could see all these stacks of bombs when you flashed your lamp, all fallen over, and you thought, well I wonder if they will go off?' Mines rescue teams rushed to the scene from around the region. One rescuer was killed when the nose clip slipped off his breathing apparatus when he stumbled, and he inhaled poisonous fumes. It was said to have been the biggest man-made explosion ever in Britain, and during the Second World War it was surpassed only by the atomic bomb explosions in Japan. Seventy people died, including thirty-one at Ford's plaster works and six Italians. Of eighteen of the dead, no remains were found.

A German news agency claimed that one of the Führer's V weapons had hit the dump, and some wondered whether the Italian prisoners of war, or perhaps the IRA, were to blame, but a court of inquiry (held in secret) heard evidence of lax working practices. An electrician testified that when changing light bulbs, men would sometimes stand on a stack of bombs. An armourer who was injured in the blast saw another worker chiselling explosive pellets from a defective 1,000lb bomb with a brass chisel and hammer, when it was known that brass striking steel could cause sparks. It seemed that there had, in fact, been two explosions; the second, and more powerful, coming a few seconds after the first. The inquiry found no evidence of sabotage, and concluded that chipping away at the defective bomb with a brass chisel was the probable cause of the first explosion. This then triggered the second, in which nearly 4,000 tons of bombs exploded. Supervising staff had been negligent 'due either to lack of knowledge, lack of a proper sense of responsibility, or lack of proper direction from senior authority', while senior people did not know what work was being done and did not have 'adequate records or control'. In an echo of the conclusion of the Faversham inquiry, this one noted: 'There are obviously mitigating circumstances during wartime when urgency is a keynote, manpower is of poorer quality and more work is expected of a unit than that for which it was designed.' In July 1945, the dump was again declared fit for use, and it continued to store bombs during the Cold War. The fields around the crater were rented out as farms, but they did not yield much because the drainage was ruined. Many years later, a farmer out ploughing came across an upturned oak tree embedded in the ground, its roots pointing to the sky.

As progress in weaponry brought new hazards, so did progress in industry. In 1973, the Nypro chemical works opened in the village of Flixborough, 4 miles from Scunthorpe. It was the only place in Britain that could make caprolactam, a crucial ingredient of nylon fibres. This was made by heating cyclohexane (a derivative of coal tar similar to petrol) under pressure to oxidise it. At seven minutes to five on the afternoon of Saturday 1 June 1974, a devastating explosion destroyed much of the works. Some of the seventy workers ran for their lives and managed to take cover behind a railway embankment, but many were still seriously injured by the blast. A reporter from *The Times* said the plant was left 'like a mangled, futuristic Meccano set, blackened and smoking'. Twenty-four hours later, the smoke could still be seen 20 miles away as it drifted ominously across the Lincolnshire plain.

Closest to the blast were the sixteen houses in Stather Road, 600yd away. Their roofs were stripped of slates, window frames were smashed to matchwood, gables were blown away, while walls cracked from top to bottom then billowed out, and personal belongings were strewn everywhere. One resident said: 'There was one small explosion, then it went up like a fireball.' He was thrown across the room and hit the piano, which ended up embedded in the wall. His 15-year-old son had to be treated for head injuries after being flung through the French windows. Outside, their steel garage was blown apart. Hundreds of houses were damaged, and about 3,000 people from six other villages within a 5-mile radius were evacuated to reception areas for fear of poisonous fumes. A chemist at the plant said: 'Many people round here just did not realise the potential hazards they were living by. They thought it was still a fertiliser plant, which part of it was some years ago. What they were really doing was, in effect, like boiling petrol. We knew something like this was bound to happen one day.' On the other hand, a similar plant was said to have been running in Holland for twenty years without ever having had a serious accident, and the British Chemical Industries Safety Council tried to reassure those who had a chemical works for a neighbour by pointing out that during the three years leading up to Flixborough, there had been no known deaths among those living near chemical works as a result of accidents. It was true that twenty-seven workers had been killed, but the council said the industry had a better safety record than average.

It became clear that in addition to the thirty-six workers injured at Flixborough, twenty-eight had been killed in the worst chemical accident in British history. Firemen had enormous difficulty reaching eighteen bodies in the control room, where the roof had collapsed, and from which no one escaped alive. They were held back by a 'vast lagoon' of water contaminated with acids and other chemicals, and the danger of charred and buckled steelwork collapsing on them. Three days after the explosion, a small tank of benzene exploded, and fires were still burning ten days later. The official inquiry into the disaster concluded that the explosion was caused by the failure of a 20in temporary pipe in part of the plant that oxidised cyclohexane. Nypro accepted that the pipe did not meet the required standard, admitting that: 'The company's internal procedures did not provide explicitly for design and testing standards in these circumstances.' The pipe had been put in as a 'rush job' two months earlier to bypass a defective reactor in what was otherwise a well designed and well built plant. There had been 'no proper design study . . . no safety testing, no reference to the relevant British Standard'. A desire to resume the oxidation process with the minimum delay had led the management to fit a pipe that might rupture at far lower pressures than those set for safety valves, and at lower temperatures than those reached in the section. From that moment on, the 'disaster might have occurred at any time'. The inquiry said the blame must be shared by many people at board level and below, but not the workers who actually fitted the pipe: 'they carried out the work they had been asked to do, properly and carefully.' As the pipe ruptured it released cyclohexane which mixed with air to form a cloud of vapour, then ignited, causing an explosion of 'warlike dimensions'. The law at the time of the accident did not cover the state of the temporary pipe, and there were no grounds for prosecution.

CHAPTER TEN

# MINING DISASTERS

Coal mining has always been dangerous. In the mid-nineteenth century, according to *The Times*, 1,000 coal miners a year were being killed. At that time, many new seams were being opened in the pits around Barnsley, where the deposits were rich, but the mines were 'fiery' – prone to escapes of gas from the coal seams. The Oaks colliery, about a mile south of the town and 850ft deep, was one of the biggest in Yorkshire. Below ground, the most distant workings were around 2 miles from the bottom of the shafts. In 1847, it had been the scene of a disaster in which 73 men and boys had been killed, and explosions in 1849, 1857 and 1862 at three other mines in the area had killed another 300.

On the whole, the Oaks was regarded as a well-run colliery, and, knowing its 'fiery' characteristics, the owners, Messrs Firth, Barber and Co., had tried hard to provide adequate ventilation. In those days, that meant lighting a furnace at the bottom of the ventilating shaft to create a strong draught and drive up air that had become laden with gas from the mine, while fresh air was sucked in from outside. Methane, known as 'firedamp', which could be lethal when mixed with air, was constantly escaping from a fault in the mine, but it was piped along to the bottom of the fresh air shaft, and used for lighting lamps there. In December 1866, the miners complained about a defect in the ventilation system, but the management said they had rectified it. Industrial relations were still poisoned by a strike two years before during which the owners had taken a very hard line, bringing in blackleg labour under police protection, and expelling miners from tied cottages, so that many families had to camp in tents in conditions so desperate they were described by a local newspaper as 'partial famine'.

At about twenty past one on the afternoon of Wednesday 12 December, in the words of the *Barnsley Chronicle*, a 'convulsion shook the whole neighbourhood as if the earth had been rent by an earthquake'. Dense black smoke and clouds of dust rose from the mouth of the pit as from 'a suddenly ignited volcano', and up to 5 miles away people found themselves covered with coal dust and soot. According to the miners' union, 340 men and boys were down the mine at the time. The management had no proper record. The explosion destroyed the cage in Number 2 Shaft, and that in Number 1 was shattered and disconnected from its rope, which was left badly chafed. Hurriedly a new cage was fitted, and because time was precious, one of the managing partners, a mining engineer and a deputy decided to go down in spite of the danger of poisonous gas. They were not equipped to make an extensive search, but they hoped to find men who might have been able to pick their way to the pit bottom. When they 'rapped' on the rope before descending, they got no response, but huddled at the foot of the shaft they did find twenty or thirty survivors, badly affected by 'afterdamp', the poisonous gases left after an explosion.

By now, all roads leading to the colliery were crowded with friends and relatives of miners with, in the words of the *Chronicle*, 'the most frantic terror and anxiety depicted on the countenances of those whose husbands, fathers, sons, or brothers had that morning descended the fatal shaft'. The survivors who reached the surface did not present a reassuring sight; many were fearfully burned. Each time the cage came up, onlookers surged forward. If the management could recognise the victim, they would call his name until someone claimed him. Often it was plain the miner had no chance of recovery and all loved ones could do was to take him home to die, often in terrible agony. Of the 340 men and boys who had gone down the pit that morning, only half a dozen were to survive. A few had lucky escapes. Two men had overslept that morning, and failed to go down; two others had to stop work because of a roof fall and came up 10 minutes before the explosion, while another set off towards the cage early to go to a funeral. Still underground, he was almost knocked unconscious by the blast, but managed to battle his way through the debris and choking fumes to safety.

Soon, about eighty volunteers were involved in the rescue, including miners from neighbouring pits, but a deadly cloud of poisonous gas prevented them from reaching anything more than a small part of the workings. In the space of 50yd, they found thirty-eight bodies burned beyond recognition, though in other parts of the pit, the dead had scarcely a mark on them and had plainly died from suffocation. The rescuers were courageous men. Everyone knew there could be another explosion at any time. 'Napoleon and

Wellington never commanded braver or more willing soldiers', opined the
*Chronicle*, 'men more fearless of danger – than those who rushed to the Oaks
Pit.' By nightfall, those waiting by the pit for news of loved ones clustered
around great bonfires, while the rope in Number 1 Shaft was replaced, and,
as ventilation improved, the rescuers were able to press on further into the
mine, even though the roof was beginning to collapse in some places. Then
the pit began to get hotter and experienced miners among the rescuers said
there would soon be a second blast. Sixteen fled to the surface, and were
reproached for cowardice when they reached the top. Seven others went
down to join the twenty-one still below, but within minutes there was another
violent explosion heard up to a mile away, and once again clouds of dense
smoke and showers of debris shot up the shafts. The cage was lowered to the
bottom of the pit, and raised again, but it was empty. It seemed that twenty-
eight rescuers had now been lost, too.

'The loss of life at Barnsley', lamented *The Times*, 'is equivalent to that in a
pitched battle, and as married men are far more numerous among miners
than among soldiers, the misery entailed by it on wives and families is
probably much greater.' A third explosion on Thursday evening sent flames
and sparks spurting out at the pit head, so it seemed clear that the mine was
well and truly on fire, and that there could be no hope of anyone else
emerging alive. Then, at about half past four on Friday morning, the signal
bell suddenly rang in Number 1 Shaft. On the surface, the general belief was
that this must be some strange effect of the underground inferno, and when
people shouted down the shaft, there was no reply. Still, just to make sure,
they lowered a bottle of brandy and water on a rope. When they raised the
rope again, the bottle had gone. The explosions had damaged the pumping
equipment, and by now, torrents of water were pouring down the shafts, but
mining engineer John Mammatt and another man volunteered to go down on
a pulley. After a perilous descent, they found a solitary survivor named
Samuel Brown. He was one of the rescue party who had gone down the pit
early on Thursday morning, and had seen others rushing back to the shaft.
With two companions, he had tried to take shelter, but the blast had killed
both of them. Brown himself had been knocked unconscious, but when he
came round he found he had only slight burns and bruising to his head.
When he had recovered enough to move, he struggled to the bottom of
Number 2 Shaft, stumbling over corpses as he went, but found it engulfed in
flames. At first, he sat down and resigned himself to death, then he told

himself, 'this will not do', and dragged himself through the darkness. If he tripped over a body, he would listen for sounds of breathing, but he never found any. Finally, he reached Shaft 1, where there was just enough light from the fires in the mine to enable him to see the bell, which he rang. When the rescuers asked him where the others were, he replied: 'No there's no more; I am the only one.' He said that he had heard no sound that might indicate that anyone else was alive.

Brown's rescue was the last piece of good news from the Oaks. Early on Saturday morning, there was a fourth explosion, followed by another thirteen over the next three days, and the owners decided to seal up the mine to stop the fires. The death toll was 361, of which 334 were miners and 27 rescuers. It was at the time the worst disaster in British mining history, but what had caused it? Was it the firedamp, which would have escaped as the seams were worked? Or had there been a sudden rush of gas into the mine, of the kind that had been known before at the Oaks? Either of these things could have led to a dangerously explosive cocktail. Another factor might have been that blasting was going on in order to improve ventilation. The man in charge of this had lived just long enough after the blast to tell rescuers that the first explosion had come a split second after they had fired their last shot of powder to pierce the barrier of rock for the new drift. The drift had previously been found to be gas-free, but had the flames from this shot, which was more powerful than earlier ones, ignited some unexpected pocket?

At the inquest, the government's inspector of coal mines, Joseph Dickinson, said there seemed no lack of care in the way the colliery was run, and that there was no question that the explosion took place while a shot was being fired. John Kenyon Blackwell, the government commissioner appointed to attend the inquest, said it had been recommended for a long time that pits should be divided into completely isolated sections to prevent an explosion ripping through a whole mine, but no attempt had been made to do this at the Oaks. He said the evidence did not allow him to come to any clear conclusion on the cause, and the jury agreed, adding that they thought it 'unnecessary to make any special recommendations as to the working of mines, seeing that the Government are collecting information, no doubt with a view to the better protection of life, but they think a more strict inspection is desirable'. After the disaster, a miners' union deputation tried to get the Home Secretary to speed up the tightening of the law, but it failed, and miners had to wait another six years for legislation.

More than 350 men and boys might be dead, but there was still lots of money to be made from the coal at the bottom of the Oaks, so fresh shafts were sunk, new miners were recruited, and new workings opened. Giving evidence to the Royal Committee on Accidents in Mines a decade later, John Mammatt said that eighty bodies at the Oaks were still unaccounted for: 'We sometimes come across some bones, we did the other day, and we sent them up to the top, but nobody claimed them, and they were buried.'

Forty years later, again in the days before Christmas, disaster struck at another pit across the Pennines. The Pretoria, 5 miles from Bolton, produced good house coal, and was operated by the Hulton Colliery Company. The workings were on three levels; the highest was the Yard mine at 900ft deep, in the middle was the Arley, while the lowest was the Trencherbone. The pit was only a dozen years old, and its managing director claimed it was 'one of the safest collieries in the country'. On 21 December 1910, at about eight o'clock in the morning, flames shot from the main shaft, a sign that down below there had been an escape of gas followed by an explosion. Before long, six bodies were brought up from the Arley mine, including the under-manager, who was found in his office, but what of the other 440 men working there and in the Trencherbone? They began to emerge in a very disciplined way; first came those suffering from the effects of afterdamp, who were quickly revived by doctors and nurses at the pit head. Then came the boys, then the men. Survivors spoke of having been lifted off their feet by the explosion, but fortunately the ventilation fans kept working, and most were able to grab their belongings and rush to the bottom of the shaft. The rescue parties found that only six men had died in the Arley, but when they entered the Yard mine, they discovered that it had been devastated by an explosion, and that here the fans had stopped, leaving the men at the mercy of poisonous gas. A 15-year-old youth who had three brothers working down the mine was allowed to leave his job in the local mill, and go to the pit. He ran across fields, leaping hedges and ditches until he found 'a depressing sight, women and children without hats and coats, children clinging to their mothers' skirts all crying and sobbing'. The Bishop of Manchester arrived with other local clergymen, and got them to sing 'Jesu, lover of my soul', as he delivered a sermon and prayed for those underground. One of the young man's brothers died. Another suffered severe gas poisoning, but survived. As the bodies were recovered, some once again had been dreadfully mutilated by the explosion, while others, who had been overcome by fumes, were virtually unmarked. Some of the dead looked as if they had fallen asleep; one was found with his breakfast can between his legs, another was leaning on his shovel. Four men had apparently left their lamps, run on 10yd, and then collapsed. To escape, they would have had to negotiate 180yd of poisonous gas.

The rescue parties searched the Yard sections all night, but found no sign of life. When they got back to the pit head, the government's mines inspector, Mr Gerrard, said that just before they reached the coal face, they found a concentration of afterdamp and other poisonous gases which stopped them going further, but which also showed there was no possibility of anyone being left alive. Of the 344 men and boys in the Yard mine at the time of the explosion, the only survivor was a 16-year-old youth, who had gone with the fitter to whom he was apprenticed to the pump house, 200yd from the bottom of the Yard shaft and 100yd from the Arley shaft. They had just got inside as the explosion came. He said: 'It sounded like a cannon going off. It knocked me to the ground, but the fitter kept his feet. We made our way along to the Arley Pit, when the fitter fell, and I fell over him. We had smelt the gas very strongly.' He lay unconscious for about an hour. 'When I woke up I found the fitter was dead.' The youth reached the Arley mine by following some water pipes, then he heard voices. 'I shouted for about an hour. About ten o'clock a party came down and brought me up the Arley shaft. I saw nobody else alive in the Yard Mine, and I did not think that I should be saved.' The death toll made it the second worst mining accident in British history.

As with most mining disasters, the majority of victims came from small, tightly-knit communities. This time places like Atherton, Chequerbent, Daubhill, and Wingates around Bolton and Leigh, were the ones to suffer, and few families escaped without the loss of at least one member. 'General' Booth of the Salvation Army offered help in placing fifty children in suitable homes. One street in Daubhill was left mourning fifty victims. A Wingates family lost a father and five sons; one Chequerbent family a father and three sons, the youngest making his first descent into the mine. A foreman from the lower levels was killed when he went into the Yard mine to try to find his two sons.

Three weeks after the explosion, a reporter from the *Leigh Correspondent* went down the pit. He found tons of debris lying around: 'Rails were bent and twisted, tubs had been driven into each other and telescoped, the stout beams forming the roof were bent . . . the props had been forced out of their positions and were standing at angles approaching 45 degrees . . . huge slabs of rock had been wrenched from the roof.' Every so often, there was a chalkmark showing where a body had been found. Sometimes, near it, 'was an orange, a can containing drink, and a tin of food that had all gone mouldy'. The cause, though, was a mystery. Sir William Hulton, the head of the mining firm, rejected suggestions that the pit was 'fiery'. He said they had never had an explosion, 'though they had a few of the accidents which were inseparable from mining'. Besides, coal was cut hydraulically instead of by blasting as in many mines. Experts from Austria said there had probably been escapes of gas caused by recent seismic 'unrest'. Others suggested the cause was a defective light, or perhaps someone had lit a match.

Sitting on Christmas Eve, the inquest heard evidence from some relatives saying that miners often complained of being made 'dozy' by the effects of gas, and the coroner noted that a roof fall about 20yd long had happened the day before – something that could well have released it. In the end, the jury concluded that a defective or overheated safety lamp had ignited gas and coal dust, which was widespread on the haulage roads in the mine. It called for an investigation into the dangers of coal dust and the design of lamps, but the Miners' Federation conducted its own inquiry, and decided the explosion was caused by an electrical spark coming into contact with gas and coal dust. The union complained that the pit had not followed regulations for watering dust. It produced a catalogue of other deficiencies: the manager was overloaded – he had no less than seven pits to supervise – and this meant he was unable to inspect the workings at the Pretoria as often as he should; the pit firemen were young and inexperienced, and, in contravention of the law, the fans, instead of being put in a place where they would be likely to survive an explosion, were sited where they would be among the first things to be destroyed. The Federation also said that electrical machinery was being used in a part of the mine where there was a risk of gas. Its representatives pressed Winston Churchill, then Home Secretary, to appoint more inspectors, claiming that if the mine had been inspected properly, the gas would have been detected, and men would have been got out in time to save their lives.

High-quality Welsh steam coal was sought after by ships all over the world, and during the 1890s, a pit was established where several good seams had been found in Senghenydd, about 5 miles from Caerphilly. By 1913, the Lewis Merthyr Consolidated Collieries Group's pit was producing 1,800 tons of coal a day, while overall that year Wales's 300,000 coal miners extracted a record 56.8 million tons. There was a downside. Many of the seams released gas, and as long ago as 1846, the *Mining Journal* had warned that if greater care was not taken, 'South Wales would undoubtedly become a huge charnel-house'. The words seemed prophetic, as between 1867 and 1905 there were eight explosions that each killed more than 100 men in Wales, the worst accounting for 290 at the Albion colliery, Cilfynydd, in 1894. In 1901, there was an explosion at Senghenydd. Fortunately it happened between the night and day shifts, so that only eighty-two miners were below ground at the time, but all but one were killed. The cause was never ascertained, though it could have been coal dust in the mine's atmosphere. The pit was also prone to sudden leaks of gas. One that followed a serious roof fall in 1910 was so severe that all the men were withdrawn for a time.

The mine had two shafts, the Lancaster and the York, both just short of 2,000ft deep, and some faces were more than 2 miles from the bottom of the shaft. The main shift went down between five-thirty and six o'clock in the morning, and worked until two in the afternoon. For an hour and a half beforehand, firemen checked the mine for gas, though it was questionable whether this gave them enough time. At ten past eight on the morning of 14 October 1913, just as the miners' children were leaving to go to school, the unmistakable sound of an explosion issued from the top of the shaft, and the cage was flung into the air. The women came running in time to see columns of smoke rising. The manager, Edward Shaw, himself a former miner, raced across the colliery yard and found a mass of wreckage at the top of the Lancaster shaft, with the dead body of the man responsible for loading and unloading the cage. At the time, there were more than 900 men underground, about half in the eastern districts and half in the west. Rescue teams from all over the South Wales coalfield descended on the pit, as well as individual miners who tramped from their own villages to join Senghenydd's rescue workers, who were highly trained, but not equipped with breathing apparatus.

Shaw himself quickly descended the York shaft with another man, but that too had been damaged, and the cage got stuck at a seam 300ft from the bottom. They shouted down to a lower seam, which was worked only on the east side of the pit, and heard answering voices, suggesting that the men there had escaped the explosion. In fact, many men on the east side had not even been aware of it, until officials told them to go straight up in the cage, evacuating more than 450 in batches of 20. On the west side, though, Shaw found a different story. The mine was blazing 'like a furnace', and the ventilating fans that usually provided life-giving air to the men underground were now feeding the fires. Lack of water made it impossible to fight the blaze, though even with water, it may have been too fierce to combat. As one inspector commented, a burning pit was more dangerous than any battlefield. Shaw told the man accompanying him to round up the miners on the east side, and then tried to explore the west himself, but he found fiercely burning timbers as far as the eye could see, and was beaten back by the smoke and poisonous gases.

Soon rescuers began to descend the pit, but the fire put up an impenetrable barrier behind which the men, alive or dead, were trapped. Often firefighters could only work for a minute at a time because of the gases and the heat. By now, big crowds had appeared, but the police kept all except a few hundred wives, relatives and friends out of the colliery yard. The remainder stood on the surrounding hillsides. All were quiet and dignified. Blood on the coal was a fact of life. *The Times*'s correspondent had 'never seen so silent a throng . . . They waited for news and the only news they got was bad news . . . The women particularly seemed to be steeling themselves against the knock-down blows which are the lot of miners' wives.' He found himself captured by the drama of the event: 'the setting of the tragedy is grand and wild . . . The colliery is surrounded on three sides by mountains, and bare of trees or shrubs, they are stern and rather gloomy hills that frown down on the valley as it descends to the uniform streets of the colliery town.'

All the oxygen cylinders that could be found in Cardiff were rounded up and rushed out to Senghenydd by car to supply the rescuers' breathing apparatus that had now arrived, though even then nine were overcome by fumes. The Rhondda brigade managed to fight its way into a section that had not yet been explored, but it found only twenty-five dead horses before being beaten back by fumes and heat. After a while, though, the fire abated, and one rescue team managed to reach another western area late on Tuesday evening. Three-quarters of a mile from the pit bottom, they found a boy unconscious but groaning, who was 'almost gone'. After two hours of artificial respiration, they managed to revive him. Nearby, they discovered a man also alive. In spite of their exhaustion, the rescuers managed 'a sort of cheer', and over the next few hours, they found a total of eighteen survivors. Most were in a bad way, but a couple were remarkably well, including one 'who looked as if he was taking his daily walk', and a boxer, who asked for a cigarette as he stepped out of the cage, and then walked home with two friends.

From the accounts of those rescued, it seemed they had heard the explosion clearly, but had often been overcome by afterdamp as they tried to reach safety. One set off with a group of other men, but lost them one by one, until he was too weak to go on. 'At midday I sat down on the side of the road and gave up all hope . . . I must have lost consciousness for I remember nothing more until I saw the rescue party.' One young miner was eating his breakfast in a manhole, when the blast whisked the bread from his hands, and he saw sparks fly past 'as fast as motor cars', but he was virtually unhurt, and stayed put until the rescue team came. After these small successes, though, the rescuers found their progress to other areas barred by heavy roof falls or poisonous gas. In the area where they had found survivors, it seemed the air had stayed good for about 50 minutes after the explosion, meaning that many more men might have been saved if only the pit rescue team had had breathing apparatus, and had been able to go down immediately after the explosion. Now things were much worse. One rescuer who returned to the surface blackened beyond recognition was asked about conditions below ground, and replied: 'If you have got some idea of what hell is like, this is it.' It was terrifying work. The local MP went down to see the rescue effort and commented, 'nobody knew whether the floor and ceiling would not come together like a trap at any moment'. As ever, there were many tales of individual heroism. An underground manager had led a group of men to safety, and then gone back into the foul air to try to rescue two more miners whose position he knew. His body was found the next day.

As at the Oaks and Pretoria, some of the dead had been terribly injured by the blast, while those overcome by fumes had scarcely a mark on them, like a man and his son found in each other's arms. The crowd at ground level was still 'silent, but no longer expectant . . . Every few minutes the lines of people break and a little procession files between them. In the midst is a plain coffin, borne on the shoulders of the dead man's comrades.' The final death toll was 440, including one rescue worker from a neighbouring village who was killed by a falling timber, and a 73-year-old man who had worked underground for sixty years. He was brought out alive, but died in hospital. It was the worst mining disaster in British history. Most of the dead had succumbed to carbon monoxide poisoning. Families were as devastated as ever. One woman lost her husband, her four sons and her three brothers. Nearly two weeks after the explosion, fire was still raging underground, and it was another month before miners returned to the stricken pit. Then followed the search for an explanation, led by the chief inspector of mines, Richard Redmayne, who said there was 'no doubt whatever that coal dust existed on the roof, sides and timber in dangerous quantity', though Senghenydd was by no means the worst pit in South Wales in this respect. The pit employed men to shovel up dust from the floors but not, unfortunately, from the roofs and sides, and although the mine was watered every night, the water supply was probably inadequate. The problem was aggravated because the trams that carried the coal were of a design that would be outlawed from 1916, which allowed dust to escape easily. Redmayne did not believe coal dust had caused the explosion, but it did cause fire to spread. He also complained that the daily tests for gas were inadequate.

After the fires were put out, heavy roof falls were found in the west of the pit; these could have released methane, as they did in 1910, but if they did, what was the origin of the spark that ignited the explosive mixture of gas and air? Was it from a lamp station, where a naked light was kept to relight lamps that had gone out? Could falling stones have provided it? Or had it come from the electric signalling equipment? To make the bell ring, the operator had to bring together two naked wires, or bridge them with a piece of metal like a knife. Every time he did it, he caused a spark, but was it strong enough to cause the explosion? Tests showed that in some conditions it could be, and certainly, it was believed that an explosion at Bedwas colliery in 1912 had been caused in this way. After the Bedwas disaster, a letter had been sent to all the coalowners in South Wales alerting them to the risk from sparks caused by signalling, and Redmayne considered the attitude of the Senghenydd owners in not eliminating this risk 'astonishing', though he stopped short of saying it caused the disaster. He considered the manager, Shaw, 'honest and industrious', and said he had done all he could with the means at his disposal, but overall he detected 'a disquieting laxity in the management of the mine'. He also declared that if the colliery's own rescue team had been equipped with breathing apparatus, 'a few more lives might have been saved', and that if there had been an adequate water supply, the fires might have been put out much earlier.

Summons were issued against Shaw and the owners. At Caerphilly court, the charges against the owners were dismissed, while Shaw was fined £24 for five breaches of mining regulations. A local newspaper pointed out that this amounted to about one shilling per dead miner. The South Wales mining inspectorate appealed against the verdict, and this time the owners were convicted for not being able to put the ventilation equipment into reverse immediately, though it is by no means clear whether this line of action would have saved lives.

# CHAPTER ELEVEN

# SHIPWRECKS

Few disasters were witnessed by as august an assembly as that before which the *Mary Rose* sank on 19 July 1545. England was once again at war with France, and there was a French fleet in the Channel threatening an invasion of the Isle of Wight. The danger brought Henry VIII to the south coast, where a great army was already encamped at Southsea. When he heard that French ships were rounding the island, he rushed to Southsea Castle to watch the battle. The *Mary Rose*, one of the greatest vessels in the navy, was the flagship of Henry's Vice-Admiral, Sir George Carew, who until very recently had been Lieutentant-General of the Horse. She had originally been built in 1511, but was transformed in 1536 into a 600-ton, four-masted carrack, one of the first to be equipped with opening gunports, bristling with ninety-one guns.

The ship's normal complement was 415, but that July day, there were also nearly 300 soldiers, often wearing heavy armour, in case the French should attempt to board her. Many would have been on the bow castle on the upper deck, and their presence alone would have been enough to make the ship top heavy and unstable. At least some of her gunports would have been open as she prepared for action. It was a still day, and the English fleet was at a disadvantage against the French, who had more galleys. So, as the *Mary Rose* passed Southsea Castle, she hoisted her sails to try to use a light wind blowing off the land. Immediately, she began to heel over to port. Soldiers and sailors were sent tumbling down and guns may have broken loose and hurtled across her decks. Soon the gunports dipped beneath the waves. From that moment, the ship was doomed. She had no watertight bulkhead, and the hold would have filled very quickly. In his memoirs, the French commander, Marshal du Bellay, claimed that 'the *Mary Rose* one of their principal ships was sunk by our cannon'. In fact, the French did not have the firepower to damage her at a distance, and there was no sign of the *Mary Rose* having been hit.

The sad truth is that the ship went to the bottom in 6 fathoms without firing a shot because of poor seamanship, leaving the Lord Privy Seal, Lord Russell, to bemoan 'such rashness and great negligence'. As she began to founder, the Vice-Admiral's uncle, Sir Gavin Carew, had come past in his own ship and shouted to his nephew to find out what the trouble was. Sir George had called back: 'I have the sort of knaves I cannot rule.' Perhaps there were too many experienced sailors aboard, each with his own prescription for getting the ship out of difficulties, and there could have been panic and indiscipline among the hundreds of men who were unused to the ways of the sea, but beyond that, we do not know what the trouble was. The topmasts of the vessel were left sticking out of the sea, and about thirty men managed to save themselves by clinging to them. Few others survived. Those trapped below had no chance, while some of those on deck got tangled in the rigging or were knocked out by falling spars. Those wearing armour would have sunk like stones, while of the rest, many could not swim, and even if they could, they risked being sucked down by the sinking ship. The King was said to have heard the cries of the drowning men as he watched. Vice-Admiral Carew went down with his ship, as did the Captain, Roger Grenville. His death was seen by his 4-year-old son, who grew up to be that great English maritime hero, Sir Richard Grenville of the *Revenge*, immortalised in Tennyson's poem.

Strenuous attempts were made to raise such a valuable wreck. At one point, so much effort was going into trying to salvage her that the superintendent of the royal dockyard complained that its shipwrights had 'no leisure to attend any other thing', but in the end the project was abandoned, and the ship lay undisturbed until 1836, when two brothers looking for another wreck happened upon her. It was not until the 1970s, though, that divers began a systematic exploration of the *Mary Rose* in the biggest marine archaeological project in history. One hundred and seventy-nine bodies were found still in the wreck, mostly men in their early twenties. The remains of the vessel were raised to the surface in October 1982, and today they can be viewed in a Portsmouth dry dock, where conservation work on the hull continues.

Just over forty years after the *Mary Rose* sank, England survived the fearsome invasion that Philip II of Spain had intended to launch with the Armada of 1588. In defeat, the ships were driven by storms around the coasts of Scotland and Ireland and wrecked as they desperately sought a way home. With their own vessels destroyed, 1,300 men clambered aboard the

*Girona*, a three-masted galliass, but just before midnight on 30 October, a northerly gale blew her on to the Antrim coast at Lacada Point in view of the Giant's Causeway, and she split apart. Only nine of those aboard survived. Another ship became known as the 'Tobermory galleon' when her crew took a local man hostage as they looked for food and water on the Isle of Mull. He blew up the ship's magazine, killing himself and 500 Spaniards.

In 1691, Britain was again at war with France. In late August, as the fleet tried to lure the enemy out of the safety of the Channel ports to join battle, it was buffeted by some nasty storms, and many vessels, including the 90-gun man o' war *Coronation*, had to take refuge in Torbay. The ship was six years old, and weighed more than 1,350 tons. Aboard were about 600 crew and two companies of Royal Marines. After a couple of days, the weather took a turn for the better, and the *Coronation* and other ships ventured out, but on 1 September the storms got up again. This time the ships sought refuge in Plymouth Sound, but soon winds approaching hurricane force were blowing, while rain lashed down, making communication between vessels impossible. With the entrance to the Sound partly obscured by mist, most of the ships anchored off Rame Head. Of those that tried their luck in the Sound, the *Northumberland* was driven ashore in the Hamoaze, and the *Harwich* on to Mount Edgcumbe where she broke up, while the *Royal Oak* also went aground, and was only saved after all her guns were lifted out to lighten her.

Now the *Coronation*, commanded by Captain Skelton, began to be driven towards land. She may have had a small vessel that she had taken as a prize secured alongside her, which would have added to her problems. As she listed heavily to port, the crew cut down all her masts to try to stabilise her. For a moment, a squall obscured her from view, and when it cleared again, the *Coronation* was no more to be seen. Even though she was close to shore, only about twenty of the crew managed to escape, some in longboats, others clinging to wreckage. It had been a disastrous day for the navy, but there would be worse to come.

Sixteen years later, Britain was still at war with France, and late on the afternoon of 22 October 1707, Admiral Sir Cloudesley Shovell, Commander-in-Chief of the Mediterranean fleet, was leading home eighteen warships from a successful summer campaign. A favourite of Queen Anne, Sir Cloudesley had been born in the obscure Norfolk hamlet of Cockthorpe, where three hovels provided three boys who were to become admirals, while Nelson himself was born a few miles away at Burnham Thorpe. As a cabin boy, Shovell was said to have swum under fire carrying despatches in his mouth. Three of the ships in the fleet, the *Association*, the *Eagle* and the *Firebrand*, had narrowly escaped destruction in the Great Storm four years earlier (see Chapter 16). This time, on their voyage back, they had been persecuted by storms from every point of the compass, and by now they were hopelessly lost. In the darkness, they hove to in order to take soundings, and came to the conclusion that they were just off Ushant at the tip of Brittany, and that the English Channel lay before them. Conveniently, there was a south-westerly gale to blow them home. Rather than wait until daybreak, Sir Cloudesley decided to press on. In fact, they were just off the Isles of Scilly, which were beset by some of the most dangerous rocks on the entire British coastline, and appropriately boasted a well named after St Warna, the patron saint of shipwrecks. The local people were said to murmur: 'We pray thee, O lord, not that wrecks may happen, but that if they should, you wilt guide them into the Scillies for the benefit of the poor inhabitants.'

In just an hour, the ships found themselves surrounded by rocks. They fired cannons to warn of the danger; some steered north, others south and west. Only one man, the master of the *Panther*, appears to have assessed his position correctly, keeping his ship out of trouble. Sir Cloudesley's vessel, the *Association*, in the leading position, was first into danger. The most south-westerly of the main islands, St Agnes, had a coal-burning lighthouse, but few saw it until they were in mortal danger, and then they sometimes confused it with the stern light of the *Association*. Captain Finch Reddall of the *Isabella yacht* made this mistake: 'we steered after it till we perceived it to be a fixed light . . . and we perceived ye rocks on both sides of us.' He immediately headed west, 'and by God's mercy we got clear of them'. A similar report from Sir George Byng's flagship, the *Royal Anne*, said that the *Association* fired a danger signal when she was half a mile away. Then Byng's ship saw the *Association* strike the rocks, 'and in less than 2 minutes disappear. The *Royal Anne* was saved by great presence of mind both in officers and men, who in a minute's time set her top sails, one of the rocks not being a ship's length to leeward of her.' Others were not so fortunate.

The *Association* had crashed on to the fearsome Gilstone Ledges, and went down almost immediately, with the loss of the entire crew of 739. At about a quarter to eight, Captain Francis Percy of the *Firebrand* said he 'heard the Admiral fire a gun, and immediately lost sight of his lights'. The *Firebrand* also hit the Gilstone and was then carried off again by a huge wave, with her hull severely ripped and water pouring in fast. Captain Percy set his men to work the pumps and steered along the southern edge of the Western Rocks, heading for the lighthouse, but before he could reach safety, the vessel sank in 10 fathoms, not far from the Menglow Rock. There were forty-five men aboard, and the Captain and about twenty-five others escaped by clinging to wreckage. Percy is said to have come ashore on a hencoop. He had a reputation for being lucky. In one battle with the French, he had bent down to buckle his shoe, just in time for a cannonball to fly over his truncated form, instead of crashing into his torso. The *Phoenix* also mistook the light on St Agnes for the rear light on the *Association*, and she too struck rocks, but the captain was able to run her aground and not a single member of the crew was lost. The *Eagle* and the *Romney*, though, went down. A wreck found on the Tearing Ledge close to the Crebinicks is thought to be the *Eagle*. There were no survivors from the crew of 500. What happened to the *Romney* is not known, but among her complement of 365, there was only one survivor, the quartermaster, who was said to be 'a lusty fat man'. He survived by clinging to an oar until he was swept on to the Hellweathers Rock off Annet Island, where he was found the next day. The story goes that when he came ashore, officers and doctors all crowded around to ask him questions, but no one bothered to dress his wounds, and he would have died if a merchant ship's doctor who lived on the island had not taken him in and attended to him.

The *St George* also hit the Gilstone, but a big wave floated her again, and she escaped with just a smashed stern gallery. The next morning the sea was full of all manner of floating debris, and up to 1,800 men had been lost. Sir Cloudesley's body was found in a sandy cove on St Mary's. There was a story that he was alive when he was washed up, and that a local woman confessed on her deathbed that he had been killed so that he could be robbed of, among other things, an emerald ring, but this seems doubtful. Although the only visible injury on Sir Cloudesley's body was a small scratch above the eye, the currents and the gales had carried his body 8 miles, and it is unlikely that an obese 57-year-old man could have survived this ordeal, especially when you consider that scarcely any out of hundreds of younger, fitter men came through it.

A navigational error was the cause of another major shipwreck off the south-west coast of England half a century later. The 92-gun, 1,700 ton *Ramillies* had been launched as long ago as 1696, since when she had been rebuilt twice, and had given honourable service in almost every major naval action of the time. On 15 February 1760, she had been on blockade duty against the French – who else? – when a violent south-westerly gale got up. Her hull began to leak, and the captain decided to seek shelter. In thick fog, he sighted land, which he assumed to be Looe Island, and headed east thinking this would take him to Plymouth Sound. In fact, what he had seen was Burgh Island in Bigbury Bay, and instead of reaching safety, the *Ramillies* crashed into the unforgiving 200ft-high cliffs of Bolt Tail. The impact was so fierce that her masts broke. The crew managed to drop two anchors, but both snapped, and her stern rammed right into a large cave at the bottom of the cliffs, smashing her to pieces. Of the 734 aboard, only 26 managed to survive.

Another man o' war that had done sterling service against France was the *Royal George*. At more than 2,000 tons, with 108 guns, she was one of the biggest ships of her day. During the Seven Years' War, she had been with Admiral Hawke when he virtually annihilated the French fleet at Quiberon Bay. By 1782, though, the *Royal George*'s great days were behind her. For sixteen years, she had virtually been pensioned off, but then when war broke out with France again in 1778, she had answered her country's call. In October 1781, her rudder dropped off, and when she put into Plymouth for repairs, Vice-Admiral Millbank commented: 'I found her so bad that I do not recollect there was a sound timber in the open.' The officers in the dockyard, however, felt they could make her last a bit longer, and four months later she set sail again. In the late summer of 1782, she was in the Solent preparing to take part in an expedition to relieve Gibraltar, when she sprang a leak. There was not enough time to take her into dry dock, so on 28 August, the crew had to heel the ship to bring the area the caulkers needed to work on out of the water. The safest way of doing this was to attach ropes to the mast and then tie them to another ship which would pull over the ship being worked on, then, if there was a problem, the ropes could be cut and the ship would return to an upright position.

On this occasion, however, the *Royal George* was tilted by moving the guns to the side opposite the leak. When the work began, on board were not only the 850 crew and the workers, but also visitors, friends and family. After a couple of hours, water began to enter the ship. The captain ordered the guns to be put back to their original positions, but it was too late. The vessel turned on her side and sank. Gunner's yeoman John Smart testified: 'She gave a great jerk or crack first, and within a moment . . . went down, and I jumped out of the starboard stern port.' About 320 escaped death, but between 800 and 1,000 were drowned, including Rear-Admiral Richard Kempenfelt, who was in his cabin. No less a versifier than William Cowper composed a lament 'On the Loss of the *Royal George*', which included the lines:

> It was not in the battle;
> No tempest gave the shock;
> She sprang no fatal leak,
> She ran upon no rock.
> His sword was in its sheath,
> His fingers held the pen,
> When Kempenfelt went down
> With twice four hundred men.

The second half of the nineteenth century saw a number of serious shipwrecks with heavy loss of life. In September 1853, the sailing ship *Annie Jane* left Liverpool for Canada with 45 crew and 450 passengers, most of them Irish families heading for the New World. She immediately ran into a storm, and had to return to port for repairs. The ship sailed a second time and was smashed by wild weather again. Among the passengers were carpenters and other craftsmen with their toolkits, and they managed to make her serviceable, but the storms had not abated, and the *Annie Jane* was driven north until she sighted land on 28 September. It turned out to be Barra Head in the Hebrides. Most of the passengers were asleep when the ship was driven aground at Vatersay, and were woken up by the hammer blows of the rocks against her hull. Two hundred were crushed to death as the poop deck collapsed. As women clung to their menfolk and their children, a huge wave broke over the vessel, sweeping off about 100 people and all the boats. Within an hour, the breakers had smashed her into three sections, and passengers trying to huddle among the cargo of railway lines were crushed and mutilated.

At first light, local people came to help, and used the remains of the mainmast as a bridge from the wrecked poop to get survivors ashore through water up to their armpits; 102 people were rescued, including twenty-eight crew, twelve women and just one child, who was with an Irishwoman going to join her husband in America. Her other child had been torn from her by the sea. The nearest churchyard was 10 miles away, and there was neither timber nor carpenters to make coffins, so the 393 victims were buried in great pits dug close to the shore, which are marked today by a memorial.

Six years later, it was a ship bringing emigrants back to Britain that was wrecked. The 2,700-ton, iron-hulled steam clipper *Royal Charter* tried to use her engines as little as possible, instead relying for speed on her streamlined build, and boasting that she could make the journey from the goldfields of Australia to Liverpool in sixty days. On 26 August 1859, she left Hobson's Bay, Victoria, with 388 passengers, a crew of 112, and cargo that included perhaps £600,000 in gold, much of it carried by individual passengers. As the ship reached Holyhead, Captain Taylor saw the weather was worsening dramatically. He could have put in to shelter, but that would have jeopardised the sixty-day timetable, so the *Royal Charter* sailed on into winds of 100 miles an hour. Twice the Captain asked for a pilot, but none dared venture out among the now terrible breakers. By eleven o'clock at night on 25 October, the vessel was out of control off Port Lynas. Captain Taylor dropped the port and starboard anchors and, for a time, this held her, then at about half past one in the morning, the chains parted, and after a voyage around the world, only hours from Liverpool, the clipper ran on to rocks, where she broke in two just 50yd from shore. Waves over 60ft high washed passengers and crew away, while some filled their pockets with gold dust and leapt into the sea to try to swim to land, but it was hopeless.

At daybreak, those watching on shore saw the sea still battering the helpless, immobilised wreck. Then, to their astonishment and horror, they witnessed a man let himself down on a rope from the deck into the breakers. He was a Maltese Able Seaman named Joseph Rogers, who had volunteered to swim with a hawser to the shore to try to secure what was left of the ship. Three times he was beaten back, but on the fourth occasion, he managed to secure the vessel to a rock. Then twenty-eight men from Moelfre formed a human chain to bring ashore as many people as they could. Sadly that amounted to just forty-one of the nearly 500 on board. Altogether during that dreadful night, sixty-nine ships were wrecked around the British Isles, killing a total of 795 people, but the gold on the *Royal Charter* met a kinder fate than the passengers and crew. More than £250,000 of it was salvaged.

As ironships and ironclads appeared, wooden ships began to be withdrawn from front-line duties. HMS *Eurydice* had been launched in 1843 as a 900-ton 26-gun frigate. She was designed to be fast with her sleek wooden hull and her broad expanse of sail, and had been considered one of the finest vessels in the Royal Navy, but in 1861 she was converted into a training ship. In March 1878, she began a voyage from Bermuda to Portsmouth, with about 340 people on board. Most were young seamen under training, but they were supervised by a highly experienced crew. She seemed in fine fettle following a refit two years before, and crossed the Atlantic in just sixteen days. On Sunday 24 March, she was off the south coast of the Isle of Wight, a couple of miles from Ventnor, with the coastguard reporting she was 'moving fast under plain sail'. Just after half past three she was beside Sandown Bay. There were only two other vessels in the area, a fishing boat returning to Sandown, and the schooner *Emma*. Suddenly a violent snow squall burst on the bay. The fishing boat took shelter, and the schooner pulled in her sails, but eyewitnesses said the *Eurydice* sailed on at full sail with her gunports open before disappearing in the blizzard. Why she was sailing with open gunports has never been resolved.

It seems that when sailors climbed the rigging to try to take in the sails, Captain Hare ordered them down for their own safety. He then ordered the main sheets and halyards to be cut to ease strain, but it was too late. The *Eurydice* was thrown over on to her starboard side, the sea poured in through the open gunports, and within 5 minutes she sank. Although there were many strong swimmers among the crew of 366, most were trapped on board or sucked down with the ship if they got clear. Of those who did manage to swim away, many perished in the freezing waters. The training ship sank in 11 fathoms just over 2 miles from shore, with her mastheads showing above the surface. Astonishingly, a quarter of an hour after the disaster, the squall had passed, the snow had stopped, and the sun was shining. The *Emma* was then able to launch a boat and pick up the only five survivors, but three died from exposure before they could reach hospital. This wreck too found its laureate. Gerard Manley Hopkins wrote of her loss:

> Too proud, too proud, what a press she bore!
> Royal, and all her royals wore.
> Sharp with her, shorten sail!
> Too late; lost; gone with the gale.

Later that same year, there was an even more disastrous shipwreck, but this one happened not on jagged rocks, or in high seas or during a violent storm. Instead, it was on the River Thames on a lovely September evening.

The *Princess Alice*, one of the biggest pleasure steamers on the river, was carrying home about 750 passengers from a day out at Rosherville pleasure gardens near Gravesend. At a quarter to eight on 3 September 1878, the vessel was approaching Tripcock Point on the south bank of the Thames. A band was playing, and the passengers were dancing and singing. The Captain, William Grinstead, had allowed the helmsman to stay behind at Gravesend, and an able seaman among the passengers was hired to take his place, though he had never steered a vessel as long as the *Princess Alice*, and had little experience of the Thames. At the same time, the *Bywell Castle*, an 890-ton collier, was approaching from the opposite direction on her way to Newcastle with a cargo of ballast. Her master, Captain Harrison, who was unfamiliar with the river, had hired a pilot to steer her to Gravesend. As the vessels met, the question of which ship should do what was confused. New rules introduced in 1872 said that when steam vessels met head on, they should pass port to port, but these rules were not widely publicised, and had no force in law. Many captains were more likely to follow conventions established over many years. One was that pleasure steamers rounding Tripcock Point would hug the southern shoreline, which is exactly what the *Princess Alice* did, even though it meant passing the *Bywell Castle* starboard to starboard.

As a vessel passed the point, the tide would first carry her out into the centre of the river, then swirl her back towards the shore. Seeing the steamer's initial move, Captain Harrison presumed she had turned to starboard in order to pass him port to port whereas, in fact, she was being pulled by the tide, and would soon turn back to port. The *Princess*'s first mate, George Long, said he saw the *Bywell Castle* approach through the evening haze 'like a great black phantom'. The pleasure steamer carried just two lifeboats and twelve lifebuoys. Long raced to one of the lifeboats and tried to free it, but there was no time before the ships collided. Another crewman did release a boat, but, in the panic, it was let down into the water without a single passenger aboard, and drifted away. The *Princess Alice*'s steward, William Law, was in the saloon with about fifteen people at the time of the accident. He felt a light crash, then a heavier impact. 'I ran upon deck, and amid the confusion and screams of the passengers I heard the water rushing in below, and saw that we were sinking.' He shouted to the people below to come on deck, then he tried to rescue his young lady: 'I took her on my shoulder, being a good swimmer, and jumped overboard and swam to the shore, but as I was going my poor girl slipped off my shoulders, or was dragged off, and I lost her, although I dived for her.'

Another survivor spoke of the Captain shouting at the vessel bearing down on them. He saw her change course, but it was too late. The collier ripped through the pleasure boat 'just as you would push your fist through a bandbox'. As the *Bywell Castle* reversed away, water rushed into the breach. Within seconds, the *Princess Alice* broke in two. In 4 minutes she had sunk. One man said it felt like being flung down a shaft. Most of the passengers could not swim, and *The Times* reported that the Thames 'for a hundred yards was full of drowning people screaming in anguish and praying for help'. The water in which so many people were to spend their last moments of life was full of putrid, raw sewage. One man grabbed a lifebuoy in the water, then told his wife to throw the children to him and jump herself, but he lost them all. The crew of the *Bywell Castle* threw down ropes, but it was hopeless. One man did manage to grab one, and tried to climb up the side of the ship with his wife clinging to his neck. He had almost reached the top when she said she could not hold on any longer, and fell back into the water. He slid back down the rope, but never saw her again. Members of the crew heard his cries for help, and hauled him up.

A number of barge owners lowered small boats. One managed to rescue eleven people, but his boat was nearly swamped by others desperately trying to clamber aboard, and he had to use his oars to knock them off its sides. The *Princess Alice*'s sister ship, the *Duke of Teck*, following behind, had seen the collision, and arrived just 10 minutes after. She managed to haul some people aboard, but time was running out. The *Bywell Castle* launched three of her own boats and brought back about forty people, but when the boats went out a second time, 'all was still,' said Captain Harrison, 'and there was nothing to show how many hundred death struggles had taken place there just before.' Within 20 minutes of the accident, the only things to be seen bobbing about in the water were hats, caps and cloaks. Captain Grinstead went down with his ship, along with his son, his brother and his sister-in-law.

There was no record of who was on board, so the final death toll will never be known, but in the weeks that followed, about 640 bodies were recovered. Just over 100 people were known to have survived. Fifty members of a Bible class had been on board, and only one escaped death. Many whole families were wiped out. The inquest into the accident was highly critical of the lack of life-saving equipment and of the manning levels on the *Princess Alice*. She had a crew of just fifteen, including four firemen and two engineers, and a perfect stranger had been allowed to take the wheel. The jury blamed both ships for the disaster, and added that collisions like it 'might in future be avoided if proper and stringent rules and regulations were laid down for the regulation of steam traffic on the River Thames'. The vessels' respective owners sued each other, but the law put the blame squarely on the *Princess Alice*, saying she should have passed the *Bywell Castle* port to port. Two years later, rules for navigation on the Thames were given the force of law. The *Princess Alice*'s engines were salvaged, but the wreck was broken up at Greenwich, while the *Bywell Castle* went down with all hands in the Bay of Biscay in 1883.

# CHAPTER TWELVE

# TRAIN CRASHES

Shipwrecks may have inspired their Cowpers and their Hopkins, but for a train crash, there was William McGonagall:

> Beautiful Railway Bridge of the Silv'ry Tay!
> Alas! I am very sorry to say
> That ninety lives have been taken away
> On the last Sabbath day of 1879,
> Which will be remember'd for a very long time.

And so on and so on. The Tay Bridge had opened on 31 May 1878, and at 2 miles was the longest in the world. It was crucial to the marketing strategy of the North British Railway Company. Its passengers had been having to get out of the train and take ferries across the Forth and the Tay, while on the rival Scottish west coast route, there were no estuaries to interrupt the journey. The bridge's designer was Thomas Bouch, who, by the time the Tay Bridge was completed, was already working on the design for the last piece in the east coast jigsaw, the Forth Bridge. As soon as work on the Tay Bridge began, though, a problem appeared. The original design assumed that the river bed was of solid rock, but it soon became clear it was gravel. So Bouch modified his plan. After fourteen brick pillars had been built to support the bridge girders, he decided to reduce the weight on the foundations by using clusters of cast-iron columns bolted together and filled with concrete for the remaining seventy-one. To provide as much room as possible for ships to pass under the bridge, the southern section was built on a rising gradient, then the rails ran downhill to the northern shore. In the tall middle section of the bridge, the 'high girders', the rails were laid inside the girders, rather than on top of them, as they were on the rest of the bridge. A government inspector, Major-General Hutchinson, tested the structure before the railway company was allowed to bring it into service by coupling together six locomotives and running them over the bridge at 40 miles an hour. Hutchinson then agreed that trains could use the bridge, but imposed a 25 miles an hour speed limit. Some still had their doubts, but generally the Tay Bridge was acclaimed as a masterpiece. Queen Victoria herself travelled across it, and awarded Bouch a knighthood.

The last Sunday of 1879, 28 December, was coming to a stormy end. Passengers on the afternoon train to Dundee crossed the Firth of Forth by ferry, then, at about eight o'clock, they changed to the six-coach Sunday mail train that would take them to their destination. On this occasion, it would be pulled by Engine Number 224, a much bigger and more powerful locomotive than usually made the journey. By now the weather was ferocious, with winds probably gusting to 100 miles an hour, hitting the bridge head on; the worst conditions to which it had yet been subjected. It was so bad that after signalman Barclay had got out of his cabin at the southern end of the bridge to talk to the driver, he had to crawl back on all fours. As the tail lights of the mail train moved off into the darkness, the signalman saw sparks on the bridge, as he had when the previous train had gone through an hour before. Then a violent burst of wind shook his cabin, there was a brilliant flash of light and, when it had gone, there were no sparks and no tail lights to be seen. Barclay and another railwayman tried to make their way along the bridge to find out what had happened, but they were beaten back by the storm. Then they went down to the shore of the firth. To their horror, they saw that the high girders had vanished. They could only hope the train had made it safely to the other side of the section before it had collapsed.

Meanwhile, on the north side of the firth at Dundee station, they were waiting more and more anxiously. Then a man came rushing up. His house overlooked the estuary, and as a fierce gust of wind blew, he had seen three separate streams of fire fall from the bridge. When he looked through his telescope, he saw that part of the bridge was gone. There was no communication between the two banks. So while those on the south were still clinging to the hope that the train had reached the other side, those on the north were praying that it had stopped short of the collapsed section. Then word came that the Broughty ferry had found mail bags washed ashore, and that a fisherman had seen a carriage ventilator and a destination board from the train in the sea. By ten o'clock, a boat was venturing out to look for survivors, but the storm was still too severe for it to approach the broken stumps and the mass of twisted metal that now stood where the high girders had once towered nearly 90ft above the water.

When the firth had calmed enough for a diver to go down, he quickly found the train lying within the southern section of the collapsed girders. In other words, it had not fallen into an abyss that had already been formed; train and girders had gone into the water together. There were no survivors from the seventy-five passengers aboard.

Sir Thomas Bouch told the committee of inquiry his analysis of what he thought had happened. Pointing to the sparks the signalman had seen, he argued that the gale had caught the last two coaches and blown them off the rails into the high girders, bringing down the complete section. The experts who formed the committee of inquiry, though, were sceptical. They pointed out that sparks had also been seen when the previous train had passed. Then a maintenance worker testified that structural weaknesses in the bridge appeared almost as soon as it opened (though he acknowledged he had not drawn this to the attention of his superiors). It was clear that the 25 miles an hour speed limit was widely ignored, but the bridge had probably also been weakened by the effect of the wind. It was of very rigid construction, and therefore vulnerable to the high winds to which the estuary was known to be subject, but Sir Thomas had to admit that he had not made any particular enquiry into the potential effects of wind. The committee declared that once it was clear that the bridge was not going to rest on solid rock, it should have been completely redesigned. Their devastating conclusion was that it 'was badly designed, badly constructed and badly maintained and that its downfall was due to inherent defect in the structure which must sooner or later have brought it down. For these defects both in design, construction and maintenance Sir Thomas Bouch is in our opinion mainly to blame.' Sir Thomas's reputation lay in ruins, he lost the Forth Bridge contract, and a year later he was dead.

A couple of months after the crash, in February 1880, some fishermen on the north-west coast of Norway saw what they thought at first was a sea monster. They managed to haul it on to the beach, and found it was a railway carriage. The wheels had come off, the windows were smashed, and a door was hanging off its hinges, but the name 'Edinburgh and Glasgow Railway' was plain to see. It was one of the wagons that had fallen from the Tay Bridge. There may have been no human survivors from the crash, but Locomotive 224 was raised from the firth minus its chimney and cab. It was repaired, and pulled east-coast expresses until it was scrapped in 1919. The Tay Bridge was rebuilt too, using some of the iron girders that survived the disaster, but for many years no driver would take 224 across it. Then on the twenty-ninth anniversary of the disaster in 1908, the engine once again pulled the Sunday night mail across the Tay.

If the Tay Bridge disaster was the most memorable of the nineteenth century, the one that happened at Armagh ten years later had the greatest influence on safety. Britain's railways had grown rapidly and rather randomly, with safety seldom the priority, and in 1889, the single track line that climbed steeply from Armagh for 3 miles to Dobbins Bridge Summit on the way to Warrenpoint was still working on methods devised fifty years before. At ten o'clock on the morning of 12 June, a Sunday school excursion was preparing to make the trip. There was great excitement. For most of the children, this was the only time they ever got to the seaside, and they had looked forward to it for months. A band led them from the Methodist church to the station, and the Great Northern Railway of Ireland had provided thirteen coaches and two brake vans, but only a small engine. Now, so many trippers appeared that the stationmaster sent for another two carriages. The driver, who was not familiar with the line, protested and demanded a bigger engine. The stationmaster suggested transferring some of the coaches to the scheduled train that would be arriving shortly, or getting it to help push him up the hill, but it seems not to have been an amicable discussion. So at a quarter past ten, in something of a huff, the driver turned down the offer and started the climb. There were about 940 passengers aboard, two-thirds of them children, and the train was so packed that it was standing room only in many of the coaches; there were even people travelling in the brake vans. As usual, the carriage doors had been locked to prevent 'unauthorised access'.

At first the engine steamed along nicely, but gradually it began to lose power, and on a 40ft embankment within sight of the summit, it stalled. Travelling on the footplate with the driver was the chief clerk to the line superintendent, who was in charge of the excursion. He and the driver discussed the options. They could send someone down the hill to warn the scheduled train and then get it to push them up to the summit, or they could divide the carriages, and pull the front portion to sidings beyond the summit. Then the engine could come back to pick up the remainder. A vacuum brake line ran through all the carriages, but it would not work once the train was broken up. Each brake van, though, had a handbrake which locked its own wheels. The two men decided to split the train, and the chief clerk told the porter who was acting as guard in the front brake van to uncouple the fifth coach from the sixth. Then he ran down to the back of the train to see the guard, who was wedged with fifteen standing passengers in the other brake van, telling him to screw his handbrake down hard, and then block his wheels with stones.

In the middle of the train, the porter was already wedging the wheels of coach six with stones. Then he began unfastening the screw coupling between it and coach five. But just as he disconnected the two carriages, the engine eased back a little. It was only about a foot, but it was enough. The sixth coach lurched over the stones, and the back ten carriages began rolling slowly downhill. There was panic. The rear guard leapt back into his van and with the help of two passengers tried desperately to screw the handbrake down harder, but to no avail. The chief clerk exclaimed: 'Oh, my God, we will all be killed,' then rushed off to remonstrate with the driver. Now the driver eased back further to try to catch up the receding coaches while the porter struggled frantically to recouple the coaches. Twice he nearly achieved it, but each time he tripped over old rails lying by the side of the track. He also thrust stones under the turning wheels, but they were just pushed aside or ground to powder. By now the ten runaway coaches were inexorably gathering speed. The passengers in the brake van started to jump out, and those trapped in the carriages by locked doors were able to pass some children out of the windows, but soon they had picked up too much speed for anyone else to escape, and 600 people were racing down the hill.

Back at Armagh station, the 1025hr scheduled service was preparing to leave, with everyone blissfully unaware of the dramatic events going on near the top of the hill. The rules required a 10-minute gap between trains to prevent any danger of collision, and with this interval elapsed, the second train, consisting of a horsebox, two brake vans and three coaches, set off. It reached about 30 miles an hour and was a mile and a half from the summit when the fireman suddenly shouted out 'Hold!' as he saw the runaway carriages bearing down on them. The driver immediately shut off the steam, applied the brake and managed to slow his train to about 5 miles an hour. Unfortunately, the runaway coaches were by now hurtling along at 40 miles an hour; coaches that were, in the words of a local priest, 'not much stronger than a garden shed'.

Fortunately, the brake van at the front of the runaways was now empty, because as it crashed into the locomotive, it was crushed to matchwood, but the same fate met the next two carriages, and debris was flung down the embankment, with the remaining carriages piling up chaotically behind. The engine of the scheduled train was flung on its side, and the train behind it broke up and began rolling back towards Armagh in two portions. The leading section consisted of three coaches and two vans, while the front part was made up of the horsebox and the engine tender. The impact had flung the driver on to the tender, and even though he was injured, he managed to screw down the brake and bring it and the horsebox to a halt, while the guard applied the brake on the other carriages to stop them after a quarter of a mile. By now, a scene of dreadful carnage had been revealed, with bodies strewn beneath the wreckage on the embankment. Eighty people were killed, including 22 children, and another 262 were injured. Most of those who died were in the last two carriages of the special.

Once again, Major-General Hutchinson was called in to investigate. He ran a trial which showed the excursion engine was capable of pulling a train of this length to the top of the hill. However, he felt that it was operating very close to its limit, and questioned the railway company's judgment in leaving such a small safety margin. He also criticised it for rostering an inexperienced driver, and took the driver to task for splitting the train, but the heaviest condemnation was reserved for the chief clerk, who was in charge of the special, and who had authorised such a risky procedure. For many years, the railway inspectorate had been pressing for a tightening of safety, but now the public was outraged over the Armagh crash, and particularly over the number of children killed. Parliament had to act. Before the year was out, a new law required trains to have brakes that would automatically bring them to a halt if they were split, and signal boxes to be linked by telegraph and to operate a system that did not allow a train to enter a section of track until the one in front had left it, thus establishing some fundamental principles of rail safety.

Britain's worst railway disaster happened during the First World War, a mile and a half over the Scottish border at Quintinshill near Gretna. At a quarter to four on the morning of 22 May 1915, 500 soldiers from the Royal Scots Regiment had left Larbert in Stirlingshire for Liverpool on the first leg of their journey to Gallipoli. Most were asleep. The troop train was made up of old wooden carriages lit by gas. They would not normally have been regarded as suitable for a journey of this distance, but there was a war on. At six o'clock in the morning, a new signalman was due to come on duty at Quintinshill.

It was around the time when two sleepers from England came through, and there was a local train to Beattock due at ten past the hour. If the sleepers were running late, this local service would be switched on to one of the loop lines at Quintinshill while the express overtook it. That morning, both expresses were running half an hour late. The signalman coming on duty, James Tinsley, lived at Gretna Junction, and if his colleague, signalman Meakin, knew that the local train was going to be held up at Quintinshill, he would tip him off so that he could catch it. It meant Tinsley arrived half an hour late for duty, but Meakin would cover for him by noting train movements from six o'clock on scrap paper so that Tinsley could copy them into the official register in his own handwriting later. That morning when Tinsley arrived, a goods train from Carlisle was already occupying one of the spare loop lines. When an empty coal train arrived, it had to be parked in the other loop, and the signalmen held the local train on the main line to London 65yd from their box. Meakin handed his notes over to Tinsley so he could copy them into the register, and then sat back to read the morning papers that Tinsley had brought.

The first of the sleepers passed through safely at 0638hr. Neither signalman remembered giving the appropriate signal to authorise the troop train to proceed, but certainly neither sent a signal to the next box to warn it that the local train was blocking its way. Ten minutes later, the troop train appeared, travelling at about 70 miles an hour. Suddenly, the driver saw the big engine of the local train in front of him, but there was no time to do anything. He crashed into it, driving the coaches back more than 130yd, while his engine ended up on its side across both main lines. One of its coaches was flung clean over the engine and the train's 213yd length was reduced to just 67yd of wreckage. Meakin shouted 'whatever have you done, Jimmy?' to his colleague. Then he remembered the second sleeper rushing towards them from the opposite direction and flung the signals to danger. At the same time, the guard of the local train and the engine crew of the empty coal train started running along the side of the line towards the oncoming sleeper with its thirteen carriages drawn by two engines: 600 tons of train running at 60 miles an hour. As soon as the driver saw the men's frantic waving, he slammed on his brakes, but it was too late. He ploughed into the wreckage, killing some of the survivors of the initial crash who were trying to rescue their comrades. The leading locomotive crashed into the tender of the troop train and drove it on its side for 30yd, then smashed it into the wagons of the goods train on the loop line. The first three coaches were derailed and telescoped into one another.

Gas escaping from the broken tanks under the coaches of the troop train was quickly ignited by live coals flung out of the engines, and fire spread with nightmare speed the whole length of the train, so that many of those who had not been killed by the impact were now burned to death in the locked carriages. *The Times* reported that one engine, 'battered and bent, was tilted grotesquely in the air', while the second express engine 'looked as though it had been bent in some mighty grip. Of the engine of the troop train nothing could be seen. Somewhere under the piled wreckage it lay mangled and broken.' Among the first on the scene were Mr and Mrs Dunbar, caretakers of the blacksmith's shop at Gretna Green, where runaway couples from England went to get married. Mrs Dunbar had been so terrified by the noise that she had shouted: 'The Germans have come.' When she and her husband realised what had actually happened, they hurried across the fields to the railway. Their shop would be turned into a charnel house, as they lamented: 'It was only yesterday we had a wedding here.' Mattresses from sleeping cars and cushions from carriages were requisitioned as stretchers to carry the injured down an embankment into fields that had become improvised first aid stations. The fire brigade from Carlisle arrived at nine o'clock, but the flames burned all that day and through the following night.

One of the survivors from the troop train, Lieutenant Lang of the Royal Field Artillery, said he had been sleeping, and was woken when he was thrown on to the floor and pinned under his seat. The roof had collapsed 'like a concertina', but he managed to clamber out and, with the help of another soldier, saved five of their comrades. Fifteen coaches of the troop train, four carriages of the sleeper and five goods wagons were all destroyed. Of the soldiers, more than 200 were killed and about the same number injured. The driver and fireman of the troop train also died, while eight people were killed and fifty-four injured on the sleeper, and two perished on the local train. One soldier travelling in the sleeper said the scene was worse than anything he had seen in the trenches.

The inquiry had no difficulty in pinning the blame squarely on the carelessness of the two signalmen. There was technology available that would have prevented two trains occupying the same section of track, but the inspector, Colonel Druitt, felt it was unreasonable to ask the Caledonian Railway to go to the expense of providing it in places like Quintinshill, where the layout was simple and the signalman had a good view of the trains. He did, however, suggest abolishing gas lighting on trains, and called for the introduction of steel rolling stock. Tinsley and Meakin were both convicted of culpable homicide. Tinsley was sentenced to three years' hard labour, and Meakin to eighteen months in gaol. The remnants of the battalion eventually arrived in Gallipoli on 13 June, and took part in the attacks on Gully Ravine and Achi Baba.

England's two worst train crashes both happened in thick fog in the 1950s. The first came on the morning of 8 October 1952, when there were about eighty-five passengers aboard the Perth to London sleeper. Because of the weather, when driver Jones reached Watford around eight o'clock, he was about 80 minutes late, but by then the sun was breaking through and visibility around Harrow and Wealdstone station was about 200 to 300yd, though it was more restricted in the open country between Watford and Harrow. The local train from Tring to Euston had also been delayed by fog, and had arrived about 7 minutes late at the station. At 0819hr, it was waiting at Platform Four on the fast line to London. The local train was usually transferred to the fast line at this point, and the rule was that it should be given precedence over any night expresses running late. It was crowded, with about 800 passengers packed into its nine coaches.

Now the Harrow signalman was horrified to see the Perth express hurtling out of the fog on a collision course. He immediately sounded the alarm detonators. Meanwhile, the local train had just released its brakes, and was waiting for the guard's signal to move off. The whole train bolted forward, and carriages were flung on to their sides, as the Perth express ploughed into it and was then derailed by the impact. The sleeper's engine came to rest more or less upright about 80yd on, with five carriages behind it, but on the neighbouring track along which the 0800hr Euston to Liverpool and Manchester express was thundering from the opposite direction. Within 2 seconds of the first collision, it struck the sleeper at 60 miles an hour. Both of the Liverpool train's engines were catapulted across one of the platforms, and came to rest 75yd from the point of impact. Three passenger coaches from the local train, three from the Perth express, plus seven from the Liverpool express were now compressed into a heap of wreckage 45yd long and 30ft high, having ripped a hole two tracks wide in the footbridge overhead. People crossing had been flung down into the twisted metal. At the bottom of the heap was the sleeper's engine, *City of Glasgow*. The wooden coaches at the back of the commuter train had been smashed to pieces.

The emergency services arrived within 3 minutes, but, by modern standards, the rescue effort was pretty haphazard. One injured man got out of the wreckage, took the bus to Watford and at about eleven o'clock presented himself at the local hospital, where they still had not heard about the crash. Firemen pulled at the wreckage with their bare hands or cut with hacksaws, and detached train doors had to be used as makeshift stretchers. One of the first ambulancemen on the scene said: 'We were inundated with injured people crying "Help!" We opened the back of the ambulance and it was swamped.' People were grabbing bandages, and loading casualties in on train seats. They had only a basic first aid kit, and the key objective was to get people to hospital as quickly as possible. 'The ambulance crews were just seen as removal men,' said one crew member. 'People would hand us the injured and we would take them to hospital. It was known as "scoop and run".'

Doctors were found by touring the area with a loud-hailer. They climbed into the wreckage to give morphine injections, but once victims were released, they were often whisked away without proper information accompanying them on what painkillers they had been given, or whether they had had anything to drink. At half past ten, medical teams from the US Air Force base at Ruislip arrived. One of the British rescuers noted in awe: 'the Americans had everything . . . they were performing operations on site.' From experience in World War Two, the USAF had learned the value of giving some basic life-saving treatment on the spot. Once they had done what they could, they would label each person carefully before sending them off to waiting ambulances. Local women had been tearing up sheets to make bandages. The Americans opened a proper dressing station.

It took until half past two to free the 157 injured people and get them to hospital. Of the dead, 98 were passengers, and 4 were railway workers, including the driver and fireman of the Perth express and the driver of the leading engine of the Liverpool express. Ten more passengers died later in hospital of their injuries. Sixty-four of those killed were from the local train. The locomotives from the Liverpool train had to be scrapped, but the City of Glasgow was repaired and pulled trains for another decade.

The driver of the Perth express should have seen a signal showing yellow and begun slowing down almost a mile and a quarter from the station. Then there were two further semaphore signals set at stop. The guard said the brakes had worked normally throughout the journey. He had felt sharp braking, which was followed within 2 seconds by three violent lurches, followed by an equally violent rebound. Investigations suggested that all the signals were working normally. With visibility at about 100yd, going at 50 miles an hour, the driver would have seen one of the crucial signals for only about 4 seconds. Steam and smoke from a passing goods train might also have restricted his view, and the morning sun, breaking through at an angle, would have been in his eyes as he searched for it, but the driver was regarded as methodical and reliable, and these were the normal hazards he had to face. Perhaps there had been some unknown calamity in the cab, except that we know the brakes were put on at the last minute. The inquiry's conclusion was that: 'Driver Jones must have relaxed his concentration on the signals for some unexplained reason.'

Five years later, fog was to cause another disastrous railway accident in the London area. On 4 December 1957, a thick 'pea-souper' had been playing havoc with services all day and, as darkness fell, things got worse. The eleven coaches of the 1656hr Cannon Street to Ramsgate express left London 45 minutes late, packed with about 700 commuters and Christmas shoppers. As the train entered the three-quarter mile cutting between New Cross and St Johns, visibility was reduced in places to as little as 20yd. The main line through St Johns was one of busiest in the world. Every day, an average of 990 trains travelled on it, and another 125 took the bridge that carried the Nunhead to Lewisham loop line overhead. On average there was a signal every 490 yards.

As the express approached St Johns, it passed a signal known as L16, which was showing double yellow to notify the driver that the next signal but one, L18, just over half a mile away, was at red. It gave ample warning for a train travelling at 50 miles an hour to stop at L18, and the express was going a good deal slower. These signals, though, were sited to the right of the track, while the engine was driven from the left of the footplate, so they had to be observed from a distance, because the boiler obscured them once the driver came close. L16 could be seen from more than 300yd away, but the driver lost it for the last 80yd. Similarly, L17 was invisible for the last 95yd, and L18 for the last 238yd. In dense fog, the driver would not see them at all. The fireman, on the other side of the footplate, did not see the signals until the engine came close, but then they stayed in sight until it had passed them.

The fireman was used to being asked to look out for signal L18, but not L16 and L17. So once they left New Cross, he had begun firing for the long climb up to the top of the North Downs until, approaching L18 at about twenty past six, he paused from his shovelling to check the signal, and shouted to the driver 'You've got a red!' The driver applied the brake, but to no avail. Ten seconds later, at about 30 miles an hour, he ploughed into the back of the Charing Cross to Hayes electric train that was stopped at the next signal. The last two coaches were of stronger build than the front eight, and the impact drove coach nine right through coach eight in front of it. A woman who had been Christmas shopping said: 'we were one struggling mass of tangled arms and legs. It seemed we had been there an age before the silence was broken by one man who said: "Let's have cigarettes all round." When the rescue workers arrived with the arc lamps, I could see that both his legs were badly torn and bleeding.'

The crash happened beneath the girder bridge that carried the loop line. The Ramsgate train brought down a stanchion supporting the bridge, and 350 tons of steel girder collapsed on to it, completely destroying the first coach and crushing the front half of the next. Fortunately, the driver of the Holborn Viaduct to Dartford train that was then approaching the bridge spotted the track falling away in front of him in time to apply the brakes and prevent his train toppling off. Someone living in one of the houses by the line raised the alarm, and the first ambulances and fire engines were on the scene within 5 minutes. Ninety people were killed, and 109 seriously injured. The last of the injured was removed from the wreckage by half past ten. He was not seriously hurt, and was found still clutching his briefcase.

Driver Trew from the Ramsgate train was taken to hospital with severe shock. He was 62, had been a driver for eighteen years, and was regarded as conscientious and reliable. He told the coroner's inquest that he had caught glimpses of yellow signals at L16 and L17. When the fireman said he had a red light at L18, he 'was a bit surprised because we never stop there'. He said he trusted his fireman, and could not explain why he had not asked him to look out for L16 and L17. Trew was charged with manslaughter, but at his trial, he said he had not seen either signal in the fog, and that, after getting a green light at the signal before L16, he believed he 'was all right up to St Johns'. The fireman confirmed that the driver did not ask him to look out for L16 and L17. He was looking out for L18, but he knew when he told the driver it was red that there was no chance of stopping. The guard further back along the train said 'visibility was nil'. He could only see signals at a coach's length. At the first hearing, the jury could not agree, then at a re-trial, Trew was acquitted.

# CHAPTER THIRTEEN

# AIR CRASHES

When the seventy-eight passengers and five crew boarded their Avro Tudor V charter flight on Sunday 12 March 1950 to return home from Belfast after the Ireland v Wales Rugby Union international, they must have been in a jubilant mood. Wales had won 6–3 to take their first triple crown for thirty-nine years. The Avro Tudor had a rather chequered history. Powered by piston engines similar to those fitted to the Spitfire and the Hurricane, it had played a crucial role in the Berlin airlift. Indeed, the pilot flying it that day had commanded Tudors during the airlift. The prototype, though, had crashed, killing the designer, and in one year, two Tudor IVs had disappeared without trace on flights to and from Bermuda – mysterious events that had helped spawn the legend of the Bermuda Triangle. It was never established that there was anything wrong with the aircraft's design, but it was withdrawn from scheduled passenger services, and confined to charter operations.

The flight to Wales was perfectly normal until the Tudor had almost reached its destination of Llandow airport. Then three brothers playing football in a field by the village of Sigingstone saw it 'coming in so low we thought it was going to hit us'. They ran for their lives, as 'suddenly the engines seemed to cut out, then started again, and the machine rose slightly, but immediately nose-dived into the ground'. After a few minutes, they bravely approached the wreckage, and saw 'one of the passengers staggering towards us. He was cut on the head and called out "Try and help them."' The aircraft had broken into three pieces, and the brothers managed to pull out two passengers. Soon virtually every one of the village's population of 150 had turned out to help, while men from RAF St Athan arrived to take charge. Altogether, rescuers managed to get five people out alive, but two died in hospital. One of the survivors said the stewardess had just told them they would soon be landing. 'It seemed a normal approach . . . then there was a steep climb. I thought there was something wrong so I ducked,' he said, 'and the next thing I remember was the bump.' Clods of earth flew around, then the aircraft came to a standstill. He said that most of the seats gave way, and the passengers were flung forwards, but he and his brother-in-law managed to get out through the back door. At the time, the death toll of eighty made it the worst disaster in civil aviation history.

The aircraft was operated by Fairflight, which was run by Air Vice-Marshal Donald Bennett, CB, CBE, DSO, a bomber pilot with a distinguished war record. The inquiry into the crash was told that on the journey out, a member of the cabin crew had taken some hand baggage into the forward part of the aircraft, but when he had asked passengers on the return trip if he should do the same, they had declined his offer because they were quite comfortable, even though a number of them were bringing back additional things they had bought. The approach was normal, but 800yd from the end of the runway, when it was about 50ft above ground, the Tudor went into an abrupt climb, then stalled at about 150ft. Its starboard wing dropped and it fell in a steep sideways dive. The inquiry's verdict was that the aircraft had crashed because it was incorrectly loaded, with too much weight at the back. Bennett disagreed vehemently. When he inspected the wreckage, he noticed that the pilot's seat, unlike the co-pilot's, had not been properly locked down, and argued that the pilot must have lost control as his seat moved, but the inquiry dismissed his argument. Fairflight was prosecuted for wrongly loading the aircraft and fined £50.

Seventeen years later, at ten past ten on the morning of Sunday 4 June 1967, a British Midland Canadair C-4 Argonaut was approaching Manchester airport at the end of its flight from Majorca. The aircraft, which was on charter to a Liverpool holiday firm, had been registered in 1949, and had just had a major overhaul. It was powered by four piston engines, and on board were five crew and seventy-nine holidaymakers. When he was over Stockport, about 5 miles from the end of the runway, the pilot, Captain Harry Marlow, radioed that he was 'having a little bit of trouble'. On the ground, a teenage boy listening to aircraft frequencies had heard the pilot's voice saying 'six miles to run'. He went outside and saw its approach was very low: 'I went back to the radio and heard a voice say: "Keep on rolling", and after that there was silence.' A former RAF air traffic controller who also lived nearby said he realised the aircraft was in trouble: 'The engines were going on full boost. Then suddenly they cut out and I saw the plane dip into the centre of Stockport.' In the town, people watched in horror as the Argonaut lost

height. It managed to struggle over the roof of Stockport Infirmary and some
blocks of flats, then skirted a gasworks and a factory. As the aeroplane hit the
ground, it demolished a disused warehouse and an electricity substation,
before it broke into pieces in a yard full of cars at the back of a garage,
narrowly missing underground tanks holding thousands of gallons of petrol.
The pilot had managed to bring it down in one of the few empty spaces in the
centre of Stockport.

Police were soon on the scene from their headquarters nearby, as were
members of a Salvation Army band who had been due to play in an old
people's home. Flames were already licking at the wreckage, and some rescuers
were burned when the aircraft's fuel tanks exploded. Sadly, it was not just
rescuers who flocked to the scene. There were so many sightseers that all the
main roads into Stockport had jams up to 3 miles long, and the army had to
be called in to set up road blocks. As crowds gathered in the old cobbled streets
around the stricken aircraft, police struggled to clear a way for ambulances.
The chief constable said 'it was like a football crowd'. A dozen of those aboard
had survived, including the pilot, a stewardess who had been in the galley
getting water for a passenger, and two teenage boys. Seventy-two people were
dead. In hospital, Captain Marlow got a note signed 'O.A.P.', saying, 'Thank
you for a brave pilot who saved our town and averted a worse disaster.'

The official inquiry said the Argonaut had a serious design fault in its fuel
system, and that it failed to conform to regulations that had come in as long
ago as 1948, but the Air Registration Board considered it safe. The board had
put the aircraft that crashed through flight tests that year, but had renewed
its certificate of airworthiness without waiting for the results. Although
Captain Marlow had survived, he had no recollection of the events leading up
to the crash because of a head injury. The inquiry praised him for bringing
the aircraft down in an open space, but it noted that he appeared 'to have
had little sleep during the 24 hours before the crash.' The crew had been on
duty for almost 13 hours at the time of the accident, below the existing
maximum, but above a new limit to be introduced in January. The pilot had
made slips talking to radio stations en route, once giving the wrong call sign
and once the wrong time. Because of problems he was having with the
engines, he abandoned his first approach, and took the aircraft around to the
right. Then it began to lose height and, after doing an almost complete circle,
it hit the ground. The flight recorder showed that both starboard engines had
failed at the same time.

The aircraft's controls allowed pilots to transfer fuel between its tanks during the flight, but because it was hard to see the levers properly, it was easy to select the wrong one, and if the lever was not returned precisely to the 'off' position, it failed to close the valve. This meant that sometimes a tank might contain much less fuel than a pilot expected, and near the end of the flight, it might be dry, causing any engines being fed from it to fail. If this happened at high altitude, there was room for correction, if not, the consequences could be disastrous. The inquiry report said that an error of a fraction of an inch in setting one or more of the fuel cock levers had caused an 'inadvertent fuel transfer in flight', which led to the engine failure and the crash. Three other airlines had discovered that this kind of transfer could happen, but British Midland pilots had had no warning. Nor was there any reference to the potential problem in any of the Argonaut's flight manuals, even though it was easy to overcome if the crew identified it in time. Five days before the crash, another British Midland pilot had reported that fuel seemed to be running surprisingly low in one of the tanks, but this information seemed not to have been passed on. 'Had the facts been reported, they were of such a striking nature', concluded the inquiry, that there would have been an immediate warning to pilots, giving Captain Marlow a much better opportunity to avoid or at least cope with the problem that caused the crash.

An even worse disaster came five years later, also on a Sunday – 18 June 1972. At the time, the pilots' trade union, BALPA, was threatening strike action against British European Airways, later to form part of British Airways, over pay and conditions, and a crucial meeting was due to be held the next day. Opinions were bitterly divided, and that afternoon, 51-year-old Captain Stanley Key, who was highly critical of proposed strike action, lambasted a colleague who spoke in favour of it in what was said to be the worst outburst of temper ever seen in the BEA Heathrow crew room. Key immediately apologised, but it is not clear what effect the spectacle had on Jeremy Keighley, who was to be his co-pilot on BEA's Flight BE548 to Brussels an hour and a half later.

Keighley was 22, and had just passed out of training school. He was regarded as promising, but lacking in self-confidence. The other member of the Trident crew was Second Officer Simon Ticehurst, aged 24, whose job it was to monitor the other two. At the last minute, a BEA freight crew boarded the flight, and Captain John Collins, who was also a qualified Trident pilot, took the jump seat behind Key in the cockpit. While the aircraft was on the runway, the crew reported a 'slight problem' to the control tower, but it was never clear what this was. The Trident jet took off at 1608hr in blustery conditions with low cloud and rain. After 83 seconds, Captain Key reported 'Climbing as cleared.' Ten seconds later, he reduced power to comply with noise abatement rules. One minute and 48 seconds into the flight, Key said 'up to 60', acknowledging that he had climbed to Flight Level 60. This was the last that was ever heard from the aircraft. When Ticehurst's log was found in the wreckage, the final entry noted that they had been cleared to this level.

Moments later, two young brothers out walking the dog near their home in Staines saw the Trident fall 'like a stone' and just miss the A30 dual carriageway, landing at a 60-degree angle in a field – one of the few open spaces in the area. They ran half a mile to fetch help. The tail had broken off, and there were bodies hanging out of windows and lying around the fuselage. The first people on the scene started pulling passengers from the wreckage, or walking around the aircraft shouting 'Anybody alive?' But there was a strong smell of kerosene, and everyone was afraid it might explode at any moment.

A police constable from Feltham was the first person from the emergency services to arrive. He had been radioed about a plane crash by Scotland Yard. As he headed down to the aircraft, he thought he was walking on luggage, but realised he was stepping on dead bodies too. The Trident had hit the ground nose first, so the back was empty, while the front was jammed with people and seats. He found a stewardess still strapped to her jump seat, dead, and a man complaining that his legs were hurting. He dragged him out on to the grass: 'I said, "Don't worry, you'll be all right," but he died within seconds.' One man was actually taken alive, though deeply unconscious, to hospital. He died 3 hours later. Sightseers were soon congregating at vantage points, often carrying children on their shoulders. Even when police shouted 'ghouls' at them through loud-hailers, the spectators were not deterred. If there had been many survivors, it would have been difficult to get them to hospital through the crowds. In fact, all 112 passengers and 6 crew died.

The Trident had not been fitted with a cockpit voice recorder, but the flight data recorder revealed that 1 minute and 54 seconds into the flight, the droops had been retracted, when the aeroplane was at around 1,750ft and its speed was 186 miles an hour. Droops are devices on the wing that give additional lift while the aircraft is taking off and climbing to cruising altitude.

They should not have been retracted until the aircraft had climbed another 1,300ft and was going another 70 miles an hour faster. To do it at this point could cause a disastrous stall, but the flight crew had plenty of visual and other warnings to urge them to take remedial action. An amber light would have come on in front of each pilot, a 'droops out of position' warning would have lit in front of the central pedestal, the steering column would have started shaking, and the control panel would have been pushed forward with considerable force. To correct the problem, they could have applied more power to increase speed, or extended the droops down again, or held the steering column forward. It was not clear who was responsible for retracting the droops, but what was more baffling was why the crew repeatedly failed to recognise what was wrong and take action to correct it. Indeed, 2 minutes and 8 seconds into the flight, the automatic stall recovery system was switched off. The Trident then lost speed and height, went into a deep stall, and crashed 22 seconds later.

When the aircraft was examined, it seemed that all its systems were in working order, so what of the crew? Captain Key was regarded as a punctilious and experienced pilot, as well as a fit and healthy man, but pathologists who examined the bodies after the crash discovered he had a serious heart problem and had suffered a ruptured blood vessel within the 2 hours before the crash. He would probably have been suffering chest pains before he climbed into the cockpit. Had this led to errors and misjudgements? The Trident was the first British aircraft to be fitted with droops, so it had two levers, one for the wing flaps and one for the droops, while other aircraft had a single lever. Could Key or Keighley have pulled the wrong lever? Did Keighley misunderstand an instruction from Key? They would have been buffeted and thrown about by the bad weather and, for much of the time, they would have been in cloud and unable to see the ground.

Another discovery was a set of offensive remarks, some about Key, some about BEA management, scribbled on one of the flight crew's tables. Had there been a row in the cockpit about the pay dispute? The official inquiry by the UK Air Accident Investigation Branch dismissed the graffiti as a factor, believing it was unlikely that either of the other officers had written it, and that it was not clear whether Key ever saw it. So what of the other two pilots on the flight deck? Did either of them spot that Key was making errors? Had Keighley's fragile self-confidence been further damaged by witnessing Key's outburst in the crew room, making him less likely to question the captain's actions or judgement? And what of Ticehurst, who was supposed to be monitoring the actions of the other two, and who should, according to one witness at the inquiry, have been screaming 'Speed!' at the Captain? Was he busy filling in the log? Or was he distracted by the presence of Captain Collins, who was found after the crash with a can of air freshener in his hand? The inquiry concluded that Key's heart condition led to a lack of concentration and poor judgment, so that he had failed to correct the stall, and had possibly confused the droops and the flaps, but that his incapacity was probably not noticed by the others on the flight deck. The absence of a cockpit voice recorder meant, however, that this could only be conjecture. One of the results of the disaster was that from then on, recorders were fitted to all BEA airliners.

Jet engines compress air as it enters, mix it with fuel and then burn the mixture in a series of combustion chambers, producing a stream of very hot gases that flow at high speed out of the tailpipe and drive the aircraft along. In 1985, the most widely used jet engine in the world was the American company Pratt & Whitney's JT8D. Just before quarter past seven on the morning of 22 August, two of them were powering a British Airtours Boeing 737 as it sped along the runway at Manchester airport preparing to take off on a charter flight to Corfu, with 131 passengers and 6 crew aboard. The aircraft had reached 144 miles an hour and was 4 seconds away from lifting into the sky when there was, in the words of passenger Michael Loftus, 'a loud bang. It was as if we had hit something on the runway.' The captain thought it was a tyre burst or a bird strike, and shouted 'Abort take-off!' The crew steered the aircraft off the runway, halting it just 200yd from the airport's fire station.

In the control tower, they had already seen the red flash of an explosion, and flames licking the fuselage. They radioed a warning to the crew, and recommended evacuating the passengers from the right-hand side. A stewardess had opened one of the emergency doors on the opposite side before the 737 even stopped rolling, but passengers close to the left-hand wing could see it was on fire, and several stood up. Michael Loftus said: 'The pilot came on the tannoy and said "Stay in your seats and keep the seat belts fastened," but it was too late because everyone was panicking.' The purser rushed to the right front door and hit it hard, but it jammed. So he gave the opposite door a crack, and had a look outside. He could see fuel was beginning to flow forward from the wing and some of it was alight, but he judged that it was far enough away to let down the slide. In the rush to escape, some passengers got stuck by the forward galley where the aisle narrowed to less than 2ft, but a stewardess managed to pull a young passenger bodily away to clear the blockage. It was still less than half a minute since the aircraft had come to a stop, and already fire engines were spraying foam at it.

By now the aft right door had been opened, but it quickly became impossible to use it because a light wind was blowing fire and smoke into that area. Within 80 seconds of the aircraft stopping, flames broke through the cabin floor, and the rear section was filled with thick, black, hot smoke. A woman said that at first people obeyed the command to sit down, but 'then the flames got worse and some people started to rush for the front . . . people were crushed and lying down in the aisles. I went over the seats and just fought my way out. I could hardly breathe because of the smoke.' Another passenger said: 'There were lots of kids on board but everyone was trampling over everything and anybody to get out. It was like being in hell.' A 21-year-old man seated near the front could not see past the middle of the aircraft because of the smoke, but he heard terrible screams and shouting: 'One of the stewards grabbed me and threw me down one of the chutes.' Two young girls seated by the emergency over-wing exit on the right-hand side tried to open it, but it weighed 3½ stones, and it fell inwards, trapping one of them in her seat. A passenger behind managed to manhandle it out of the way, and the girls and others escaped over the wing as the windows started to melt, and the overhead lockers blazed.

As poisonous gases like ammonia, hydrogen cyanide and carbon monoxide filled the aircraft, the dense smoke made the overhead lighting useless, and in any case irritated people's eyes so much that many could not keep them open, while breathing it made passengers feel their lungs had solidified. One survivor said 'getting through the smoke was like trying to go against a brick wall'. Another said his mouth, nostrils and ears were blocked with brown debris 'with the consistency of Oxo cubes', and all the time passengers were wondering when the engines were going to explode. Meanwhile the purser had now managed to open the right-hand front door, and the forward stewardess dragged out two young women overcome by smoke and threw them on to the slide.

Despite the thousands of gallons of foam that the tenders sprayed on to the aircraft, the flames burned right through the top of fuselage, and within 2 minutes, the heat had become so intense that most of the tail sheared off and crashed to the concrete. Michael Loftus had carried his 4-year-old daughter away from the aircraft to safety. Now he went back to see his wife on the wing holding their 2-year-old son. There appeared to be no chutes there. She said: 'Michael appeared out of the foam and shouted "Jump". So I closed my eyes and jumped and he grabbed us.' A fireman managed to pull out a boy even though he had been in the blazing aircraft for more than 5 minutes, but many were found dead close to an exit, just a few feet from safety. One survivor said that when he fought his way to a door and got a breath of fresh air, he felt like Superman, and suddenly found the energy he needed to escape. All around the aircraft were people lying on the grass unable to breathe and coughing up huge amounts of mucus, their faces black and burned. Fortunately flight attendants from another aircraft that had just landed helped clear their lungs. Fifty-three passengers and two stewardesses lost their lives. Only twelve died of burns; the remainder were overcome by poisonous fumes.

There was a deep feeling of shock. People knew that passengers and crew would be killed if an airliner crashed, but this one had slowed to a halt in an orderly fashion at a well-equipped airport. It did not take long to establish what had gone wrong. The head section of a can from one of the engine's combustion chambers was found on the runway. The chamber had ruptured, and flung the head through the combustion casing. It hit a fuel tank access panel, and ripped a hole in the tank 3½ft wide, releasing hundreds of gallons of fuel which were set on fire by the hot exhaust gases. As it fell to the ground, it caused the thump that crew and passengers had heard. If it had not hit the weak point of the access panel, probably nothing would have happened. Three times, parts had been ejected from JT8 engines, but each time they had fallen without damaging the fuel tanks, and take-off had been abandoned safely. It emerged that in 1983, the engine of the Airtours' 737 had shown signs of cracking from metal fatigue. It was repaired by direct fusion welding, but Pratt & Whitney had warned operators that this could reduce the engine's life. The day before the disaster, the aircraft's log had recorded a problem with the idling speed, which could be a sign that the engine was suffering from fatigue, but it seemed the manufacturers had not mentioned this possibility to the airline, and maintenance staff simply adjusted the idle speed.

When these facts became known, the company announced it would no longer attempt to repair combustion chambers in this way, and following the disaster, the Civil Aviation Authority introduced a number of new safety measures. Fuel tanks would be strengthened, and seats next to over-wing exits modified so they did not obstruct the door, while smoke detectors were introduced in lavatories. Floor level lighting was also recommended to help passengers find their way to the exits in a smoke-filled aeroplane. Survivors and relatives of the dead wanted smoke hoods provided for passengers, and the authorities did run tests, but decided not to demand them. In spite of all the new safety measures, though, one of Manchester's top firemen soberingly commented: 'I don't think there is the time to escape from an aircraft. I don't think you could be sure that everyone would get out of the plane if you had that identical situation again.'

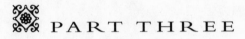 PART THREE

# ACTS OF GOD

# CHAPTER FOURTEEN

# PLAGUE

In AD 166, it is likely that Roman Britain was attacked by the Plague of Galen, a disease brought back by soldiers who had been fighting in the East, and some believe that the Plague of Galen was bubonic plague. The great eighth-century historian Bede recorded a number of epidemics which may also have been plague. In 426–7, he recorded a sudden 'severe plague' falling on the Britons, which 'destroyed such numbers of them, that the living were scarcely sufficient to bury the dead'. Then he writes that in 664 'a sudden pestilence . . . depopulated the southern coasts of Britain, and afterwards extending into the province of the Northumbrians, ravaged the country far and near, and destroyed a great multitude of men.' It helped revive heathenism, as many 'forsook the mysteries of the Christian faith and turned apostate'. The following year, pestilence ravaged the country of the East Saxons, modern-day Essex, and in 681, 'a grievous mortality ran through many provinces of Britain'.

It was in 1348, though, that plague brought the most devastating epidemic in recorded British history. The dubious distinction of being the place where it entered the country is often reserved for Melcombe Regis in Dorset, where it is said an infected German sailor came ashore in June, though it is possible that by then the disease had already arrived in Bristol or Southampton. Certainly, by July, local people in Melcombe Regis were going down with it. Plague was carried by bacteria that normally lived in the digestive tract of fleas, especially fleas of the black rat, a creature that was happy living close to humans. From time to time, the bacteria multiplied in the flea's stomach to such a degree that they caused a blockage. Then, while it was feeding, the flea regurgitated huge quantities of the bacteria into its host. If it bit a human, the human became infected. The first symptom was usually a blackish, often gangrenous, pustule at the point of the flea bite, but the most dramatic signs of the disease were the buboes, inflamed swellings sometimes as big as an apple in the groin or the armpits. Then black blotches appeared on the arm, thigh or other parts of the body, caused by haemorrhages under the skin. With the swellings came a high fever and an agonising thirst. In a small minority of cases, the victim might recover as the buboes subsided or burst, but usually they would die within five or six days. This was bubonic plague. There was another, more deadly, version, in which the fever was accompanied by spitting of blood. Sometimes there were no buboes, but death came even quicker – in two or three days. It was more infectious than bubonic plague, because bacteria were sprayed into the air every time the patient breathed out. This was pneumonic plague, which could thrive in the colder conditions of winter, when bubonic plague tended to die out. There was also a third version – septicaemic plague, in which the blood was infected and the victim died within hours, before the buboes got a chance to form. In this version at least, there was so much bacteria in the blood, it could also be transmitted by the human flea. Fortunately, it was the rarest form. Together, the three became known in the fourteenth century as the Black Death. The disease provided a fearfully painful and degrading end. The sweat, excrement, spittle and breath of victims gave off an overpowering stench, and their urine was thick black or red.

Warmth and dirt provided an ideal environment for the black rat, and in those days even the aristocracy lived in conditions we would regard as grotesquely overcrowded. An earl and countess might expect to share their bedroom with their daughter and the daughter's governess. Lower down the social scale, it was not unusual to find a dozen people sleeping in one room, perhaps sharing with animals. This made isolation of the sick practically impossible. The population about to be attacked by the Black Death was already weakened by dysentery, diarrhoea and all manner of other diseases, and when doctors tried to treat it, the treatments, such as heavy bleeding, if anything did more harm than good. The infection was believed to be passed by a 'miasma', a poison cloud, so that as far as prevention was concerned, flight was the only really worthwhile measure. Those who could not escape carried nosegays of flowers or herbs, sealed windows with waxed cloth, or tried to purify the air by the constant burning of aromatic woods or powders.

The Black Death had appeared in Asia in 1346, and had begun a remorseless advance across Europe. By October 1348, it was rife in Dorset, and it soon spread into Somerset. So many priests were dying that there were not enough to hear everyone's final confession, and the Bishop of Bath and Wells had to authorise lay people to receive them if necessary. He decreed that confession could be given 'even to a woman'. In December, the Bishop went to Yeovil to hold a service of thanksgiving, but with the death rate in his diocese running at up to 52 per cent, many local people were plainly not clear for what they should be grateful, and an angry crowd armed with bows and arrows attacked the church and besieged the Bishop and congregation until nightfall. Wherever the Black Death initially appeared, Bristol is generally regarded as the first major city to be hit. The population in those days was about 10,000, and up to 4,000 died. Once again, 'the living were scarce able to bury the dead', and grass sprouted several inches high in High Street and Broad Street. The vast majority of people in fourteenth-century Britain, perhaps 90 per cent, still lived in villages, but isolation was no protection. The plague reached even the most remote villages in Devon and Cornwall, like Templeton on the moors to the west of Tiverton. In Cornwall, tin mining almost stopped, with the amount produced falling to one-fifth of pre-plague levels.

The citizens of Gloucester saw what had happened to Bristol, and were determined to spare their city from a similar fate. They tried to halt all links with Bristol and closed the gates to anyone who might be carrying the infection, but the plague still got in. From Bristol, it also seems to have spread into Oxfordshire, Buckinghamshire and Berkshire, while from Southampton, it moved across Wiltshire, Hampshire and Surrey. Three-fifths of the clergy died in Wycombe, and the Bishop of Winchester told his priests to exhort their flocks to attend sacraments of penance, and process barefoot with heads bowed around the market place or through the churchyard. Whatever merit this idea might have had, it did not prevent the disease hitting Winchester with particular violence, and it is reckoned that at least half of the population of 8,000 died. The Bishop was dismayed to see the townspeople burying their numerous dead in a common pit outside the town.

London was by far the greatest city in Britain, with about 70,000 people. Its first cases were seen in November 1348, though the worst time was the spring of 1349, and people were dying well into 1350. Just as in Winchester, the graveyards could not cope, and although new burial grounds were found, by early 1349, 200 bodies a day were being shovelled into the pits. Food supplies began to dry up as carters grew reluctant to come to the city, so Londoners had to go out into the countryside to search for supplies. They helped to spread the disease, as did those fleeing to escape it. The Black Death proved to be the most disastrous epidemic in the capital's history, probably killing more than

20,000, around a third of the population. In the wake of the epidemic came a crime wave, with sacrilege becoming particularly common.

Around London, the disease made a devastating progress. At Standon, near Ware in Hertfordshire, thirty-two tenants were supposed to mow the lord's hay, but in 1349, no men went to mow, and the hay was left to rot in the fields. In Kent, the old and decrepit Bishop of Rochester survived, but had almost no one left to serve him, as four priests, five esquires, ten attendants, seven young clerics and six pages were all carried off. In the town, 'no one could be found who would bear the corpses to the grave. Men and women carried their own children on their shoulders to the church and threw them into a common pit.' These pits, not surprisingly, gave off an 'appalling stench', and people did not dare walk by them. A Rochester monk complained that as a result of the disease, most of the population 'has become even more depraved, more prone to every kind of vice, more ready to indulge in evil and sinfulness'. By March 1349, the Black Death was in Wales, and the poet Jeuan Gethin recorded that 'we see death coming into our midst like black smoke, a plague which cuts off the young, a rootless phantom which has no mercy for fair countenance'. By midsummer, out of 114 rent-paying tenants in Cardigan, 97 had died or fled.

East Anglia suffered especially badly, with perhaps half its inhabitants wiped out, and Norwich's population did not return to pre-Black Death levels until about 1700. Stamford was becoming an important town at this time, but the plague stopped it in its tracks, and it never recovered its lost impetus, while the mortality rate in the villages around Bury St Edmunds is estimated to have reached 60 per cent, and a Lincolnshire chronicler lamented that 'even the waters of the flood which happened in the days of Noah did not carry off so vast a multitude'. As 1349 wore on, the pestilence moved north, and in August at the abbey of Meaux near Hull, the abbot and five monks died in a single day. Pulpits were now ringing with the message that the Black Death was a punishment for people's wickedness, but congregations were growing angry that the clergy had delivered no warning to their flocks beforehand that God was so furious with them he was about to impose such a terrible sanction. In Worcester, as in Yeovil, resentment boiled over into violence, with armed townsmen breaking down the gates of the cathedral priory, chasing the prior and trying to set fire to buildings.

The Scots tried to profit from England's disarray. According to one English chronicler, as plague ravaged Cumberland and Durham, they gathered their forces in the forest of Selkirk, 'laughing at their enemies', while they awaited the best moment to invade, but the plague was no respecter of boundaries, and the Scots too began to fall sick. The panic-stricken soldiers then dispersed, spreading the disease through the country, so that in 1350 'there was, in the kingdom of Scotland', according to John of Fordun, 'so great a pestilence and plague among men . . . as, from the beginning of the world even unto modern times, had never been heard of.' He said that a third of the population died, and that people were so afraid that sons 'durst not go and see their parents in the throes of death'. He added that the sick 'dragged out their earthly life for barely two days. Now this everywhere attacked especially the meaner sort and common people – seldom the magnate.' It is true that the more eminent you were, the better your chance of survival; for example, in England the Black Death killed 40 per cent of the clergy, against 18 per cent of bishops, but the rich and powerful died too. The new Archbishop of Canterbury, John Offord, was struck down in May 1349 at Westminster, before he could even be enthroned. Thomas Bradwardine was then chosen, but he died in August. A former chancellor was also a victim, along with the royal surgeon. When the Black Death arrived, Britain's population had been about 4 million. It probably killed nearly 1.5 million of them. Whole villages disappeared, like Tilgarsley in Oxfordshire, Ambion in Leicestershire and Ringstead Parva in Norfolk, while Middle Carlton and fourteen others in Lincolnshire were said to have ceased to exist either at the time of the outbreak or in the two decades that followed. Some places recovered fairly quickly; Farnham, one of the richest of the Bishop of Winchester's estates, did so in spite of losing about a third of its population, but at Crawley, pre-Black Death numbers were not attained again until 1851.

The disease hastened the death of the feudal system. Even before it appeared, there were already some villages where tenants paid rent to their lords in money instead of working on his land, but the massive labour shortage that followed the epidemic enabled many more to do the same, and if their lord would not agree, they could simply slip off and find another who was more amenable. Plague returned to England in 1361 in what became known as the *mortalité des enfants*, because while the Black Death tended to kill more older people, this one was very hard on the young, particularly those born after 1350. Though it killed fewer people than the Black Death, it was nonetheless devastating, carrying off about one in five. There were another four severe plague epidemics before the end of the century, and it also struck regularly in the fifteenth century, so that overall some historians believe it reduced Britain's population by perhaps half.

During the sixteenth century and the first half of the seventeenth, plague continued to be a frequent, unwelcome visitor, but the authorities began to develop a more coordinated response. In 1518, Henry VIII tried to make the sick carry white sticks, and ordered that infected houses be marked. Bills of Mortality were also introduced, so that each week London's parish clerks had to list the number and cause of deaths. During some outbreaks, local quarantine measures were introduced. So in 1577, the Privy Council banned the citizens of Aylesbury, which had been stricken by the disease, from attending a fair at Thame, and two years later, the mayor of Newcastle upon Tyne forbade any ship from Yarmouth docking there, though the measure did not prevent the plague carrying off 2,000 people in the city. In 1587, for the first time, plague orders were circulated to all Justices of the Peace, telling them to quarantine infected houses and appoint watchmen to keep the sick isolated.

The first year of King James VI and I's reign in England, 1603, though, was marked by perhaps the deadliest epidemic since the fourteenth century, killing 34,000 in London out of a population of 225,000, while York lost nearly a third of its inhabitants. Bristol suffered more than 2,200 deaths, and Manchester 1,000. In 1625 James was succeeded by his son, Charles I, but the first year of his reign, too, was marked by a dreadful outbreak, when London was again very badly hit, with 40,000 dying. One rector considered 'the want and misery is the greatest here that ever any man living knew; no trading at all; the rich all gone; housekeepers and apprentices of manual trades begging in the streets.' While, according to Thomas Dekker: 'If one shop be open, sixteen in a row stand shut together, and those that are open, were as good to be shut; for they take no money.' Thomas Brewer put it in verse:

> Lies London now, bare, blasted, wither'd, shook
> Of strangers pitied, of her own forsook.

The authorities urged people to stay in the capital so as not to spread disease, but the poet John Donne recorded: 'The citizens fled away as out of a house on fire.' Not surprisingly, they tended to be unwelcome in the places where they tried to take refuge, with the 'water-poet' John Taylor versifying:

to be thought a Londoner is worse,
Than one who breaks a house or takes a purse.

The plague ranged far and wide again, killing more than 2,000 in Exeter. In Plymouth, the corporation proclaimed a public fast every Wednesday, but 2,000 died there too. The King's physician recommended further measures to combat the plague, including the imposition of a forty-day quarantine period for sufferers. He also perceptively identified 'rats, mice, weasels and such vermin' as carriers, but no one took much notice, and there was a further epidemic in 1636 which saw the burial of more than 10,000 victims in London between early April and mid-December. Glasgow faced a serious outbreak between 1646 and 1648, when the town council locked and guarded the city gates, banned the holding of 'wakes' over the dead, and ordered people with dogs to 'keep them fast or hang them'. Then, mysteriously, in the 1650s Britain suddenly found itself relatively free from this scourge.

In 1663, however, ominous reports began surfacing of a severe outbreak of plague in the Netherlands. In England, the government promptly imposed quarantine restrictions on ships coming from the infected areas, and only five deaths were recorded in 1664. Reassuringly, the winter of 1664/5 was cold, with the Thames frozen over for two months, and hard frost continuing in London into April. These seemed unfavourable conditions for the disease. The government had vessels patrolling the Thames estuary to enforce restrictions on suspect ships, but in March 1665, it declared war on the Dutch, and trade with the Netherlands declined. Perhaps the Privy Council let its guard slip, and missed an infected vessel. Certainly, by the end of April, Pepys was recording in his diary rumours 'that two or three houses are already shut up'. In fact, only three cases had been recorded during the month and, although the figure reached forty-three in May, that still represented less than 3 per cent of all deaths, and the better-off were able to note with relief that it seemed to be the poorest people who were catching the disease, in dingy alleys on the outskirts of the city.

The Privy Council closed down alehouses, put restrictions on lodgers to reduce overcrowding, and ordered a general clean-up, though not all of the measures were scrupulously enforced. Many people had an interest in playing down the scale of the disease – like relatives of the sick, who did not want to be incarcerated in their homes with the victim, and the government itself, which did not want to see other countries restricting trade with England or to provoke an exodus from London that might damage the war effort. In June, the weather was hot, and Pepys saw houses in Drury Lane marked with red crosses, and 'Lord have mercy upon us.' Then he heard that the plague had come into the City, and began thinking about 'how to put my things and estate in order, in case it should please God to call me away'. Deaths mounted steadily through the month until, in the final week, 270 fell victim.

Well over half were from St Giles-in-the-Fields, a poor parish west of the City. Neighbouring parishes put warders on the streets and passageways leading from it to try to stop people spreading the infection, but spread it did, and as the disease made its appearance in Westminster, the King and court moved out, while streets filled with the coaches of aristocrats and grandees leaving for the country. Among those who stayed were the Archbishop of Canterbury and the Lord Mayor, Sir John Lawrence, who had a glass case made from which he could receive visitors. July was the month when the Great Plague really took off. There were more than 5,600 deaths in seventy-three parishes. Pepys packed his wife and maids off to Woolwich, where he would spend his nights, though in the daytime, he continued to go to his house and office in the City. Those who could not flee were understandably reluctant to venture out too much, and the diarist John Evelyn was struck by London's 'mournful silence'. Pepys now sorted out his papers and accounts and re-drafted his will, mindful that 'a man cannot depend on living two days to an end'. He received constant reminders of the dangers when he passed close to corpse bearers or discovered that someone with whom he had been in contact had been taken ill, but that did not stop him embarking on amorous adventures in areas known to be infected.

There were many theories on how to avoid catching the plague. Puffing a pipe or chewing a plug of tobacco was supposed to help. Stories grew up that no London tobacconist had died of the disease, and at Eton College, the boys were instructed to smoke. Many potions and supposed remedies were sold. The famous physician Dr Thomas Sydenham treated victims by bleeding, followed by induced vomiting. If the patient did not vomit, Sydenham prescribed a mixture of Venice treacle, powder of crab's eyes and cochineal. This was followed by sweating for a day, during which time the victim's shirt was not to be changed, and they must be given a 'cooling diet', especially 'soup and broth', then a purge of tamarinds, senna leaves and rhubarb. Under this regime, it was said that no patient died. Other suggestions were to keep a piece of gold in your mouth, wear an amulet of toad poison, or catch syphilis. At the public health level, fumigation using a mixture of brimstone, saltpetre and amber was supposed to be effective, and it must certainly have created a stench unpleasant enough to deter some rats. At one point, all the cesspools in London were opened in the belief that the smell might drive away the disease, and many of the poor sought protection in the nauseous fumes of Bermondsey's tan pits. The Post Office was fumed so enthusiastically morning and night that the staff could hardly see each other, but up to thirty would still die during the epidemic.

As usual, there was a clampdown on animals. The city forbade the keeping of pigs, cats, dogs, pigeons and rabbits, and dog-catchers were ordered to round up and kill strays. Killing dogs and cats was, of course, a very good way of protecting the rats who were actually spreading the disease, but although their role was not established for another two centuries, there was concern about them, and people were employed to hunt them down too. During August, though, the plague advanced remorselessly. In the first week, there were 2,817 deaths, but by the last week, 6,102. Now 113 parishes were affected, and London was becoming like a ghost town. 'How sad a sight it is to see the streets empty of people,' wrote Pepys, 'and about us, two shops in three, if not more, generally shut up.' In the 1603 and 1625 epidemics, the second half of August had been the peak, but, if that was what Londoners prayed for now, their hopes were dashed, as the first week of September showed a further increase to just short of 7,000. The Nonconformist minister Thomas Vincent recorded that people fell 'as thick as the leaves in autumn when they are shaken by a mighty wind'. Death's arrows, it was said, struck the sainted wife and the spotted whore, and he rode his pale horse to every inhabited house.

The authorities tried new measures, like lighting fires in the streets for three days and nights until they were put out by heavy rain, but altogether during September, the plague claimed more than 30,000. Now Pepys noted that only 'poor wretches' were to be seen in the streets, and that if he walked the whole length of Lombard Street, he would see only twenty people. There were no boats on the river, and the city was 'distressed and forsaken'. Some parish clergy had fled, often to be replaced by ministers who had lost their livings after the Restoration because they were seen as too Puritan. Now they returned to their old pulpits, drawing big congregations with their fulminations against the licentiousness of the court, at which God's wrath seemed so severe. Many of the clergy did stay at their posts, though, and at least eleven Anglican priests died, along with a number of Nonconformists.

The flight of the better-off starved the authorities of cash. In some parishes, less than half of what was owed for poor and plague rates was collected. Some individual donors were very generous, but, as the death toll grew and the money shrank, support for the sick, such as it was, was stretched to breaking point, and normal decency began to break down. Nurses often robbed, or left to starve, the victims they were supposed to be looking after. Apothecaries were accused of strangling patients so they could ransack their homes. Gatekeepers were supposed to turn away from the city those who did not have certificates of health, but, in fact, they took bribes to let them in. 'The plague', wrote Pepys, 'made us as cruel as dogs one to another.' Not surprisingly, attempts to quarantine the sick increasingly ran into resistance. The Privy Council was told of a case where a building in St Giles-in-the-Fields had been forced open 'in a riotous manner'. By September, Pepys noted that quarantine had been abandoned.

Coffin-makers could not keep up with demand, and more and more people had to be buried in shrouds. When the shrouds ran out, bodies of victims were dumped naked in plague pits, often lined with quicklime. The predominant sounds of London now were the incessant tolling of church bells and the rolling wheels of carts collecting corpses, with the cries of 'bring out your dead', or the oaths and curses of the ruffians who manned them. The bodies of the dead, or nearly dead, were flung aboard. They were despoiled of rings, and subjected, it was said, to sexual assaults. The city was so quiet now that the rush of water beneath London Bridge could be clearly heard, and there was so little traffic that grass grew in the streets. Thomas Vincent thought he had heard of the death of someone he knew almost every day for a month, while in mid-October, Pepys found 'everybody talking of this dead, and that man sick, and so many in this place, and so many in that'.

By then, though, the death rate was actually beginning to fall. The number had declined to 4,327 in the week ending 10 October, and by the end of the month, was down to just over 1,000. There was a blip in the first week in November, when the total went up again, but later in the month, a heavy frost brought growing hopes that the disease would be killed off. On 24 November, Pepys visited his old oyster shop, and 'bought two barrels of my fine woman of the shop, who is alive after all the plague – which now is the first observation or enquiry we make at London concerning everybody we knew before it'. On Christmas Day, Pepys saw a wedding, 'which I have not seen many a day, and the young people so merry with one another'. In the first week of January, the diarist's wife returned home, as he noted, 'the town fills apace', and by February, the King and court were back at Whitehall, but the disease was not completely vanquished, with deaths running at 30 a week right into August 1666. For the whole of 1665, the official total for plague deaths in London was more than 68,000, but the disruptive effect of the disease had made it difficult to keep accurate records, and nowadays historians tend to accept a figure of anything up to 100,000, out of a population of about 500,000. What is clear is that the number who died was much greater than in the Black Death 300 years before, but that the proportion of the population carried off, dreadful though it was, was not as high as in the previous epidemic. As ever, the Earl of Clarendon noted that 'the lowest and poorest sort of people' formed most of the victims, and that 'not many of wealth and quality' had died.

London was the economic hub of the nation, and the news that the plague had reached it in 1665 created alarm everywhere. In Leicester, carriers were banned from going to the capital in case they should bring any passengers back, and when plague appeared at Lichfield in September 1665, it was blamed on the 'covetousness' of a family that took in lodgers from London. Others towns proved less hospitable. A Londoner who arrived at Dorchester was made to stay in a shed in a field, and when he died a few days later, a pit was dug next to it so that man and hovel could be shovelled in together. London, though, was not the only source of infection. East Anglia had a thriving trade with the Netherlands, and it was no surprise when the disease arrived. Ipswich and Great Yarmouth both lost about a sixth of their inhabitants, while at Colchester the pestilence carried off nearly 5,000, half the population. When it reached Norwich, about a quarter of the inhabitants fled, but the disease raged until the end of 1666, killing perhaps 4,000 people. Students were sent home from Cambridge University in June 1665, and did not return until the beginning of 1667, but even so, more than 1,400 perished out of a population of 8,000. Ports were often badly hit, with Dover losing between a quarter and a third of its people. At Southampton, the wealthy and the clergy fled. At least half of its people were said to have died, and the corporation later fined the deputy mayor and sixteen officers for being absent during the crisis. In the Midlands, Newark lost a third of its people.

This plague was more notable for the severity with which it raged in the places it struck than for its extent. Scotland, Wales, the North and the West Country largely escaped. A sample of more than 400 parishes in England outside London showed that fewer than one in ten had unusually high death rates in 1665–6, but in urban areas, the figure jumped to one in three. Some villages were hit, though. Skeffington in Leicestershire had twenty-eight burials in two months, seven times the normal average, and many of the population took to the woods, while Eyam in Derbyshire is celebrated to this day for its heroism. The disease probably reached the village in a parcel of clothes sent from London to the local tailor, who died on 6 September 1665. At first, it looked as though the infection might spread no further, then two weeks later, the second victim died. October saw 23 deaths, but in the winter, the disease died away again. Then in June 1666, another 21 perished. Many villagers wanted to flee, but the rector, William Mompesson, persuaded them to stay, and they drew a circle half a mile outside the village which no one was to cross. When outsiders left provisions for them, villagers would pay by dropping coins into a well to try to guard against spreading the disease. Eventually, another 176 people would die, bringing the total to 260 spread among just eighty-nine families. Mompesson's wife was the only member of his family to survive.

Even in the twentieth century there were deaths from plague, in Cardiff in 1900 and 1901, and in Liverpool in 1901 and 1914, but the epidemic of 1665–6 was the last major one in Britain, despite the fact that the disease continued to ravage Europe throughout the eighteenth century. The popular explanation for the end of the plague was that the Great Fire of 1666 destroyed the black rat's habitats. Those buildings of timber and thatch in which it was so comfortable were burned down, and replaced with houses of brick and tile. In fact, rats can colonise brick buildings. Besides, the area of London that was burned down was not the part where the plague had been most devastating, and the disease also disappeared from other parts of England where there was no Great Fire.

Another explanation offered for the illness's disappearance is that the black rat was increasingly driven out by the brown rat, which is supposed to avoid humans more, and rarely to act as a host for the flea that carries the plague bacteria, but this did not happen until well into the eighteenth century. Another possibility was that black rats may have built up immunity to the plague bacteria. If the rats were no longer dying, there would be no need for the fleas to migrate to human hosts. Some historians now consider that the most important factor was more stringent quarantine regulations in Britain and in other countries, though these did not prevent the many serious outbreaks in Europe over the next century, nor were the intellectual and organisational resources of the British Empire sufficient to prevent 12 million plague deaths in India in the first half of the twentieth century.

# CHAPTER FIFTEEN

# CHOLERA AND FLU

In 1830, disturbing news came from Russia. The British ambassador in St Petersburg reported an outbreak of cholera. The government responded by putting ships arriving from Russia under quarantine, while at church services congregations intoned a special prayer: 'spare, we beseech Thee, this Thy favoured land, the wrath which to our sins is justly due.' Cholera was a horrible disease. The body could lose pints of fluid in a few minutes, and become shrunken and shrivelled. There would be acute pains in the limbs and the stomach. The skin turned black or blue, and the victim found it hard to breathe, as air issued from the mouth with a low whining or moaning sound. Sometimes the pain was so severe the body convulsed almost into a ball, and could only be put back into its normal shape after death. A doctor described finding one 30-year-old victim 'shrivelled, corpsed and shattered by six hours cholera, into a torpid skeleton of 70 years. His flesh hung about him bagged, clammy . . . his eyes were coated over with a thick transparent film, as if already glazed for the dark lantern of the tomb.'

Sunderland was then a working-class town of nearly 20,000. Most of its people lived in crowded streets, with gutters down the middle, where, according to a contemporary observer, 'all the filth of human habitations is heedlessly thrown'. On Wednesday 19 October 1831, a 60-year-old man who had had diarrhoea for ten days called the doctor. After the consultation, he initially felt better. Then the symptoms returned, and a week later he was dead. William Sproat had become the first victim of the cholera outbreak. An hour later, his son, 'a fine athletic young man', was also taken ill. By the Sunday, he was throwing himself about in bed, moaning and biting the bedclothes, and by Monday, he too was dead. One of the doctors who had attended the family decided to notify the government, to the disapproval of a number of other local medical men.

To deal with the outbreak, the government despatched Lieutenant-Colonel Michael Creagh and Dr Daun, an army surgeon who had had plenty of experience of cholera in India. In the face of some local opposition, Creagh imposed a fifteen-day quarantine on all ships leaving Sunderland. The Marquess of Londonderry, who stood to lose a lot of money if the coal trade was disrupted, wrote to the London *Standard* saying it was a false alarm, and a group of anti-quarantine businessmen mounted a boardroom coup to take control of the local board of health. The authorities stopped reporting new cases to the press, and Dr Daun had to get them inserted in the newspapers at his own expense. Then, on 11 November, eleven local doctors got up at a public meeting to confess their past errors and recant, asserting that 'as to the nature of the disorder which had created unnecessarily so great an excitement in the public mind, the same is not the Indian cholera, nor of foreign origin'. The quarantine was 'perfectly unnecessary', especially as access by land to Sunderland was not limited in any way. The cholera bacteria, unfortunately, took no notice of all this and raged on regardless. Neighbouring towns responded that if Sunderland did not impose restrictions, they would take action of their own, closing their doors to people from the stricken area. A surgeon from Houghton in Northumberland had seen a Sunderland woman suffering from the disease and voiced the general alarm: 'Oh what a frightful disease it is: how different from anything I ever saw before! The sunken eyes and ghastly countenance, cold blue skin, no pulse, violent and excruciating spasms, voice weak and almost inaudible, constant moaning. . . . Was there ever before such an apparent absurdity as that which allows the inhabitants of Sunderland to travel freely throughout England on the land side with the seeds of this torturing malady ripening in their constitutions, while the intercourse by sea is shackled with quarantine restrictions?'

As the number of cases mounted, the Central Board of Health sent its own envoy, Dr David Barry, who had seen the outbreak in Russia. He pronounced that this was indeed cholera, but reduced the quarantine period to ten days, as the incubation period of the illness had turned out to be shorter than expected. Then, in December, the restrictions were removed altogether, as the disease had plainly taken hold. A cholera hospital was opened on the outskirts of the town, but many patients were reluctant to go there, because it was a long way from home, and they were afraid they might be dissected if they died. The authorities believed prevention was better than cure; that the key was to make sure that the poor were well clothed and well fed, that they should have blankets if they fell ill, and that if a breadwinner died, his dependants should not be allowed to fall into destitution. Two thousand pounds was raised by public subscription, but it was not enough to achieve these enlightened objectives. The *Sunderland Herald* reported that thirty homes in one street could muster only two blankets between them, and the great and the good worried that if the poor were given bedding they would sell it to buy food or drink. According to Dr Reid Clanny, who headed the local doctors' advisory committee, many practitioners in poorer districts worked day and night 'without one farthing . . . either from government or from the community', while their colleagues in the more prosperous areas went on their regular rounds without ever pitching in to help. Altogether in Sunderland, there were more than 400 cases, and 215 people died. The *Lancet* complained that many had died unnecessarily because of 'the suborning of medical opinion, and the recklessness and avarice of a knot of mercantile speculators . . . who . . . continued to deny the existence of an unusual disease, until the choked graveyards of their town bore witness to the deplorable fact.'

Government commissioners travelled around neighbouring towns giving advice, but no one knew what caused the disease. At Gateshead, Lieutenant-Colonel Creagh told the board of heath that cholera corpses were very contagious, while the danger of infection from the living was only 'trifling'. If cleanliness was needed to contain the disease, the signs were not good. North Shields had virtually no drainage, while Tynemouth had only a ditch in the middle of the main street, into which the inhabitants flung 'night soil' and other debris. In its Ropery Banks district, 100 homes did not have a single lavatory between them, while in the Low Town area of North Shields, there were sixty-two for 7,000 people, and from those, the sewage drained into the subsoil. The vast majority of people had no running water, and had to rely instead on standpipes, travelling water salesmen, or wells of doubtful quality. Tynemouth's first case appeared in December – a beggar who had recently arrived from Sunderland. Nationally, there was a scientific battle going on between those doctors who believed that the disease was contagious – the 'contagionists' – and the 'miasmatists', who asserted that it was transmitted by 'bad air' infected by refuse or sewage. So it was a blow for the contagionists when a number of people who had had no contact with the original victim began to fall ill. By now the disease had also reached Newcastle upon Tyne and, across the river, Gateshead was hit on Boxing Day.

'The inhabitants of Gateshead fell asleep on December 25 in perfect security and devoid of panic,' wrote one doctor, 'but before the sun rose on the 26th fifty-five individuals had been seized, 32 of whom were destined not to see it set.' By the end of 27 December, more than 100 cases had been reported, and 52 people had died. *The Times* noted that 'not a few' of the victims 'lived in clean, well-ventilated apartments; and, for working people, were in comfortable circumstances.' The worst-hit place in the whole of England was Newburn, a reasonably prosperous village of 550 people 5 miles from Newcastle, where 65 people died.

The bug had crossed the border into Scotland in mid-December, claiming its first victim in the small town of Haddington in East Lothian, then, a month later, it appeared 40 miles away at Hawick, before striking Edinburgh, then Glasgow and the Highlands. Musselburgh lost 250 people in five weeks, which was attributed to the 'vicious, immoral and miserable' character of its inhabitants. Fear was now sweeping the country. In Clackmannanshire, an ailing young woman dragged herself 5 miles to the village of Dollar to take refuge with her mother. When local people found the doctor had diagnosed her as having cholera, they dragged her from her bed and sent her back home in a cart. She died that night. The villagers then forced her mother from her home and burned it to the ground. Fifteen hours later, she too was dead. No one would help to bury her, and doctors had to carry her coffin, but even then, villagers insisted she was interred outside the churchyard. An Aberdeen surgeon tried to calm the atmosphere by deliberately allowing his clothes to come into contact with cholera victims, but at Pathhead in Kirkcaldy, when officials from the local board of health tried to remove the body of a victim, local people barricaded the house, apparently wanting to hide the fact that cholera had reached them. The next morning, one of the barricaders went down with the disease, as did his wife and mother, all of them dying within a few hours.

Edinburgh took energetic precautions, but suffered 1,000 deaths out of a population of 136,000, while Glasgow closed the theatres and banned evening sermons, but still sustained the worst death toll outside London – nearly 3,200 out of a population of 200,000. The outbreak was almost entirely confined to parts of the city dependent on old public wells, like the High Street, the Gallowgate and the Trongate. Professor Lawrie, who treated more than 1,000 victims, was tortured by 'the withering disappointment which followed the failure of remedies . . . I have tried leeches, blood-letting, blisters, warm baths, stimulants, in a word everything that empiricism could suggest without avail. I need hardly add that I know not how to cure this affection.' By the time cholera had died out at the end of 1832, Scotland had lost 10,000 of its 2.3 million people.

When cholera threatened, London had brought in rigorous controls on ships, but none at all on the hundreds of coaches arriving in the capital every day. In February 1832, the government also announced days of fasting and humiliation to be held in March, when the nation would confess its sins and beg for God's forgiveness. Four days after the announcement, cholera arrived in the capital. The government passed laws requiring doctors to notify all cases, and local boards of health were empowered to set up dispensaries for the poor, to fumigate homes and to clean up environmental hazards, but by the time the first national fast day was held on 21 March, there had been more than 538 deaths in London. Response to the fast days was said to be disappointing. By the time the epidemic died down in the autumn, official figures for the capital put the number of deaths at just under 5,300. Many believed the true number was more like 7,000, and the disease returned in the summer of 1833 to carry off another 1,500.

In other cities, the sad tale was repeated. In Leeds, the authorities tried to clean up the poorest areas, but when they tried to improve the living conditions in Boot and Shoe Yard, they found themselves having to remove sewage that had accumulated over thirty years. Seven hundred died in the city. In Lancashire, Liverpool with its notorious back-to-back houses and cellar dwellings lost 1,500 out of a population of 230,000. One elderly man in the port died on 19 July 1832. *The Times* reported that his wife was drunk, and that she removed his body, then 'boldly entered the bed, sleeping between the same coverings under which her husband had died'. She suffered no harm. Neighbours said she lived entirely on gin and gooseberries, but the newspaper emphasised that it was making no medicinal claims for this diet. Thirty miles away, Manchester's half-hearted attempts to protect itself were likened by a local doctor to those of 'the country gentleman described by Addison, who thought to keep out the crows by nailing up his park gate'. Allen's Court, which had a tripe boiler's works on one side, a catgut manufactory on the other, and was bounded by the River Irk 'dyed and defiled by impurities of every kind', was nicknamed 'Cholera Court' after fourteen people died there in 48 hours. As the death toll in Manchester and Salford mounted to 900, a mob appeared outside the cholera hospital carrying a coffin containing the headless body of a small child. It had died in the hospital and had been examined *post mortem*. The body had then been exhumed, and was found to be, according to *The Times*, 'unaccountably mangled'. The rioters claimed the child had been murdered. They broke into the hospital, wrecking the wards and carrying off patients to their homes. A nurse escaped their rage by leaping into bed, covering herself with a blanket and writhing and groaning as if she was suffering a violent cholera attack. Outside, the military had to clear the streets.

Bilston in the West Midlands was to lose 750 people, one in twenty of its population, in spite of being well drained, having wide and airy streets, with well spaced houses, and a very efficient board of health. The head of the board of health was the local vicar, the Revd William Leigh. He recorded that cholera was 'literally sweeping every thing before it, neither age nor sex, nor station, escaping . . . the hearse carrying the dead to the grave, without intermission by night or day'. He mounted an appeal that raised more than £8,500, some of which was spent on a 'cholera' school for orphans. Leigh remarked on the great generosity shown by the poor in helping each other and in taking in orphaned children. In the west, 600 people died in Bristol, and more than 1,000 in the Plymouth area. In Exeter, a man is said to have set off for work one morning leaving his wife and daughter in good health, only to find them both dead on his return. The local board of health wanted to set up a special burial ground for cholera victims, but had to give up in the face of local opposition. Then, when it tried to inter them in the normal cemetery, that produced a riot. Cholera appeared in Northern Ireland in April 1832. At Coleraine, some of the inhabitants fled to the countryside, while in Belfast the streets were deserted, and the few people to be seen were wearing mourning, as all day long the hearses clattered past.

This first epidemic reached every corner of Britain and killed about 60,000 people, but still no one knew what caused cholera. The *Lancet* mused: 'Is it a fungus, a miasma, an electrical disturbance, a deficiency of ozone, a morbid off-scouring of the intestinal canal? We know nothing; we are at sea in a whirlpool of conjecture.' The contagionists, who had the support of the *Lancet*, thought quarantine was the best defence, while the miasmatists believed in cleanliness, and campaigned for sanitary improvements. Exeter offered cash prizes for the best plan for improving the city's water, and laid 13 miles of new sewers, but for the government such things were of lower priority than other reforms, like factory regulation and the new Poor Law that would introduce the workhouse. So it was not until 1842 that the official *Report on the Sanitary Condition of the Labouring Population of Great Britain* by Edwin Chadwick appeared. It may not have had the snappiest title, but it was a best-seller, being bought by more people than any other government publication up to that time. It showed that in Leeds, cholera cases were clustered around the worst-drained districts, and that in Derby, life expectancy for a member of the gentry was forty-nine years, for a tradesman, thirty-eight, while for a workman, it was just twenty. Chadwick knew how to reach the Victorian heart, and declared that the failure to fight preventable disease was costing money. In response the Home Secretary set up a Royal Commission to look at the fifty towns with the highest death rates in the cholera epidemic. It found that only one had a satisfactory sewage system and only six an adequate water supply, while pressure groups like the Health of Towns Association began agitating for improvements, claiming that black slaves in America lived better than the poor in the cellars of a British city.

Finally, in 1848, after fierce debate, Parliament established a National Board of Health, and towns with the highest mortality rates were ordered to set up their own boards, while others could if their ratepayers wanted to. By now, though, cholera was back, with the first case, that of a seaman from Hamburg, diagnosed in September, while the board faced constant attacks from *The Times*, the *Lancet*, the Royal College of Physicians and numerous local organisations over its interference. Its members worked like Trojans, but they did not understand cholera; Chadwick, for example, believing 'all smell is disease'. Much of their effort, therefore, was misdirected, as when they told people not to eat green vegetables. By October the infection had appeared in Edinburgh, and by December in Glasgow and Belfast. In the village of Carnbroe, near Coatbridge, forty people fell ill on New Year's Day, and one man, convinced he was going to die, cut his throat rather than wait for the agonies of cholera. Sunderland was struck again, but at first the epidemic was relatively mild. Then in May 1849, it appeared in other parts of England and in Wales, where Merthyr Tydfil was struck with great violence. Industry had been developing rapidly in the green valleys and Merthyr was based around iron mines and a smelting works. It had 50,000 people crammed into tiny cottages, many of them along a stream used as an open drain. The inhabitants flocked to incessant prayer meetings, as the disease carried off 1,700. Cholera also broke out at Mevagissey in Cornwall, another place where there was no proper drainage. Local doctors borrowed tents from the government and evacuated 1,300 people to a camp half a mile away with a good supply of fresh water. Not one of them caught cholera, while almost all of those who stayed in the village contracted the disease, and nearly 140 of them died. The board of health reluctantly conceded that 'much evidence has been elicited proving the influence of the use of impure water in predisposing to the disease'.

London suffered once more, with 14,000 deaths out of a total for the whole country again of more than 60,000. The worst single outbreak of the whole epidemic occurred in a huge boarding school at Tooting, popularly known as Drouet's Baby Farm, the only place in the area that was affected. It was a place where the authorities dumped pauper children from all over the capital to be over-worked, badly clothed and under-fed. More than 180 died. Dickens wrote that the establishment was 'brutally conducted, vilely kept, preposterously inspected, dishonestly defended, a disgrace to a Christian community, and a stain upon a civilised land'. The proprietor was charged with manslaughter, but acquitted. One writer said cholera had become 'a health inspector who speaks through his interpreter, the Registrar-General, in a language which reaches all ears'. Much, indeed, was said and written about it; more than 700 works were published in London alone between 1845 and 1856. The most important, though, was the pamphlet *On the mode of communication of cholera*, by Dr John Snow, published in 1849. Snow was a Yorkshire farmer's son, who had been apprenticed to a series of village surgeons, and then, in 1831, at the age of 18, had single-handedly fought a cholera epidemic at a local colliery. Five years later he set off for London on foot to make his fortune, qualified as a Member of the Royal College of Surgeons and opened up a general practice in Soho. A serious young man of great determination, he became an authority on chloroform and would achieve fame when he prescribed it for Queen Victoria to reduce the pain of childbirth in April 1853. Snow had wondered for some time why, when cholera was a disease of the intestines, not the lungs, it should be spread through poisoned air, as the miasmatists thought. Now he argued it was caught from drinking water, but his theory won little favour, and many felt as baffled as ever. One doctor with great experience of the disease in Scotland said, 'its nature is as unknown and its prognosis as gloomy as when it first emerged from the jungles of India to run its career of desolation'. His own study of 260 victims revealed that only 82 were fair and 11 had red hair, pointing to the conclusion that dark-haired people were more at risk.

While the debate went on, cholera returned in the winter of 1853/4, attacking the north of England and Scotland. The National Board of Health's powers were due to lapse in July 1854 and, despite the spirited advocacy of Chadwick, Parliament decided not to renew them. *The Times* rejoiced, 'We prefer to take our chance of cholera and the rest than be bullied into health', but in the end MPs relented, and a similar body was established. In August, cholera was back in London, cutting a swathe through the East End, then spreading into Soho, where Snow had his surgery. During the space of ten days in the area around it, 500 people died, and things would have been even worse if many others had not fled. In the rest of the district, there were virtually no deaths. Snow described it as 'the most terrible outbreak of cholera which ever occurred in this kingdom', but he thought he knew why it had happened. Conquering his natural shyness, he steeled himself to demand that the authorities remove the handle from a water pump in Broadwick Street. Reluctantly, they agreed.

When the handle was removed, the epidemic abruptly ended. Today, the pump is marked with a plaque, and the site of his surgery is occupied by a pub that bears his name. (A few hundred yards from Snow's surgery, Florence Nightingale, then 33, was working at the Middlesex Hospital, and became celebrated for the tireless and compassionate care she gave the cholera victims. Two months later, she would go out to the Crimean War, and become the most famous nurse in the world.) More evidence that Snow was right emerged from South London. During the first four weeks of the epidemic, 286 people had died in houses supplied by the Southwark and Vauxhall Water Company, but only fifteen in those served by the Lambeth Water Company. The Southwark was still drawing water from a polluted stretch of the Thames at Battersea, while the Lambeth was supplying cleaner water from Surrey, but still many medical men rejected Snow's theory, and the new General Board of Health dismissed contaminated water as the cause of the outbreak. Sadly, Snow would never see his vindication. He died of a stroke, aged 45, in 1858. Altogether, this third epidemic killed 20,000 people, including 10,000 in London and 6,000 in Scotland.

Still the disease was not done, and there was a fourth outbreak in 1865. On the whole it was a small one, except for parts of East London, where a contaminated water supply killed more than 900, but miasmatists like the principal medical officer of the Great Western Railway had still not given up. He claimed that areas affected by cholera were marked out by a 'thin transparent bluish haze'. One of the worst-hit places was Liverpool, where 2,000 died out of a total of 15,000 for the whole country. This was the last major epidemic in Britain. In 1875, Disraeli's Public Health Act compelled all local authorities to provide drainage, sewerage and an adequate water supply, and by 1896 cholera was rare enough to be classified as an 'exotic disease'.

The next major epidemic would arrive in Britain in the final year of the First World War, though it may have claimed its first victims in the last year of the Wars of the Roses. The 'Picardy Sweat' came to England in the autumn of 1485, killing three lord mayors of London in as many months. Altogether, 'a wonderful number' of people died, and there were five further epidemics of 'sweating sickness' over the next seventy years. Nowadays it is believed that at least some of these outbreaks were influenza, an illness that can present itself in more than 300,000 forms. During the epidemic of 1517, it was recorded that people would suddenly fall ill as they sat at home or walked in the street. They would sweat profusely, and might be dead within 4 hours. They could, as one contemporary put it, be 'merry at dinner and dead at supper'. If they survived for 24 hours, apparently they would recover quickly. Medical advice was to lie down, wrapped up well in warm blankets, in a moderately heated room. Those who took cold drinks to soothe their fever, it was said, always died. By the end of July, the sickness was claiming many victims; 400 died in Oxford in a week. One chronicler claimed that some towns lost half of their inhabitants, though this is almost certainly an exaggeration.

In London, the Michaelmas law term was cancelled and court functions were abandoned, but King Henry VIII rejected the idea of cancelling all fairs, as he felt they were among the few consolations people had. He himself took every possible precaution (especially after his Latin secretary died of the sweat in August), cancelling the Christmas festivities, refusing to receive ambassadors, and isolating himself from everyone except three or four servants. Eleven years later, the sweat was back. By now, Henry had fallen in love with Anne Boleyn. One of her servants caught it, as did Cardinal Wolsey and a number of courtiers. It broke Henry's heart, but he sent Anne away to Hever Castle, where she caught the illness. The King despatched his physician to look after her, and she recovered, though her brother-in-law died. Meanwhile, Henry again kept himself to himself and attended mass three times a day. When the sickness struck again in 1551, Henry's successor, the precocious young Edward VI, took refuge at Hampton Court and offered his diagnosis: 'if one took cold, he died within three hours . . . if he slept the first six hours . . . then he raved and should die raving.' Six years later the affliction returned, as Wriothesley's *Chronicle* recorded: 'this summer reigned in England divers strange and new sicknesses . . . as strange agues and fevers, whereof many died.' This epidemic was accompanied by bad harvests and severe food shortages, and may have contributed to killing about one in twenty of the population.

If there is doubt about how often 'sweating sickness' was actually flu, there is no question about the great epidemic of 1918. It became known as 'Spanish flu', because this was the European country where it seemed to strike first – infecting 8 million people, including King Alfonso XIII. It reached London in the spring, where King George V caught it, and in May it laid low more than 10,000 sailors of the British Grand Fleet, preventing the ships from putting to sea for twelve days. Birmingham had ninety-six deaths in a week, Belfast ninety-seven. In Sunderland, the figure was twenty, and output was badly hit in the Northumberland and Durham coalfields. *The Times* noted the suddenness of its progress: 'persons who feel perfectly well and are able to go about their business at ten o'clock in the morning being prostrate at noon.' It was also highly infectious; one sneeze could leave 85 million bacteria suspended in the air for more than half an hour. The symptoms would begin with a cough, then pain behind the eyes and in the back, until eventually every fibre in the body ached. A fever would take the temperature as high as 104°F, and the victim would be unable to take food. Fortunately, it was fatal in only about one case in twenty.

From mid-June to the end of August, flu caused up to 1,700 deaths in London, before seeming to die away. Then, in October, it reappeared. Manchester's medical officer of health visited schools, and found children collapsing 'like poisoned flowers' across their desks. The schools were shut down. In Nottingham, carts were despatched to wash down the gutters with disinfectant. Now the virus seemed to have mutated into a more sinister form, with flu turning to pneumonia within a few days, or even a day, of symptoms appearing, and the skin turning a deep plum colour. It could be a horrible end, with victims gasping desperately for breath, their lungs full of fluid, and oddly the death toll was higher for those aged between 5 and 45 than for those over 45, while flu was normally a bigger killer of the old. Cockermouth had been free from flu, but one thanksgiving service at the church was enough to infect almost every family in town, and houses would carry signs saying: 'Walk in – don't knock – all in bed.' At Dover, a stoker married a

Woolworths counter-hand, then 24 hours later found himself standing in his wedding suit by her grave. In Wimbledon every fireman except the chief was off work ill. Southampton, Leicester and Glasgow all had death rates running at three times or more above their normal level, and during the early part of November, 289 people collapsed on London's streets and had to be taken to hospital. Later in the month, seventy-eight people died at Basford workhouse in Nottinghamshire. With the country in the grip of wartime food shortages, rumours spread that the rich were hoarding all the food, and that the poor were dying not from flu but from starvation.

In Belfast, they closed schools, Sunday schools and pubs, but most picture houses stayed open, and the Panopticon was kept 'flu-proof' by frequent spraying with a mixture of phenol and lavender ('the finest germ-killer in the world'), while in Glasgow there was 'much irritation' when the military authorities decided to put mass entertainment out of bounds and many wounded soldiers and men home on leave were banned from going to a football match. Altogether, in the week following the armistice on 11 November 1918, 19,000 people died of flu in Britain. It seemed especially cruel that so many who died were soldiers who had survived the horrors of the First World War. The government admitted that the Medical Research Committee had given a warning back in August that the autumn would probably see an epidemic of great severity, and the Local Government Board admitted that 'some lives might have been saved, spread of infection diminished and suffering avoided if the known sick could have been isolated from the healthy'.

As ever, there was debate about how individuals could avoid catching the disease. Some doctors thought open windows were an open invitation to the virus, while others urged the entire population to sleep in the open air, as this helped to wash away the infection from the lungs. The *Lancet* mused: 'If persons entering densely crowded underground lifts and cars were to keep their mouths closed – by preference upon an antiseptic lozenge . . . the spread of influenza would be much abated.' The medical correspondent of *The Times* recommended tobacco in moderation as a means of combating infection, and many workplaces dropped 'no smoking' rules. For some, the epidemic represented a business opportunity, and an advertisement suggested a way of helping others: 'Refrain from buying Bovril if you have a stock in the house. . . . In this way you will leave the available Bovril in the shops for those who have illness at home. Bovril Ltd recognising that those who are deprived of the body-building power of Bovril may more easily fall victims to the epidemic are doing their utmost to increase the supply.'

Despite these interesting remedies, in December deaths were up again, and in Manchester funerals were being delayed because undertakers could not keep up with the demand for coffins. *The Times* speculated that it might all be because of the end of a cold, dry spell: 'In hot, damp weather, perhaps, the resisting power of the individual is lowered, he becomes depressed, and less well able to ward off the danger threatening him.' Whatever the reason, the disease continued to wreak havoc into the following spring, with 580 people dying in Glasgow in one week in March. Any nurses being released from military service were urged to look after flu victims 'even at the expense of deferring taking a well-earned holiday at the termination of their strenuous labours during the war'.

Altogether nearly 229,000 people died of flu in Britain, a similar total to Germany, but many fewer than in Italy, and in India there were 12.5 million victims. Among the victims were Sir Hubert Parry, who wrote the music for 'Jerusalem', and Captain William Leefe Robinson VC, who shot down the first German airship over Britain during the First World War. Although many Britons lived in poor overcrowded housing, it is not clear that class and money were a factor in who lived and who died, and in London, the death rate was as high in fashionable Chelsea and Westminster as in working-class Bermondsey and Bethnal Green. Nowadays, many believe that 'Spanish flu', like so many other strains, originated in Hong Kong or China, but the exact nature of the organism that caused it remains a mystery, and is still the subject of energetic research, particularly as many scientists believe the world is now due for another devastating flu epidemic.

# CHAPTER SIXTEEN

# STORMS

There must have been many outbreaks of wild weather in Britain before recorded history began, but thanks to the Anglo-Saxon Chronicle, we know that in 876 there was a great storm which probably produced very little lamentation, because it smashed up a fleet of Viking raiders: 'the pirate host . . . were caught in a great storm at sea, and there off Swanage one hundred and twenty ships were lost'. In 1091, a tornado destroyed a church and 600 homes in London. Then, in 1287, a fierce wind made the sea burst its banks near Hickling in Norfolk, flooding towns by the coast: 'Issuing forth about the middle of the night it suffocated or drowned men and women sleeping in their beds, with infants in their cradles, and all kinds of cattle and fresh water fishes; and it tore up houses from their foundations, with all they contained and carried them away. . . . Many, when surrounded by the waters, sought a place of refuge by mounting into trees; but benumbed by the cold, they were overtaken by the water, and fell into it and were drowned.' It is said that at least 300 people perished.

The deadliest British storm arrived in the early hours of Saturday 27 November 1703. The wind had appeared on the Lizard Peninsula between nine and ten o'clock the previous evening, and the vicar of St Keverne said that by midnight it was blowing so fiercely that 'the country hereabout thought the great Day of Judgment was coming.' Fourteen miles south of Plymouth Hoe, a 60ft wave demolished the Eddystone lighthouse, built just five years before, killing the man who built it, Henry Winstanley. Meanwhile, in London, the writer Daniel Defoe saw a reading on his barometer that was so low he assumed his children must have been playing with it. In fact, he would become the chronicler of the storm, gathering eyewitness accounts from all over the country.

On land, winds reached more than 70 miles an hour, and the area from Milford Haven to the Severn Estuary and around the shore of the Bristol

Channel suffered especially badly. Most houses in Swansea lost their roofs, while in Cardiff, a huge breach was made in the city wall. In Bristol, a number of buildings were blown down and several people were killed, while shipping was damaged in the harbour. Defoe reckoned 15,000 sheep were lost around the banks of the Severn and a 'multitude' of cattle. Indeed, most places to the south of the Trent suffered some damage. In Kent, more than 1,000 buildings were flattened, including the church spire at Brenchley, said to be the tallest in the county at nearly 200ft. At Cambridge, many pinnacles were blown from King's College Chapel, and a chimney stack crashed through the roof of the bishop's palace at Wells, killing the bishop and his wife. In Shoreham, the ancient Market House was 'blown flat to the ground and all the town shattered', while waterspouts ripped through Oxfordshire, uprooting trees and haystacks.

There were many stories of astonishing individual tragedies and escapes. At Highbridge on the Somerset Levels, water poured into the ground floor of a house. The man and woman inside tried to escape, but the house collapsed and they were killed. Their baby, though, floated out in its cradle, and was found alive when the floods abated. At three o'clock in the morning, a furious gust of wind blew a stack of chimneys on to a house in London, in which there were seventeen people. A nurse, a maid and a baby fell through three floors to the kitchen. The baby was found unharmed hanging in the curtains, and the nurse and maid escaped with slight bruises. Indeed, everyone got out without serious injury. At Charlwood in Surrey, a miller was woken up by the storm, and decided he must save his windmill. When he got to the mill, though, he found he had left his key at home, and went back to get it. By the time he returned, it had completely disappeared, just one, according to Defoe, of hundreds that were destroyed. At a Northampton mill, 'the mighty upright post below the floor' was 'snapt in two like a reed'. In the same town, 'an honest yeoman, being up on a ladder to save his hovel, was blown off, and fell upon a plough, died outright and never spoke word more', while lead on the roof of All Saints' and other churches was 'rolled up like a scroll'.

In London, the *Post Man* newspaper reported: 'there is hardly any house but has had a share in the calamity.' Westminster Abbey had its roof torn off, and many other churches were damaged, as were the Inns of Court. Lead from roofs was often carried 'an incredible distance'. People had to wrestle with a cruel dilemma. Should they stay inside a house that might collapse, or go outside and risk being hit by flying debris like tiles, which were being flung

40yd through the air? A 90-year-old woman who moved out of her house was killed by a brickbat, and a watchman died on his rounds when a chimney stack fell on him. A carpenter and his wife decided to stay indoors. She asked him to read a chapter of the Bible and he refused, whereupon the chimney promptly collapsed and killed him, leaving her 'miraculously' unhurt. Part of St James's Palace was blown down, killing a woman outside, and many of Queen Anne's favourite acacias, limes and elms in the park outside were torn up. The Queen herself was taken down to the presumed safety of the cellar. On the Thames, the arches of London Bridge were said to have been blocked with wrecked vessels. A 'great number' of boats and lighters were smashed to pieces, their remains piled together. Defoe reckoned he saw about 700 ships wrecked 'in heaps . . . the bowsprits of some drove into the cabin windows of others . . . there was hardly a vessel to be seen that had not suffered some damage'. Some were reduced to firewood bobbing up and down on the water. About 20 people were drowned in the Thames and, altogether in London, more than 200 were killed or seriously injured.

After the storm, the writer tried to calculate how many trees had been destroyed. He began a circuit of Kent, and had counted 17,000 lying on the ground before he gave up. According to his tally, twenty-five parks lost more than 1,000 each, and in the New Forest the figure was more than 4,000. John Evelyn had 2,000 blown down at his house at Wotton in Surrey, and commented philosophically: 'I thank God for what are yet left standing.' The total number lost must have run into millions. Up to 25 miles inland, farmers found their fields had been so contaminated with salt, they were unfit for grazing, and when desperate sheep on the South Downs ate the grass, they 'drank like fishes', while at Hastings, the leaves of trees and bushes looked as though 'they had been dipped in the sea.'

Those on land escaped lightly compared with those at sea. November had been a very windy month, and by the time the storm broke, ports and harbours were already crammed with vessels waiting for better weather, while others were lying at anchor outside. Off the Kent coast were many naval vessels just returned from the summer campaign against the French in the War of the Spanish Succession. Observers said they had never seen such a concentration of shipping. A couple of days before the main storm, a Dutch craft had already been stranded on the Goodwin Sands, and lost with all hands. Now, as the storm howled its worst, wind speeds in the Channel reached more than 100 miles an hour, with gusts touching nearly 140.

Many smaller ships foundered from the sheer weight of water as the sea washed over them, while the bigger ones had to cut away their masts to try to avoid dragging their anchors, but by two in the morning, virtually every vessel in the area was adrift. With so many crowded together, collisions were inevitable. The warship *Prince George* was being held by her anchors when, through the storm and spray, the crew suddenly became aware of another vessel bearing down on them. It was the *Restoration*. They managed to avoid a collision, but the two ships' cables became entangled. For more than half an hour, the vessels were driven along together, as the crews tried desperately to cut the ties that bound them, then suddenly the *Restoration* broke free, and went down with all 386 hands. The *Prince George* escaped, and as day dawned she saw a dozen ships stranded on the Goodwins, including the 70-gun *Northumberland*, which was to be lost with its entire crew of 253.

Another was the 60-gun *Mary*, which broke up leaving only one survivor from the crew of 273, a man named Thomas Atkins, who managed to cling to a piece of floating wreckage until a freak wave picked him up and flung him down on the deck of another man o' war, the *Stirling Castle*. As she was grounded, he was flung overboard again, but this time, he fell into the only ship's boat that managed to float free, and in it he reached the shore, unconscious, suffering from exposure, but alive. Of the *Stirling Castle*'s crew of 349, only 70 survived. At daybreak on Friday, the section of water had looked like 'a goodly forest'. By Saturday, it was 'reduced to a desert'. Altogether on the sands, it is estimated that nearly 1,200 men lost their lives. One merchant ship cut away her masts, and put out to the open sea. She was blown north for four days, with the crew having no idea of their whereabouts until they met a pilot boat which took them into a Norwegian port. As the tide receded, men could be seen walking on the sands and waving for help, but the people of Deal and Walmer, it was alleged, were much more interested in spoil from the wrecks than in saving their fellow human beings, until the mayor spent his own money assembling a group of rescuers who commandeered boats by force and managed to rescue about 200 men 'almost dead with hunger and cold, naked and starving'. He asked the Queen's agent to provide for the sick and wounded seamen, but the agent 'would not relieve them with one penny', so the mayor paid for their board and lodging from his own pocket. When a number of them died, the mayor had to finance their burial, while he also paid for survivors to travel to London. He eventually got his money back, but only after 'great obstructions and delays'.

The master of the *John and Mary* exclaimed, 'Such a tempest as this, there never was in the world', as his vessel was driven 150 miles from Great Yarmouth to Scarborough. In Yarmouth Roads, the 48-gun *Reserve* was swamped by huge seas while at anchor, and 190 men were drowned. Among other warships lost were the *Newcastle*, which went down off Sussex, and the *Canterbury*, lost near Bristol at a total cost of 255 lives, while the *Portsmouth* sank with 40 crew near the mouth of the Thames. The *Association* disappeared as the storm drove her from her anchorage at Harwich. She was close to a sandbank named the Galloper, and as the wind carried her over it, she lost her rudder. The waters broke in and made her list alarmingly. Her commander, Sir Stafford Fairborne, rose from his sickbed to take command. This was no easy task, for, as Defoe put it, 'words were no sooner uttered than they were carried away by the wind'. She had struck her mainmast and had only a scrap of sail as, day after day, she was driven helpless across the North Sea. Her stores began to run out, the men were put on short rations, and many started to fall ill. Back in England, the Admiralty was convinced she was lost. In fact, she had managed to limp to Gothenberg for repairs, and not until 3 January was she able to set sail for Britain. Then she had to fight off attacks from French privateers and another gale before, to general astonishment, she reached the Medway on 23 January, by which time twenty-eight of the crew had died. Among other vessels that, like the *Association*, escaped the storm, were the *Eagle* and the *Firebrand*, only for all three to come to grief on the Isles of Scilly four years later (see Chapter 11). Total losses from the storm were 13 men o' war, and more than 2,000 sailors.

Merchant vessels sank too. Three ketches went down off Brighton with the loss of all aboard, except for one man who clung to a floating mast for three days. East of Lyme Regis, a Guernsey privateer foundered with the loss of forty of her crew, three merchantmen were sunk off Plymouth, while at Grimsby, almost every vessel in the harbour was driven out to sea, and twenty never returned. In spite of the difficulties the mayor of Deal ran into, the government acted with unusual urgency to make payments to the widows and families of drowned sailors, treating them as generously as if they had been killed in the service of the Queen. The *Observator* newspaper wrote: 'never was such a storm of wind, such a hurricane and tempest known in the memory of man, nor the like to be found in the histories of England,' and many of Defoe's correspondents considered it a 'miracle' how few had died, though the number must have run into thousands. The Queen felt people should realise they had been so wicked that the storm could easily have been much worse, and that 'it was the infinite mercy of God that we and our people were not thereby wholly destroyed'. A national day of fasting was called on 19 January 1704 'for the imploring of a blessing from Almighty God . . . as also for the humbling of ourselves before Him in a deep sense of his heavy displeasure shewed forth in the late dreadful storm and tempest'. Evelyn reported 'the churches so crowded few could get into them'. The disaster would be known as 'the Great Storm' for the best part of the next three centuries.

The events that we are more likely to refer to now by that name happened in 1987. During the evening of 15 October, the temperature rose an extraordinary 9 °C in 20 minutes, then the winds grew fiercer, and at half past one on the morning of 16 October, the Meteorological Office warned the Ministry of Defence to expect a storm of such ferocity that the civil authorities might have to ask the military for assistance. By then the winds were attacking a similar area to the storm of 1703, and again doing widespread damage, though, mercifully, this time the loss of life was much less. Altogether, though, something like 15 million trees were felled, a toll made higher because the earth was saturated from the wettest start to October on record. Kent was especially badly hit and, at Sevenoaks, the seven trees that gave their name to the town were reduced to one. At 500-year-old Knole Park, two-thirds of the trees were brought down, while at Churchill's home at Chartwell, a spectacular horseshoe of beeches, much loved by Sir Winston, was demolished, as were trees that Kipling had planted at Batemans in Sussex. Kent County Council contractors had to remove an estimated 400,000 tons of fallen timber from the A25 alone. In London, Kew Gardens lost hundreds of trees. The deputy curator Ian Beyer declared: 'This is the worst day in the entire history of Kew.' At Hampton Court, more than 800 trees came down, including avenues of centuries-old limes, and walls dating back to Henry VIII were reduced to rubble. In the words of Sevenoaks District Council's chief executive Bruce Cova: 'A hundred years of our heritage disappeared in a few minutes and our countryside will never be the same again in our lifetime.'

Power cables started arcing with flashes of 1,000 volts. As millions of homes lost electricity, Sevenoaks District Council's emergency team assembled, and Cova told them these were the nearest conditions they might ever see to a nuclear attack, a sentiment echoed by a local journalist whose first reaction was: 'My God! They've finally done it. They've dropped the bomb!' At Rotherfield in Sussex, the 360-year-old church spire was brought down, while in Hampshire and Dorset, virtually every road was blocked by trees. At Gatwick, the wind speed reached almost 100 miles an hour, and on the coast at Shoreham, a gust of 115 miles an hour was recorded. More than 900 passengers were stranded for up to 12 hours as their ferries tried to dock at Dover and Harwich. In London, a racing skiff from the Serpentine was flung into a tree, as was a car at Upper Norwood. At Kennington in South London, all eighty-four families living in a block of flats had to be evacuated after brick walls were sucked out of a thirteenth-floor flat, leaving a gaping hole just feet from where a couple had been sleeping. They watched in horror as their stereo and drinks cabinet disappeared into the void. The flats were so badly damaged, it would be eight months before it was safe for the residents to return. The storm sent corrugated iron sheets flying through the air, and hurled scaffolding poles like javelins.

As in 1703, there were some dramatic escapes. One Kent family spent the night in the garden in lashing rain because they were afraid one of their beech trees looked threatening. They were right. It crashed down on the house, splintering the roof, and one limb pierced the bed where the daughter would have been sleeping. In North London, a woman's bed plunged 40ft from her second-floor bedroom into the basement. It took firemen 3 hours to rescue her, but she suffered nothing worse than severe bruising. A police officer remarked: 'Thank God it happened at night.' If the storm had struck during the day, the death toll would surely have been higher. As it was, many people simply slept through it all, including a family at Putney Heath in London whose chimney stack fell through their roof and into the kitchen, and the tramp who lived in a North London bus shelter. A tree missed him by inches, but the first he knew of it was when a policeman woke him at nine o'clock the next morning. The tramp asked who had been chopping down trees in the night. Eighteen people, though, were killed, and hundreds injured. Two firemen died at Highcliffe in Dorset when an 80ft oak tree crashed on to their engine. A 49-year-old man was killed by a beach hut flung across the sea front at Hastings, while at Rottingdean a 60-year-old man perished trying to save his garage doors. Four people were killed when their cars ran into or were struck by trees and, in London, a tramp died when bricks fell on his cardboard home.

To many it seemed like a disaster, but some naturalists argued that periodic storms of this kind are necessary to clear out old vegetation and make way for new growth. Richard Mabey, chairman of London Wildlife Trust, wrote that the storm was 'an integral part of the workings of the environment, not some alien force'. The owner of Knole Park, 74-year-old Lord Sackville, also came to see the storm as a blessing in disguise. It took a year and a half to clear the damage, but then he began extensive replanting. 'The trees that were there were planted mainly in the eighteenth century, and certainly in the case of beech and oak, they were past their prime', he said. 'Before the storm, obviously we were replanting as trees came down but that was on a very small scale. The storm gave the opportunity for wholesale replanting, and we can look forward, I hope, in 50 years to something very fine again.' Altogether, 3 million homes were damaged, and the storm caused an estimated £1.5 billion worth of damage, while the government criticised the Meteorological Office for failing to give adequate warning. Still, at least everyone could relax in the knowledge that there was not likely to be another storm like it for another 300 years.

So was it global warming or malign coincidence that set the corrugated iron and scaffolding polls flying again less than three years later? Whatever the reason, on 25 January 1990, Burns' Day, the winds were back. At eleven o'clock in the morning, gusts of 87 miles an hour were recorded in London. Many buildings had their roofs torn off, and cars were crushed by trees. Over a million houses were damaged, and the new developments in London's Docklands were particularly badly hit, as construction materials were blown around and dashed into buildings. Though the winds were not as strong as they had been in 1987, this time the death toll was higher, because they came during the day when people were out and about. Forty-seven were killed, including seven children, a dozen of the deaths resulting from falling buildings. The actor Gordon Kaye, star of the television series 'Allo, 'Allo!, was hit on the head by a plank of wood that crashed from a hoarding near his home by the Thames in West London, and had to undergo brain surgery. Once again, the trees suffered, with an estimated 3.5 million being destroyed, and the total cost of the damage was estimated at £2 billion.

# CHAPTER SEVENTEEN

# EARTHQUAKE, FAMINE AND FLOOD

In 1348, the monks of Meaux Abbey, near Hull, were flung violently from their stalls by an earthquake, while on 6 April 1580, falling masonry claimed the life of an apprentice cobbler named Thomas Gray during a tremor in central London. He is one of only a dozen people believed to have been killed by earthquakes in Britain during the last 500 years. The strongest of the last century struck Lleyn in North Wales in 1984, bringing down chimneys, while the most destructive of recent times happened 100 years before at Colchester, where it destroyed a church spire and damaged houses.

For most of Britain's history, hunger was a much more present danger. In 426, with a variety of barbarian invaders menacing the ancient Britons following the Romans' departure, Bede records that famine 'obliged many of them to submit themselves to the depredators'. The Anglo-Saxon Chronicle reported that 'terrible' portents over Northumbria in 793 – 'exceptional flashes of lightning, and fiery dragons were seen flying in the sky' – were followed by a 'great famine'. In 1116, the Chronicle noted: 'This was a very hard year and disastrous for crops, because of the very heavy rains that came just before August and which proved very vexatious and troublesome', while the 1150s were 'days of want and grief' according to the Walden Chronicle. There was 'severe famine' in 1153, and people were forced to eat dogs. Fields and villages were left empty, so that even when the harvest was good, there was no one to bring it in. Henry of Huntingdon said thousands died, and many were reduced to begging; 'there had never been greater misery in the country.' In the last decade of the thirteenth century, the wheat harvest failed three times, but the years 1315 to 1319 saw perhaps the worst famine of all. Horsemeat, normally shunned even by peasants, was now too expensive for all but the aristocracy, and ordinary folk were reduced to living on cats and dogs, the dung of doves, and, according to one chronicler, even their own children. King Edward II tried to fix the price of staple foods, but all that happened was that dealers withdrew their produce, and the ordinance was repealed. As people grew desperate, the number of robberies in Kent rose by a third, and in the countryside, it was said that men were murdered for food. When the King visited St Albans in 1316, it was scarcely possible to buy bread for his household, and even when the harvest improved in 1317 and 1318, there were terrible livestock epidemics, so that Inkpen Manor in Berkshire, for example, lost more than two-thirds of its sheep. Then the harvest failed again in 1321 and 1322. Between 1309 and 1325, it was reckoned the population of England fell by a quarter.

Scotland was badly hit in the fifteenth century. The winter of 1431 was so bitterly cold that nearly all the animals died, then three years later a bitter frost lasted for three years, so that water mills could not grind corn, while in 1435 there was great famine in Teviotdale. In 1482, famine was aggravated by an English blockade, and 'many poor folk died of hunger'. In England, there were a number of bad harvests during the last decade of Elizabeth I's reign, with 1596 being perhaps the worst of the century. The death rate jumped by up to a fifth, and there were food riots in London, Oxford and Kent. Desperate people flocked to the towns, and in Newcastle upon Tyne, it was reported that there were 'sundry starving and dying in our streets and in the fields for lack of bread'. In Scotland, the 1690s saw a series of harvest failures, with perhaps a seventh of the population dying, while in 1727 hunger came to what is now Northern Ireland, and the Archbishop of Armagh found 'all the roads full of whole families that had left their homes to beg abroad'. Ulster was also hit by famine in 1741, when there was 'want and misery in every face . . . the roads spread with dead and dying bodies . . . and many buried only in the fields and ditches where they perished'.

Just over a century later, Ireland was to suffer the worst famine that Europe has seen in modern times. Although Ulster suffered less than the rest of the island, its privations were terrible enough. In 1846, a strange and dreadful thing happened to what was for many the staple diet. Potatoes that looked normal were actually rotten under the skin. James Brown of Donaghmore, County Tyrone, drove with his sister through County Fermanagh in August, and saw 'fine crops of potatoes in the fields. We spent three days in Bundoran and, returning, found these same crops blackened and useless.' The Revd Samuel Montgomery, rector of Ballinascreen, County Londonderry, wrote:

'The tops were first observed to wither and then, on looking to the roots, the tubers were found hastening to decomposition . . . The whole atmosphere in the month of September was tainted with the odour of the decaying potatoes.' The crop had been attacked by a microscopic fungus known as *Phytophthora infestans*, about which nothing could be done.

An official report on County Armagh was soon declaring, 'the misery and destitution of the people is extreme', and there were growing signs of unrest, with talk of withholding rents in Newry, while in Belfast, bakeries were attacked. Some landowners complained at the cost of helping the starving, but others were more generous. The Marquess of Waterford, who owned 8,000 acres in County Londonderry, sent £300 for free distribution of soup and bread, and told his agent, 'set the pot a-boiling as soon as you can', while there is evidence that landlords in Ulster were more forgiving about unpaid rent than those in the rest of Ireland. The crisis soon grew to such immense proportions, though, that private charity was overwhelmed.

The winter of 1846/7 was very cold, and from all over the six counties, there were stories of worsening distress; even where food was available, it was so expensive that people could not afford it. In power in London were the Whigs – fanatical believers in the free market. In the words of one historian, 'Even the most Thatcherite of European politicians today would be deemed "wet" compared with those in power and influence in Westminster during the Famine.' Their creed said that any interference with the workings of the market was dangerous, so destitute, starving people could not just be given money or food, they had to work for it. Not only that; when the government put them to work, they were paid by results. So those who were weakest, and presumably in most need of help, got least. The other problem with this system was that at the end of a day working for government relief schemes, smallholders were too exhausted to go and work on their plots, so even less food was produced. Sometimes the poor were made to go to the workhouse, but in the one at Lurgan, the number of deaths mounted to ninety-five in the first week in February. The chaplain blamed it on stew made from putrid beef, while the medical officer said most new arrivals were already at the point of death: 'many have been known to die on the road, and others on being raised from their beds to come to the workhouse have died before they could be put into the cart, and numbers have died in less than 24 hours subsequent to their admission.'

Finally, that same month, the government had to suspend dogma, and allow boiled Indian corn, or rice when available, to be handed out free to the queuing masses. By now, people were dying in their thousands, not just from starvation, but from typhus, bacillary dysentery (often aggravated by contaminated soup), or scurvy. In Belfast, Dr Andrew Malcolm worked day and night treating the sick: 'Famine was depicted in the look, in the hue, in the voice and the gait', he wrote. 'The food of a nation had been cut off.' The *Belfast Newsletter* reported it was commonplace to see 'haggard, sallow and emaciated beings, stricken down by fever or debility from actual want, stretched prostrate upon the footways of our streets and bridges'. There was a good grain harvest in 1847, but most of the poor still faced starvation because of the absence of potatoes. Even so, the government stopped soup being given out in September. Once again, the destitute had to go into the workhouse if they wanted help. Many workhouses, though, had no money, because bankrupt landlords could not afford to pay the poor rates, and it cost four times as much to keep someone in the workhouse than to give them help at home, so Newtownards petitioned for the law to be relaxed. Parliament said 'no.' Disease began to cut alarming swathes through the enfeebled occupants of packed workhouses, and in 1848, dogma once more had to give way, and MPs were forced to modify their hard line. By the time the famine ended in 1851, something like 200,000 people had died in Ulster, with County Fermanagh the worst hit. Many who survived were driven from their land, especially in Armagh and Antrim and, in addition, hundreds of thousands emigrated.

Britain's worst recorded flood came at nine o'clock on the morning of Tuesday 20 January 1607. According to a contemporary account, farmers in fields by the Severn estuary 'perceived far off huge and mighty hills of water tumbling one over the other'. The area was very vulnerable to flooding, with much of the land below sea level, and it had been protected by walls for 600 years. The inhabitants never knew what hit them: 'the waters ran with a swiftness so incredible that no greyhound could have escaped by running before them. Whole houses were removed from the ground where they stood and were floating up and down like ships half sunk which came in such swiftness that the fowls of the air could scarcely fly so fast.' Mistress Van, a 'gentlewoman', who lived 4 miles from the sea at Llanwern, did not even have time to get into the upper rooms of her house before the waters engulfed her. One of the many pamphlets that recorded the event said, 'everyone prepared himself ready to entertain the last period of his life's destruction'. Twenty-six parishes in Monmouthshire were inundated, while on the eastern side the area flooded stretched from Minehead to Slimbridge. At Brean Down in Somerset 'stood nine houses, and of those, seven were consumed, and with them 21 persons lost their lives'. One man managed to cling to a beam as his house was dashed to pieces. He was swept along for 4 miles, but survived. His wife and children were drowned. Altogether, 200 square miles were under water, and 2,000 people were drowned, as were hundreds of thousands of sheep and cattle. Many of those who survived found themselves ruined, and 'men that were rich in the morning when they rose from their beds were made poor before noon of the same day'.

A very high tide had been expected that morning, and some accounts refer to 'the sea being very tempestuously moved by the winds', conditions which could have produced the flood. Other accounts, though, say the weather was fine and sunny, and some experts, citing the violence of the waves, say this was a tsunami. There are precedents in Britain. Geological evidence suggests the east coast of Scotland was battered by such a phenomenon 7,000 years ago, and an earthquake off Lisbon in 1755 produced a 10ft wave in Cornwall. The theory is that this one was caused by a fault off the south-west coast of Ireland. Those who support it lean on geological evidence and eyewitness testimony, which spoke of the waves being accompanied by 'such smoke as if all the mountains were on fire – the like have never been seen or heard of in the memory of man'. Others said it looked 'as if millions of thousands of arrows had been shot forth all at one time'. Witnesses of other tsunamis have also spoken of the crests of waves sparkling with strange lights. It remains unclear whether this flood was produced by a tsunami or a storm, but it was plainly a natural disaster. Another flood two and a half centuries later was man-made.

By the 1860s, Sheffield was growing fast, as it became a world centre for steel manufacturing. Its burgeoning industries demanded water and, to feed them, the Sheffield Waterworks Company decided to build four new reservoirs in the surrounding hills to add to the eight it had opened in the previous thirty years. The first of the new batch was at Bradfield, 8 miles to the north-west. It blocked a stream called the Loxley which was quite small, but set in a deep, picturesque valley so that in wet weather it became a fast-flowing torrent. The resulting expanse of water would be a mile long and a quarter of a mile wide.

By March 1864, the new reservoir was almost full. On the wet stormy evening of Friday 11 March, a local man was crossing the slope of the 100ft embankment on his way home from work when he noticed two things – a high wind was whipping spray across the top of the dam, and there was a pronounced crack in the structure. It was only wide enough to get your fingers in, but it was about 50yd long. The waterworks' chief engineer, John Gunson, was called out from Sheffield, and arrived at about ten o'clock. He thought it was just a surface crack, but to be on the safe side, he decided to lower the water until a proper investigation could be made. The trouble was that the drain valves would take days to bring it down enough, so he instructed the navvies on duty to blow a hole in the side of the overflow, but perhaps because of the rain and the spray, they could not get the gunpowder to ignite.

At half past eleven, Gunson took another look at the crack. It did not seem to have got any worse, but by now water was coming over the top of the dam 'like a white sheet'. He was heading back to the valve house near the bottom of the embankment when he heard a shout. The engineer looked up, and saw a breach about 30ft wide appearing in the top of the dam. He felt the ground vibrating beneath his feet, and scampered up the side of the embankment just in time to escape a mountain of 700 million gallons of water that was about to crash down on to the defenceless houses and villages below. The nearest house was about three-quarters of a mile away. Fortunately, the farmer who lived there was still up. A labourer sent by Gunson came running, shouting: 'It's coming!' The farmer managed to get his wife and three children out, and up the hill just in time. 'We had not been out of the house five minutes', he said, 'when the flood came, and swept everything entirely away.'

The first village in the path of the flood was Bradfield. It swept away two bridges, a blacksmith's shop, a corn mill, a school and two houses. One man (perhaps of a literary turn) whose house was set above the rest watched the torrent, now as high as a 3-storey building, in horror: 'It seemed as if the bowels of the earth were being torn up, or as if some unheard of monster were rushing down the valley, lashing the hill sides with his scaly folds, crunching up buildings between his jaws, and filling all the air with his wrathful hiss.' Most of the inhabitants, mercifully, had been got out of their houses, though it was at Bradfield that the waters claimed their first victim. Joseph Dawson, the village tailor, was one of those who had gone from the village to examine the crack in the dam, but he decided there was no cause for alarm, and went home to bed. Half an hour later, his wife, who had given birth the previous day, woke him up. She had heard some men shouting: 'It's coming!' The tailor got his brother to carry his 4-year-old son up the hill to safety, then he tried to get another man to help him carry his wife and the baby, but the man told him to run for his life, saying, 'I cannot assist you. I have enough to do to save my own life.' Dawson had managed to carry them about 20yd when the flood knocked them down. They fought their way back to their house, but just as they reached it, the baby was washed from his wife's arms. The couple struggled upstairs, and local people laid a ladder from the bedroom window so they could climb across it to an embankment, and to safety. The baby's body was found a few days later.

No warning had reached a pair of isolated cottages that lay a mile further on from Bradfield. There, the Marsdens were awoken by the water crashing in. William Marsden knocked a hole in the ceiling of the bedroom and got up on to the roof, while his wife stood on a table and threw their 2-year-old child up to him. He then pulled Mrs Marsden up on to the roof, and they all escaped injury, even though their house was severely damaged. The next village was Damflask. The bridge, an inn and three houses were flattened, and one of the inhabitants just managed to get his wife and his 4-day-old child out on a cart before the flood arrived. A woman escaped carrying her cat under one arm and her dog under the other, but a man who believed it was a false alarm was drowned just as he had finally roused himself from his bed and got one stocking on. A 27-stone pig was drowned in its sty.

Next, the flood struck a wire mill, carrying away an 18ft-long boiler and killing four people. As the water continued its devastating progress, it washed away four more bridges, four grinding mills, a paper mill, a rolling mill and a brick works, as well as many houses and trees. In the words of the contemporary chronicler of the disaster, Samuel Harrison: 'A mighty cataract and avalanche swept down the gorge of the valley in one tremendous billow of mountainous height, which nothing could resist.' Next in its path was Little Matlock, according to legend a haunt of Robin Hood and Little John. Here a man, his wife and child, his nephew, two apprentices and a servant girl were all drowned in one house. Further along the valley, ten people were drowned in a farmhouse, including an old man who had moved in to live with his children only that day. Nearby were three cottages in which eleven people drowned, while one man was washed out of the window on his bed, and ended up safe in a field. By the time the flood reached Malin Bridge, one of the biggest villages in its path, as the government inspector would put it later, 'not even a Derby horse could have carried the warning in time to have saved the people'.

Here twenty houses were destroyed, and no fewer than 102 people killed. 'A bombardment with the newest and most powerful artillery could hardly have proved so destructive,' wrote Harrison, 'and could not possibly have been nearly so fatal to human life.' The land was turned into a quagmire of stones, trees, wrecked houses, machinery, furniture and household items, while the noise was said to be like that of 100 engines letting off steam at the same time. One man clung to a piece of timber as he was swept from his house, then he was washed against the window of another house, and managed to shout for help until the occupants pulled him in. His wife and two children drowned. The Stag Inn was destroyed with the loss of eleven lives. Altogether in the valley 270 people were killed. Fifteen bridges were completely destroyed, along with thirty-three factories and workshops, three shops, two inns, 798 houses and fifty-three other buildings, while nearly 6,000 buildings were damaged. The official report into the disaster concluded that the provision for removing excess water from the reservoir at times of heavy rain was inadequate, and that the embankment was not sufficiently watertight. The inquest jury said: 'there has not been that engineering skill and attention in the construction of the works, which their magnitude and importance demanded.'

At the pretty seaside resort of Lynmouth in Devon, it seemed that it had scarcely stopped raining during the first fortnight of August 1952, which must have been a big disappointment for the 700 holidaymakers who had crowded in to join the town's 450 residents. On 15 August, by half past three in the afternoon, it was coming down in torrents. Lynmouth lies in a deep valley right up against the heights of Exmoor, and the East and West Lyn rivers meet in the heart of the town a few hundred yards from the sea. Unlike most rivers, they descend more steeply as they near the end of their journey, with the West Lyn reaching a gradient of one in five just before the junction. Most of the buildings were clustered around the two rivers, which were fed by the streams that drained the moor. These were swollen with rainwater and bursting their banks, and as they rushed downhill, they carried with them debris that formed temporary dams which then burst, releasing walls of water into Lynmouth. By eight o'clock at night, water in some streets was 1ft deep. The electricity failed, and the phones were cut off.

As the waters rose in the car park, vehicle lights came on, then their backs rose out of the water, and they swivelled around. Then, in the words of one eyewitness, 'very slowly at first then faster, they began to move off backwards, headlights towards us, driverless down the road, swinging and swaying as if dancing to music'. In the streets, though, an altogether grimmer spectacle was being played out, as a great wall of water began rushing through the town. People linked hands to cross the rising torrent and reach the Lyndale Hotel, which was sturdily built and stood on an island between the two rivers. It would eventually provide a refuge for 150 people, including four who were washed in through the window. The shelterers had to keep moving up to higher floors as the lower ones were inundated, and when one wing collapsed, they were left wondering whether the whole hotel would go. The lashing rain meant there was almost complete darkness, except for the occasional dramatic flash of lightning, while the river roared as it swept along huge boulders. Debris now blocked the narrow Prospect Bridge at the bottom of Lynmouth Hill, and water poured into the centre of the village, creating a 30ft flood that swept away a garage, a chapel, a shop and a house.

The 63-year-old local postman was swept into the waters when his house collapsed. One of his daughters, who lived two doors away, recognised his grey and red striped shirt as she saw him being carried past: 'I managed to grab him by the braces as he went past me and I just hung on until we reached safety.' But the postman lost his wife, another daughter, his son, his son-in-law and his two grandsons. His pet Jack Russell survived. Residents from a row of ten cottages backing on to the East Lyn got out to shelter in a school on higher ground, but they could not persuade an 80-year-old man, his 72-year-old wife and her 78-year-old brother to leave their home. The people taking refuge in the school saw their tiny oil lamp until half past one in the morning, then they heard a terrible crash of boulders, and the light went out. The next morning, there was nothing left of the cottages, though a bed and breakfast sign still stood in the garden of one. Among others who died were three boy scouts from Manchester camping in the meadows above the village, two Australian nurses on a hiking holiday, and an 8-year-old boy staying with his grandmother. The final death toll was thirty-four, including eleven holidaymakers and four children.

All twenty-eight bridges over the two rivers had been swept away or damaged beyond repair. Lynmouth's main landmark, the Rhenish Tower overlooking the harbour, had been demolished, though bizarrely, deckchairs that stood beside it were still neatly stacked, apart from two found five days later on a beach 30 miles away. Two big petrol tanks that had been under the forecourt of the filling station were never seen again. Altogether ninety-three houses were lost, while all nineteen vessels in the harbour were sunk or wrecked on the shore, and more than 100 mangled vehicles were found under the sea by divers. The whole town was evacuated, but by 2 September, people were allowed back, and just four weeks after the flood, Lynmouth was open again for tourist business. The Rhenish Tower was rebuilt, while the West Lyn was given a new course, and separated from the East Lyn by a wall. Stretches of both rivers were widened, and their banks were smoothed out to try to stop debris gathering. Today Lynmouth remains a delightful resort.

Less than six months later, on the night of Friday 30 January 1953, the first sign that anything was amiss was when 125 miles an hour winds hit Costa Hill in the Orkney Islands. Then chimney stacks and garden fences were blown down at Kinloss, and forests were flattened over much of Scotland. Somewhere off Barra Head in the Hebrides, the Fleetwood trawler *Michael Griffith*, with a crew of fifteen, vanished. The next morning, as the *Princess Victoria* car ferry emerged from the shelter of Loch Ryan on her voyage from Stranraer to Larne, a huge wave hit her, smashing open the steel doors to her car deck, so that she began taking in water. The captain struggled on for a time, but eventually he had to give the order to abandon ship. The first lifeboat lowered into the seething waters broke adrift with just one man aboard. Another full of women and children was overturned by a wave, drowning all of them, and of the 174 passengers and crew, only 41 were saved. At half past eleven, the Meteorological Office gave a warning of 'exceptionally strong winds' in East Anglia. A high tide was also expected, but an hour before it was due, the Tees overflowed its banks. England's east coast is extremely vulnerable, with most of it flat and low-lying, and such cliffs as there are tend to be of soft boulder clay. Some of the land is below sea level and, over the centuries, the sea has reclaimed parts of it, like the village of Shipden, lost around the time of Henry IV. To make things worse, the south-east corner of England is dropping at the rate of about 1ft every 100 years.

Now the high winds blowing on the surface of the sea were beginning to build up a surge, a wall of water sometimes 10ft higher than the normal high tide, but no one appears to have foreseen it. A telephone operator in Essex recalled later: 'Nothing really happened to alert us to any emergency.' In the afternoon, the waters cut across Spurn Point, the narrow spit of land that divides the Humber from the North Sea, stranding the community of life-boatmen and coastguards that lived at its end, and by teatime, they were tearing at the sea walls of Lincolnshire. At Cleethorpes, the sea smashed down a railway embankment and swept away buildings on the foreshore, and large areas of Grimsby were flooded. In the coastal villages around Mablethorpe and Sutton-on-Sea, forty people died. As darkness fell, the waters hit Norfolk. Much of King's Lynn was flooded to a depth of 6ft, and fifteen people were killed.

At their bungalow on Snettisham beach, Mr and Mrs Beckerton and their four children were worried about the Waltons, who were in their sixties and lived in another bungalow a few hundred yards away with their 9-year-old foster son. The Beckertons' grown-up son Peter had seen the sea coming over the protective bank, and he and his father decided to go to warn their neighbours. When they got outside, they plunged into water waist-deep, and Peter told his father to go back. Mr Beckerton last saw his son just a few yards from the Waltons' door, but he never got there. The surge carried him and the bungalow away, drowning the Walton family. Peter's body was not found for six weeks. He was posthumously awarded the Albert Medal. By now the Beckertons were in water up to their chests. Outside was a 10ft boat Peter had been planning to repair. Mrs Beckerton grabbed sheets from the linen cupboard and turned them into makeshift ropes to hold the vessel fast while the children climbed in. As rain kept pouring down, the children bailed out with cake tins, while their parents stood up to their necks in the water keeping it afloat. Other villagers who had organised rescue parties had old people swept out of their arms within yards of safety. One woman who had been rescued insisted on going back for her fur coat, and it cost her her life. The surge would leave only twenty bungalows standing in the village out of more than 100.

Near Hunstanton, the natural bank was overwhelmed, and many of the homes built on it were destroyed, with the loss of sixty-one lives. Many USAF men and their families lived along this stretch of coast, and sixteen of them were numbered among the dead. The Americans threw themselves into the rescue effort, and USAF Corporal Reis Leming, a non-swimmer, won the George Medal for single-handedly rescuing twenty-seven people from their bungalows in his rubber dinghy before he collapsed from exposure. The Hunstanton to King's Lynn train was disabled when it hit a floating bungalow, and passengers were stranded for 6 hours. Slaughden near Aldeburgh had just taken delivery of building materials for new sea defences, but the waters surged through it, and the only building left standing was a concrete mine store.

At Sea Palling, two women in their seventies escaped on to the roof of their bungalow, but both died of exposure, and a baby was swept off his father's back as he tried to struggle through the waters. Another man managed to get his 80-year-old neighbour and her daughter on to the roof of his house by 'pushing them up the ladder with my head'. He also rescued a man in plaster with a slipped disc who had been staying with them. They clung to the chimney stack and each other for 5½ hours until the waters receded. At Great Yarmouth, nine people were killed, and about 10,000 had to be evacuated, while at Lowestoft, where a new sea wall had been built a few years before, there were no deaths. Most of the forty deaths at Felixstowe occurred on an estate of single-storey prefabs. A woman eight months pregnant and her husband were saved because the prefab lifted off its foundations and floated off like a boat, though their 3-year-old daughter died from hypothermia. At Harwich, many houses had basements which helped dilute the impact of the flood, but eight people were drowned, five of whom were over 60. A dentist was seen rowing a dinghy loaded with cats at the stern, dogs in the middle and a parrot perched on the prow.

Jaywick Sands was known for its fine beaches. It had concrete walls along the front defending some of its avenues of bungalows and chalets. Behind them was a clay wall protecting more homes, but the sea burst through and flooded much of the area to a depth of 10ft in a few minutes. Four policemen tried to rouse people, but had no way of knowing which of the 1,800 buildings were occupied, and which were empty. One elderly woman managed to climb into the roof space of her chalet with her cat, then it overturned and she was trapped in darkness with no means of attracting attention. It was 31 hours before she was rescued. A man tried to escape through his front door with his invalid wife and his 3-year-old grandchild but, as they pushed it open, 'the full force of the water hit us. I was up to my neck. My wife just disappeared.' He managed to save his grandchild by clinging to a barbed wire fence until help arrived. Another man tried to reach his parents' grocery store, but was twice beaten back by the swirling waters. Repeatedly he pleaded with them by telephone to move into the top floor of their nearby house, but they were intent on trying to move their stock on to the top shelves. The last time he rang, his father said, 'The windows are all coming in,' and in the background, his mother shouted: 'Save yourself. We're drowning.' Then the line went dead. Thirty-seven people, with an average age of 66, died.

Next in the path of the surge stood 'Southend's little sister' or 'Captivating Canvey' – Canvey Island. The whole island lay below the level reached by spring tides, and was protected by a 15-mile perimeter wall. About a fifth of the population was over 60, many of them people who had gone to the island as holidaymakers, liked it, and then retired there, while another fifth were children under 14. Most of the homes they lived in were fairly flimsy bungalows or chalets. At twenty past eleven, the local police sergeant was warned that there was going to be an exceptionally high tide, but such warnings were not unusual, and the wind seemed to have dropped since the evening. Just before midnight, though, some local people saw water starting to come over the sea wall at Sunken Marsh in the north-east of the island, where the defences were 18 inches lower than those on the south side. They ran home and started warning their neighbours, some of whom took refuge in their lofts. River board men tried to raise the alarm by shouting and blowing whistles but, during the winter, many of the bungalows on the island were empty, and with most people now in bed, once again it was hard to know which were occupied. By half past twelve, the sea had made its first breach in Canvey's 15 miles of wall, and soon it broke through in a number of places. A 70-year-old woman woken by her neighbours had to escape up her outside stairs to the attic. The sight was terrifying: 'It was a surging torrent, all manner of things carried by it, including a caravan, several sheds, and any amount of heavy timber . . . knocking against the walls and doors like battering rams.'

People living in houseboats took some fugitives aboard their craft, but most islanders awoke only when there was the sudden roar of a wall bursting or a splintering of glass. Then they had to clamber on to furniture, cookers, step-ladders or whatever they could find to try to escape the grip of the icy waters. At Sunken Marsh, there was an additional inland sea wall, which trapped the waters, turning it into a 'basin of death'. As more and more water rushed in, a man saw a shed floating by 'as fast as a bus'. The flotsam was made up of chickens, goats, cats, toilets, buckets, indeed anything that was unattached and could float. One woman was woken up by the sound of her baby crying, and saw the child's cot floating. She and her husband managed to tear up bedding to make a rope and get the family of five up into the attic. The fire brigade went out to raise the alarm, but their engines were beaten back by the water, so they had to sound their sirens and let off maroons. The telephone operator was told to ring as many people on the island as she could, but already lines were coming down, and at half past two, the waters flowed in and knocked the switchboard out of action.

All this time, the Manser family were asleep in their bungalow close to the sea wall: mother, father and ten children aged 18 months to 15 years. At three o'clock, 13-year-old Christopher was woken by their dog barking. He and the eldest child, Ian, got out of bed, and 'straightaway we were up to our waists in ice-cold water. It was pitch dark.' Now they could hear some of the other children shouting out. Christopher held one young child, Ian another, and Mrs Manser the two youngest, as Mr Manser tried to get the gas light on. It flickered for a few minutes, then went out. The children were crying and screaming. Some found pieces of furniture to stand on, but as the water rose relentlessly, these began to float away. Fortunately, the bungalow was built on stilts, but soon Christopher was submerged up to his chest. That meant that outside, the water must be about 7ft deep. Five hundred yards behind the house was a path on the top of an embankment. Ian decided to swim for it to raise the alarm, dodging debris as he went. Mr Manser tried to keep three children afloat, while Christopher supported another two, but in the gnawing cold, with the water now reaching his bottom lip, 'I started to get very tired and could not get the children's faces out of the water.' So Mr Manser smashed his fist through the asbestos ceiling and tore away some of the panels. The older children were then able to get on to the table, climb up and straddle the rafters, but the table broke before Mrs Manser was able to get up, and she was left down below with the two youngest children in a pram. She shouted up to the others to sing hymns. Andrew Manser says they sang for an hour and a half: 'quite loud because my mother would keep geeing us up.' Christopher recalled 'praying to God and promising to go to Sunday School every week if He would only help'. Then 5-year-old Keith fell asleep and tumbled down, banging his head on the iron stove. Mr Manser could not swim, so Chris dived in after him to keep him afloat. Andrew says it was the 'bravest thing I've ever seen', but he could tell that Keith was dead. As all the furniture was now gone, Christopher too was now stranded below with no way of getting back up into the roof. Mrs Manser never stopped rocking the pram with the two youngest children in it. Andrew was not aware of it at the time, but now he realises 'with the water at that level, there was no way it could have been floating. The water must have been inside the pram, and the two children had just died without making a sound.' Christopher remembers how peaceful their faces looked.

While the Mansers underwent their dreadful ordeal, the first outside help reached the island, as a fire crew from Hadleigh managed to cross the bridge that linked it with South Benfleet, but they found it blocked with flood boards, and had to abandon their engine and clamber over them. Fortunately, they saw a coach parked on high ground, and the driver gave them a lift as far as the High Street, where they had to link arms to ford the fast-flowing waters. They found a dinghy in a front garden, and shouted to the owners in an upstairs room that they were borrowing it. In the absence of a paddle, they used a floorboard to row, and headed off for bungalows where they could hear people screaming for help. With their improvised transport, they rescued fourteen people. At three o'clock, the bridgeman managed to clear enough debris to allow the first ambulances to get across, with water up to their exhaust pipes. By now, the whole island was under water apart from two roads, and some people had been crouching on roofs for hours, often in their nightclothes, with a warm chimney stack to huddle against if they were lucky, but after four o'clock, the tide began to ebb. The council surveyor broke into the premises of a local boatbuilder, and commandeered seven flimsy canoes and dinghies, while firemen set off in galvanised tin baths. The craft were very hard to control, and one rowed by a police sergeant soon sank, but they saved many people. Meanwhile, on the mainland, Southend police were assembling a motley Armada of assorted craft, and fourteen lorry-loads of soldiers were preparing to go to Canvey in high-axled vehicles. As dawn broke, fearing that the next tide might bring more floods, islanders began heading for the mainland on foot. Many were still in their nightclothes. They were barefoot and drenched. Some were pushing prams, or carrying children, pets and bundles as they paddled along the 2-mile road to the bridge. At about seven o'clock, the rescue force began to arrive in earnest, and helped frozen inhabitants into boats. One volunteer who came from Barking to help was horrified to see 'a sea where Canvey Island used to be'. The bungalows, he said, looked like matchboxes in the water. By ten o'clock, the waters were rising again, and with the sea walls breached, the outlook seemed bleak.

Now the Leigh-on-Sea cockle and shrimp boats also joined the rescue effort. An army officer said people were 'full of praise for what was being done for them, and never uttered any word of complaint or moaned about their losses'. A 70-year-old retired ladies' maid had sat alone for 12 hours balanced on the headboard of her bed before a young man from Benfleet Yacht Club rescued her, while a woman who had been standing in the water with her husband and daughter for 13 hours died an hour before the rescue boat reached them. A kayak finally reached the Manser family and ferried them one by one to the embankment path. By the time they got Christopher out, he had been in the water for 10½ hours, and was frozen stiff. He was taken to a house on high ground where 'a woman put me in blankets, hot water bottles all around, and rubbed and rubbed until I came round. How I blessed her!' With another high tide expected, though, his comfort did not last for long, and in clothes many sizes too big, he too was sent to walk along the wall to Benfleet. As he was reunited with his family at a rest centre, he found out for the first time that his brother Ian had survived. The next tide left virtually all of the island under water, though some of it was only a few inches deep. Everywhere there were bodies – one in a tree, another floating in a garden still clinging to a rose bush. The authorities decided that the entire population should be evacuated. About 10,000 people were removed, but 500 stayed. One old lady commented: 'Hitler didn't get me in the war, and I'm sure Father Thames shan't get me this time', while a man with flu stayed in bed as water oozed up through the floorboards of his bungalow.

Most islanders went first to South Benfleet primary school, the nearest reception centre to the bridge. One baby arrived almost dead with cold, but the canteen supervisor wrapped it carefully, put it by the door of the oven and thawed it out. In the assembly hall, the headmaster and his wife held up a blanket as a makeshift screen behind which people put on dry clothes. The rector, seeing a man with no trousers, took off his own and hid his bare legs with his cassock. The fact that the flood had happened at the weekend had sometimes made it hard to mobilise the relief effort. On Sunday afternoon, an Essex County Council official trying to get an emergency supply of blankets rang the Ministry of Housing and Local Government, and got no reply. For several nights, the Manser family found themselves sleeping on top of tables and desks, but they testified to the generosity of local people. Many made spontaneous gifts of clothes, often without emptying the pockets. Christopher remembered: 'I found money, cigarettes, diaries and so on.'

For a time, it was feared that hundreds might have died on the island. Now a systematic search was made, with rescue workers chalking a big 'S' on each building once it had been examined. On Tuesday afternoon, the last survivor was found – a woman of 76. In fact, fifty-eight people died on Canvey Island, forty-three of them aged over 60. The inquest jury's view was: 'We feel strongly that the consequences of this disaster might have been avoided if the warning had been sent down the east coast.' Over the week following the flood, 1,000 servicemen and civilians filled sandbags day and night to make temporary repairs to Canvey's sea defences in what became known as 'Operation Canute'. There were some minor leaks, but the improvised defences held. Then, once the sewage system was restored, people began returning to their homes, and by 8 March, more than 8,000 were back. The island was given new, bigger and stronger walls. Gifts poured in from all over the world – everything from a packet of 'dolly mixtures' to £300 from the Pope and a pantechnicon full of furniture. Sardines came from Portugal, butter from Denmark, apples from Tasmania and coffee from Ethiopia. Only two homes were so badly damaged structurally as to be a total write-off, but damage to contents was often severe, and one returning septuagenarian found 'the interior of the bungalow was an utter shambles, a lot of the furniture had fallen to pieces, and clothing of all sorts was soaked with filth and mud that fairly stank'.

Altogether on land, 307 people were killed, while around the coast, eight ships were lost at a cost of more than 300 lives. Thirty-two thousand people were evacuated and, from Scotland to Kent, 24,000 houses were reported as damaged, though householders probably did not bother to report houses that were uninsured, and the true figure was, no doubt, many more. Two hundred factories were also damaged. Nine thousand sheep were killed, along with more than 1,000 cattle, 2,600 pigs and 34,000 chickens, while 150,000 acres of agricultural land were flooded, making it sterile for at least a season. Disastrous though this was, it was fortunate that the storm that produced the surge had happened before high tide, and had not coincided with a spring tide. These factors would have made the water several feet deeper, and thousands might have drowned. The official report on the disaster noted, not very reassuringly, that 'a combination of surge and tide such as that of January 31–February 1 may not occur for many years, but it may occur next winter'. Or, presumably, any winter.

# BIBLIOGRAPHY

Bardon, J. *A History of Ulster*, Belfast, Blackstaff Press, 1992

Barnett, C. *The Great War*, London, BBC, 2003

Bede, *Ecclesiastical History of the English Nation*, London, J.M. Dent & Sons, 1954

Blackstone, G.V. *A History of the British Fire Service*, London, Routledge & Kegan Paul, 1957

Bradbury, J. *Stephen and Matilda. The Civil War of 1139–53*, Stroud, Alan Sutton, 1996

Bradford, E. *The Story of the Mary Rose*, London, Hamish Hamilton, 1982

Brayne, M. *The Greatest Storm*, Stroud, Sutton Publishing, 2002

Briggs, A. *Victorian Cities*, Harmondsworth, Penguin, 1968

*British Railway Disasters*, Shepperton, Ian Allan, 1996

Cahill, R.A. *Disasters at Sea. Titanic to Exxon Valdez*, London, Century, 1990

Calvocoressi, P., Wint, G. and Pritchard, J. *Total War. The Causes and Courses of the Second World War*, vol 1, London, Penguin, 1989

Cartwright, F.F. and Biddiss, M. *Disease and History*, Stroud, Sutton Publishing, 2000

Collier, R. *The Plague of the Spanish Lady*, London, Allison & Busby, 1996

Cooksley, P.G. *Flying Bomb*, London, Robert Hale, 1979

Donnelly, J.S. Jr *The Great Irish Potato Famine*, Stroud, Sutton Publishing, 2002

Douglas, D.C. *William the Conqueror*, New Haven, Yale University Press, 1999

Duckham, H. and B. *Great Pit Disasters. Great Britain 1700 to the Present Day*, Newton Abbot, David & Charles, 1973

Edwards, A. *Flights to Hell. The Investigation of Flying Accidents and the Development of Air Safety*, Nairn, Thomas & Lochar, 1993

Faith, N. *Black Box. Why Air Safety is No Accident*, London, Boxtree, 1996

Faith, N. *Derail: Why Trains Crash*, London, Channel 4 Books, 2000

Faith, N. *Mayday. The Perils of the Waves*, London, Channel 4 Books, 1998

Fisher, J. *The Glasgow Encyclopedia*, Edinburgh, Mainstream, 1994

Fraser, A. *The Warrior Queens. Boadicea's Chariot*, London, Phoenix Press, 2002

Gardiner, J. and Wenborn, N. *The History Today Companion to British History*, London, Collins & Brown, 1995

Garmonsway, G.N. (ed. and tr.) *The Anglo-Saxon Chronicle*, London, J.M. Dent & Sons, 1975

Geraghty, T. *The Irish War*, London, HarperCollins, 2000

Gibbon, E. *The Decline and Fall of the Roman Empire*, London, Oxford University Press, 1912

Gilbert, M. *First World War*, London, HarperCollins, 1995

Gillingham, J. *Richard the Lionheart*, London, Weidenfeld & Nicolson, 1978

Gottfried, R.S. *The Black Death. Natural and Human Disaster in Medieval Europe*, London, Robert Hale, 1983

Grieve, H. *The Great Tide. The Story of the 1953 Flood Disaster in Essex*, Chelmsford, County Council of Essex, 1959

Guy, J. *Tudor England*, Oxford, Oxford University Press, 1990

Harris, S. *Sir Cloudesley Shovell. Stuart Admiral*, Staplehurst, Spellmount, 2001

Holford, I. *British Weather Disasters*, Newton Abbot, David & Charles, 1976

Hudson, K. and Nicholls, A. *The Book of Shipwrecks*, London, Macmillan, 1979

Hyde, A.P. *The First Blitz, The German Air Campaign Against Britain 1917–18*, Barnsley, Leo Cooper, 2002

Jacob, E.F. *The Fifteenth Century*, London, Oxford University Press, 1969

Jones, P.F. *The Jews in Britain. A Thousand Years of History*, Moreton-in-Marsh, Windrush, 1990

Larn, R. *Shipwrecks of Great Britain & Ireland*, Newton Abbot, David & Charles, 1981

Larn, R. *Shipwrecks of the Isles of Scilly*, Nairn, Thomas & Lochar, 1992

Lewis, P. *A People's War*, London, Thames Methuen, 1986

Longmate, N. *King Cholera, the Biography of a Disease*, London, Hamish Hamilton, 1966

Lynch, M. *Scotland. A New History*, London, Pimlico, 1992

Macaulay, Lord *The History of England*, vol 1, London, Longman, Green & Co., 1926

Mackie, J.D. *A History of Scotland*, 2nd edn, London, Penguin, 1978

McKisack, M. *The Fourteenth Century*, London, Oxford University Press, 1959

McLynn, F. *1066, The Year of the Three Battles*, London, Pimlico, 1999

McLynn, F. *The Jacobites*, London, Routledge & Kegan Paul, 1985

Mallie, E. and McKittrick, D. *The Fight for Peace: the Secret Story Behind the Irish Peace Process*, London, Heinemann, 1996

Marriott, J. *Disaster at Sea*, London, Ian Allan, 1987

Mullett, C.F. *The Bubonic Plague and England. An Essay in the History of Preventive Medicine*, Lexington, University of Kentucky Press, 1956

Mundill, R.R. *England's Jewish Solution. Experiment and Expulsion 1262–1290*, Cambridge, Cambridge University Press, 1998

Myers, J.N.L. *The English Settlements*, Oxford, Oxford University Press, 1998

Nicholson, R. *Scotland. The Later Middle Ages*, Edinburgh, Oliver & Boyd, 1978

Ogley, B. *In the Wake of the Hurricane*, Brasted Chart, Froglets Publications, 1987

Owen, D. *Air Accident Investigation*, new edn, Sparkford, Patrick Stephens, 2001

Percival, A. 'The Great Explosion at Faversham', *Archaeologia Cantiana*, vol. C, 1985

Pollard, M. *North Sea Surge. The story of the East Coast Floods of 1953*, Lavenham, Terence Dalton, 1978

Porter, S. *Destruction in the English Civil Wars*, Stroud, Sutton Publishing, 1997

Porter, S. *The Great Plague*, Stroud, Sutton Publishing, 1999

Poulsen, C. *The English Rebels*, London, Journeyman, 1984

Prebble, J. *Culloden*, Harmondsworth, Penguin, 1977

Prebble, J. *The Lion in the North*, London, Penguin, 1981

Prestwich, M. *Edward I*, London, Methuen, 1988

Prosser, T. *The Lynmouth Flood Disaster*, Lynmouth, Lyndale Photographic, 2001

Ray, J. *The Night Blitz 1940–41*, London, Arms & Armour, 1996

Ridley, J. *Henry VIII*, London, Penguin, 2002

Rolt, L.T.C. *Red for Danger*, London, Pan, 1966

*Rothmans Football Yearbook, 1971–2*, London, Queen Anne Press, 1971

Rowe, M. *The Day the Dump Went Up. The 1944 Fauld Explosion*, Chippenham, Antony Rowe, 2004

Salway, P. *Roman Britain*, Oxford, Oxford University Press, 1988

Schama, S. *A History of Britain. At the Edge of the World? 3000 BC–AD 1603*, London, BBC, 2000

Somerset, A. *Elizabeth I*, London, Weidenfeld & Nicolson, 1991

Stenton, Sir F. *Anglo-Saxon England*, Oxford, Oxford University Press, 1987

Steven Watson, J. *The Reign of George III 1760–1815*, London, Oxford University Press, 1960

Taylor, A.J.P. *English History 1914–45*, Harmondsworth, Penguin, 1970

Trevelyan, G.M. *A Shortened History of England*, Harmondsworth, Penguin, 1959

Weightman, G. *Rescue. The History of Britain's Emergency Services*, London, Boxtree, 1996

Weir, A. *Elizabeth the Queen*, London, Jonathan Cape, 1998

Williams, G.A. *When Was Wales? A History of the Welsh*, London, Penguin, 1991

Williams, P. *The Later Tudors. England 1547–1603*, Oxford, Oxford University Press, 1995

Withington, J. *Capital Disasters*, Stroud, Sutton Publishing, 2003

Woodward, Sir L. *The Age of Reform 1815–70*, Oxford, Oxford University Press, 1962

Ziegler, P. *The Black Death*, Harmondsworth, Penguin, 1970

# INDEX